For "double duty"

Best Wishes
Rodello Hunter

ALSO BY RODELLO HUNTER:

A House of Many Rooms (1965)
Wyoming Wife (1969)

THESE ARE BORZOI BOOKS
PUBLISHED IN NEW YORK
BY ALFRED A. KNOPF

A DAUGHTER OF ZION

A DAUGHTER

OF ZION

Rodello Hunter

DRAWINGS BY ALLAN P. NIELSEN

*A*LFRED A. KNOPF NEW YORK 1972

Library of Congress Cataloging in Publication Data

Hunter, Rodello. A daughter of Zion.

1. Mormons and Mormonism. I. Title.   BX8695.H83A3   289.3
74-171116   ISBN 0-394-47032-X

Manufactured in the United States of America

FIRST EDITION

To Veronica Bettinson
and the members of Lincoln Ward

Contents

Acknowledgments

I WISH TO THANK Angus Cameron, my editor, and
John Hawkins, my agent, for their encouragement in the writing of this book, and I especially wish to thank Darrel Jenkins
of Freedom, Wyoming, who knew where to find all of the
information, doctrine, and scripture that I had to look up.

To my husband, Frank James Calkins, more than thanks is
due. He has patiently suggested, corrected, and proofread,
easing the load of producing a manuscript. I give him my gratitude and my love.

R.H.

Foreword

I NEVER PLANNED to write this book. Rather than choosing to write it, it seemed to choose me. The book had its beginning when Angus Cameron, my editor at Knopf, visited us one spring. We live in a Mormon community and I grew up a member of the Church. Most Mormons, although they've been told often enough and proudly enough by their leaders that they are a "peculiar people," don't actually realize that they *are* unusual, and that their activities are also unusual. But my editor realized it, and I think that he felt that only a Mormon can truly write about Mormons—and interpret the unwritten language that they speak.

Then my agent John Hawkins and his wife Robbin came for a visit and brought with them their enthusiasm for this particular book, and it began to take form. As the manuscript grew, it took its own course, at times moving unexpectedly off the path that I had mapped out for it. But as my research and interviews and thoughtful assessment of years of observation piled the facts up before me, I could not with integrity sweep all of them back into the dusty Mormon closets where they have been so hopefully hidden. I have not been harsh—tempered as I have been by my upbringing, how could I be? But I have tried to be thoughtfully honest.

I have tried to put the Mormon on paper, and in some measure I have succeeded, for my experiences, compulsions, guilts, enthusiasms, and fears stem from the same sources as those of every other Mormon. If in some ways I am atypical of the breed—and make no mistake, Mormonism is bred—I believe that even my differences are widely shared, but perhaps not generally admitted.

Through my own activities in this book, I have meant to convey the frenzied press of "work" of the members of every ward; however, I am really a poor example. There are thousands of members in thousands of wards who have worked much harder than I ever did, and they have continued their activities throughout entire lifetimes and in many wards. My active participation in Lincoln Ward was compressed into little more than five years.

The child of a Mormon family undergoes what must be one of the most powerful indoctrinations of any society, so that in adult life, that child is incapable of admitting publicly, and sometimes not even to himself, that he does not believe in some or even in all of the basic teachings of the Church. To do so is to drain himself of one hundred and forty years of Mormon blood. It is a familiar, personal dilemma—the indescribably painful tug of war of heritage, love, and friendship against logic—which is resulting, I believe, in the quiet slipping away of many of those whose names are recorded in the vaunted three-million membership of the Church.

Not unusual at all is a preposterous conversation that I overheard recently between two members of the Church. They had stated a mutual disbelief in the divine origin of the *Book of Mormon* as Mormons are taught it. They thought that Joseph Smith had written it out of his visionary genius and imagination, but scoffed at his ever finding a stack of gold plates left by an angel in the Hill Cumorah. Then they went on to discuss the weight, size, number, transportation, and final disposition of those "nonexistent" plates in great detail and absolute seriousness!

In this book, I have not tried to make a case for Mormon theology, nor have I attempted to proselytize; I feel that only the most dogmatic theologian can find fault with my presentation of the Mormon community. Any doubts of mine that may be evident are probably no greater than those of the most potent adherent when he consults his own heart. The difference is that I am a writer and thus I am urged to reveal those doubts, but I feel that my implications will offend none but the most narrow minded.

So many things in Mormondom have changed in recent years that there are events described in this book that could not happen now. For instance, a bishop would seldom place a woman in a responsible position nowadays—such as the one Bishop Trauffer put me in—and never without strict supervision by her Priesthood superiors. Attitudes toward women in the Church are hardening, and although such actions certainly seem untimely, women are being sternly pushed back into their subservient roles as home- and babymakers.

This has been a most painful book to write, for its writing

has brought me to realizations that I may have been happier without. Who is to say how Eve would have fared had she not eaten that apple?

But she ate, and I have written, and in doing so I have discovered something about Mother Eve—it took a lot of courage to eat that apple!

Rodello Hunter

Freedom, Wyoming
1971

A DAUGHTER OF ZION

Chapter I

THE HOUSE ON
SEVENTH EAST

THE LAND ON WHICH our house on Seventh East was built had once belonged to Brigham Young. I was surprised to learn that his holdings had reached so far south of Salt Lake City's Temple Square. Two blocks west of us was the Wells Ward Church, and two blocks east of us was Lincoln Ward,* and within a radius of two miles were no less than twelve other imposing Mormon edifices and one modest chapel in St. Anne's orphanage where the members of the Catholic parish attended Mass.

---

* A ward is roughly comparable to a Catholic parish.

When we bought the house, the previous owners told us that we were located on the borderline of Wells Ward, one of the six wards that "made up the Granite Stake of Zion." All of which didn't interest me very much. For years I'd been determinedly oblivious to the beehive of Deseret which buzzed incessantly around me. My relatives, among whom numbered Mormon bishops and patriarchs, all held Church positions and constantly urged me to become active. My husband's relatives, among whom were even more bishops and patriarchs (including a great-grandfather to whom the founder and prophet Joseph Smith bequeathed his sword before he was martyred in Carthage jail), also urged me to become active. And Papa, the grandfather whom I most dearly loved, was openly chagrined by my lack of interest in the Church—his "Way of Life," his "Light Unto the World," his "reason for which man is born."

So far, I had resisted all the artful psychology of my family of zealots, but in Utah, as well as in the other environs of Mormonism, it takes the elusiveness of a wild trout and a big assist from the Devil to escape the embrace of the Church. There are so many "activities" in which to be pleasurably caught up. Once ensnared in one of them, you find that you're soon dabbling in others, until you've forgotten which good fight you were trying to make—whether you were trying to stay in all that encircling, kindly light or were trying to rest your mortal and temptation-afflicted bones in encompassing darkness. The scales are weighted in favor of the Light.

I know that the Wells Ward Bishop didn't intend that he and his councilors call on us too soon. Someone noticed that our windows were washed and the curtains were up and had reported to him that it looked as if the newcomers to the Ward were ready for their first visitors. In Mormondom, they are usually the Bishopric or the Relief Society Presidency, for the carefully kept record of each member is sent on to the next ward he resides in. Sometimes it even precedes his arrival, even though that next ward may be three counties or three states away. The Church's knowledge of its members rivals in thoroughness, if not motive, that of the Soviet K.G.B.

Any other woman would have been neatly moved in by this time, and so would I have been, under ordinary circumstances. But I was big-as-a-house pregnant with my third daughter, and slowed physically to an exasperating pace. I hadn't had time to have my hair done for a week, and I am one of those women who visibly reflects whatever she happens to be doing. If I'm baking a cake, it is obvious to any chance visitor that it is white, or chocolate, or pink birthday. If I'm scrubbing the floor I look like a scrubwoman, if I'm washing, a laundress. That day I looked like a pregnant mover!

You cannot mistake the Mormon Triumverate. I knew who they were when I looked up from the broomstick that I was sawing to see them walking abreast down the sidewalk. I knew that they were coming to call on me; we were the newest residents in the neighborhood. I watched them come up the porch steps, dismayed and irritated as the doorbell rang. I'd snatched a clean apron from the pile of unironed laundry heaped on the sofa, pushed a jumble of children's panties and socks from one chair and carried a wobbly stack of cups and saucers into the kitchen to pile them unsteadily on a stack of something else before I answered the door.

"I'm the Bishop," one of the men announced. "These are my councilors. Brothers . . ." My embarrassment smothered the names he gave me.

"Come in," I said, "sit down." I think that I might have sounded ungracious. I know I felt ungracious. They eased themselves into the domestic jungle of dishes, egg beater, baked potato rack, mixer, stacked pictures, typewriter, sweaters, boots, sheet music, boxes of spices, piles of linens, and toys scattered loosely in the confusion.

On one end of the dining room table was a pile of Sally's

and Ann's dresses still on their hangers. Their closet had no bar. I'd been in the midst of sawing the broomstick to serve as one when I'd looked out the window to see my black-suited visitors descending upon me. The half-sawed broom and the saw now leaned against the back of the Bishop's chair. I realized miserably that a living room was no place for carpentry—but it had seemed to be until they came. I was certainly not going to go outside and saw in front of the neighbors. Windows from the houses on both sides of ours overlooked every part of the yard and most of the windows of our house, a surprisingly large house for a lot which fronted only fifty feet. Judging from the curtains, my neighbor on the south obviously had a bedroom so close that she could reach out from her bed and tap on the bricks of our house.

I think that the men welcomed us into the Ward, since that was their mission, but I didn't hear the welcome. My eyes, like theirs, kept flicking to the coffeepot standing prominently on the near end of the dining table. They were pointedly interested in my feet, too, and one or more of three pairs of eyes stared at them throughout the entire visit. My ankles were bare, but I was trying to keep them tucked neatly under my chair. I'd thought ankle fascination went out in the early 1900's.

As the brethren informed me of the location of the Wells Wardhouse and the times of the various Church services, I plucked rumpled newspaper packing from around me, rolled it into balls, and dropped them into a heap beside my chair. I moved to the couch to ease my discomfort and to reach for one of the children's stuffed animals, clutching it to my stomach in a futile attempt to hide it. Then I saw what the men had been staring at.

After the movers had dumped their last box, my husband had poured himself a glass of beer. He'd set the empty can on the floor, and it had rolled next to the chair leg.

As I sat there, that beer can grew larger and larger until it dominated the room. It was infinitely more embarrassing than the disorder, the coffeepot, or my protruding belly covered by its wrinkled apron. The beer can had grown about three feet high when the Bishop of Wells Ward and his councilors stood, took their leave, and told me to call upon them if they could be of help. I never did. When the children went to Church, they went to Lincoln Ward, where we were not members. Later I had our records transferred to that Ward, under great protest. My reason for the transfer was ostensibly that none of the children's friends went to Wells Ward, and they refused to attend that Ward by themselves. But the real reason was that I could not face the Wells Ward Bishop and his memory of our "debauchery."

Almost from the moment we moved in, we had company. Word got around fast that we had two extra bedrooms, so after the first two weeks, when the doorbell rang, I could be almost certain that it was another unexpected guest, or usually guests. Mormons are bred-in-the-bone visitors. It is part of their heritage and tradition. If they come any distance at all, their stay isn't just an afternoon. It is usually overnight or for a week-end. But I had one guest who came every day for more than six weeks, said a brief word of hello upon arriving, and slept on the living room couch all day. He would wake for lunch, take dinner with us, eat heartily, and depart. Finally, I reached the point where it was him or me, and I gave my husband one of my few ultimatums.

"I don't want Poor Cornelius here anymore."

"He hasn't any other place to go. He has to stay in town and check in at the hospital every few days. You know that. Besides, his mother is a shirt-tail relative of my folks."

"If Poor Cornelius stays, I go."

"Now, he doesn't really bother you, does he? He isn't right in the head since his accident."

"He bothers me! He sleeps on the front room couch all day.

People come to the door. They see this man asleep on my couch. They think things. I can't have my friends here. I want you to tell him he'll have to go somewhere else."

"His mother was nice to me when I was a kid."

"Well, I've amply repaid them for all the niceness." I thought about that repayment. "And then some!" I added.

"This isn't like you. The doc'll let him go home soon. It wouldn't hurt you for another few days."

"Not even one more. The neighbors are talking. He comes after you leave. You come after he goes. I know they're wondering."

"To hell with the neighbors!"

"To hell with Poor Cornelius! I told him the other day that if he would like to sleep, he could go into the bedroom and close the door so that the children wouldn't bother him. Why, I can't even have Myrtle in for coffee and be comfortable. We disturb him! He watches us all the time—balefully."

"I'll ask him to go in the bedroom to lie down."

"He won't. He said he liked it on the couch, and the girls didn't bother him at all. Besides, it's too late. I don't want him in the bedroom either. After I thought it over, I decided that would be even worse—I mean it would look worse. I don't want him *here!*" And I started to cry.

"All right. I'll tell him." And he did. Then I felt guilty for turning Poor Cornelius out. I had been terribly sorry when he lay unconscious for six weeks after he'd been in a head-on collision. Poor Cornelius was young and husky. I'm told he was a pleasant young man before the accident. I never knew him as that. The doctors didn't think he'd live, and I felt real pity for his distraught mother and sister. They stayed with us during the first few days while he thrashed constantly in his hospital bed. Someone had to be with him, and when he wore his family out, I spent some strenuous hours keeping him from kicking off the covers and exposing himself to passersby and from rolling out of bed and fracturing what the wreck hadn't. Finally, they moved him to another hospital where they thought he would be more easily restrained. He wasn't. He managed to throw himself out of bed, and the hard jolt did what the doctors hadn't been able to. It woke him up.

But his recovery was slow and his mother was needed at home, so after he was released from the hospital, she asked me if "Poor Cornelius" could stay at my house for a few days. She didn't want him to "be left alone in that hot, little rented room all day."

"Of course," I said, "he can come here and rest. I'll keep an eye on him." My lady-of-charity attitude lasted almost a month, then I endured him for a while, and after that I've already told you what happened.

Poor Cornelius was one of the worst, but there were a lot of others. My neighbors called our house the Hunter Hotel. I have never considered my relatives (of which I have very few) or my husband's relatives as company, and if any of them read this book, I don't want them to think that I'm including them in what I have, since the Hotel Period, called by authentic description—The Plague of the Locusts.

Oh, there are a few of the blood that I have considered as Plague. There was a great-uncle who came to visit with his two grown sons and grown daughter soon after we'd moved into the Seventh East house, about three weeks before Barbara was born. They came unexpectedly, as usual, and hungry, also as usual. I had disliked this uncle since childhood for making fun of my pronunciation of "water." ("La de dah! And who does she think she is!" he'd say, mimicking me. I'd always heard it pronounced "watter" with the "a" bawled out and lengthened.

I had tried to close it up. Maybe it was more like "woter.")
Blushing, I'd brought him the drink of cold "watter" for which
he'd asked. But I could never like him after that. He was the
man of whom my grandmother once told me succinctly: "Elias
has such a big mouth that when he opens it, it squeezes his
eyes—shut—so he never knows what's going on!"

My husband and I were raised in small towns, very small,
farm towns, and I was brought up to welcome any relative or
guest who called on us with outstretched arms and a loaded
table. Most rural wives are prepared to cook an unexpected
company dinner, but most city wives are not, and I had become
a city wife. Somehow you don't consider cost when you are
taking from pantry or cellar, but now I had no pantry with
heavy shelves of home-canned fruits and vegetables and boxes
and packages of staples. There was no cellar with every dark,
cool corner filled with the wherewithal for unplanned dinners.
I have never begrudged a dinner or a bed to anyone, but I'm
afraid that I did begrudge the money I had to spend—especially
at that time, when our new house needed so many things, and
especially because of the volume of bedding and boarding that
we did. When I had guests it meant a trip to the store, just
around the corner and convenient, to be sure, but it also meant
that the carefully hoarded dollars from my grocery allowance
went for GROCERIES!

Almost every weekend, we had out-of-town guests. Some of
them were people who I'd met once or twice. Others of them
I hadn't met at all. They were just friends of friends. They'd
been told how upset we'd be if they came to Salt Lake and
didn't call on us. And, well, no, they hadn't had dinner, and
by the time dinner was over, it seemed heartless to expect that
they bundle up their tired children, already sleeping on the
beds in our big, extra room and take them to a motel.

Three times a year, in April, June, and October, the Church

of Jesus Christ of Latter-day Saints has CONFERENCE, when all the Saints from far and near come to the city to attend the sessions in the Tabernacle. The hotels and motels are filled, and our house was a natural haven. Once I had twenty-two house guests for three days, and that was the time I decided to hand out sheets and pillow cases and suggest that they make their own beds. There was, I told them with consummate courage, stuff for sandwiches in the refrigerator if they wanted to make them. None of this particular horde ever returned. I had betrayed the code! But I did not betray it easily. I had sharp thrusts of conscience every time I thought an inhospitable thought, but it did not stop my thinking them.

"What are you doing in the Church, now?" is the greeting most common among Mormons who have not seen one another for some time. I repeatedly said, "nothing," and then I was either given an exhortation on the gospel's truths, or my visitor's exuberant interest in me and mine disappeared behind eyes veiled with uncomprehending judgment, while they listed their own activities and the accompanying satisfactions—and I cooked dinner.

Since I seemed to be in the boarding-house business anyway, I was pleased to accept my brother-in-law's offer of ten dollars a week each for him and three of his friends to live in our big, basement room while they worked at postwar construction jobs, and until they could find homes for their families. So for several months I prepared breakfast, lunch, and dinner for the four of them. It seems unbelievable, but I paid the grocery bills and had some money left over.

I found that boarders weren't nearly as much trouble as drop-in company. They filled my bedrooms and crowded the dinner table, so that my unexpected guests dribbled away. As soon as possible in the spring, the men moved their families to Salt Lake City and left me with the terror of the empty bedroom again. (I had only one empty bedroom now, for our baby, Barbara, used the bedroom that joined ours as her nursery.)

The big bedroom wasn't to be empty long. Papa, my paternal grandfather, came down from Heber to stay with me for the summer. He'd spent the winter in California and had come home to one of Utah's early springs. But toward the end of June, he had suffered a slight stroke, one that put him in bed for a few days. Papa's son, Ward, and his wife had cared for him, but it was difficult for them because they were suffering through the slow death of their only little girl. The child had been born with a gall bladder malfunction, and though she lived for seven or eight months, she gained only a few ounces more than her birth weight.

As soon as Papa recovered enough to travel, Ward brought him down to me. Dora and her husband, Lloyd, and Ann had left for a summer tour of Europe. Zoa and Zola were in California overseeing the care of the Larson house and grounds during their absence, and Bessie, who lived in Idaho, was not well, so none of his children were available, but I had no summer plans and I was glad to have Papa.

At first he was weak and kept to his room, but after a few weeks he was his hearty old self. He seemed to enjoy being with my children, and he visited cheerfully with my neighbors.

He did what I had considered impossible. He made friends with my bedroom-window neighbor, whom I considered an ogre. I called her Les Galleon, from the way she sailed down the street from the bus stop. She wore overpowering hats that shadowed a vast, protuberant bosom. Then, oddly, she trimmed down and had a skinny waist, which slid without benefit of hips into long, shapeless legs. I never saw her coming toward me without thinking of a sailing ship thrusting its ominous figurehead in my direction. My first conversation with her is memorable. She was watering her lawn, clad in a Japanese kimono that gaped from the waist down, showing her stockings sagging below the garters which were rolled above her knees. She came over to the edge of her lawn and accused me.

"My God, you're pregnant!"

She caught me off balance. I was prepared to say, "Good afternoon," and I said, "Well, yes . . . I . . ."

"I have a mean dog," she warned. "He's trained to keep kids off my lawn. You better keep yours off. If I had one wish, I'd wish that I could push a button and destroy every kid on the face of the earth!" She looked malevolently at my stomach and turned away, jerking her spray of water fiercely as she walked.

But by his special magic, Papa made her his friend. She would see him on the porch and come over to it, carrying a huge orange, or a banana, or a bag of fresh macaroons. And once, she bore down on me with a plate of strawberry shortcake.

"This is for the old man," she said. "Tell him I sent it over to him. You can set the plate on the porch when he's through. And don't give any of this to your kids, either!"

Somehow, I couldn't be angry at her. I thanked her but she was already sailing away and probably didn't hear me. Something about the thrust of her arm as she forced the dish at me made me know that she really liked Papa.

Although Papa had recovered from his spring illness, he still had some bad headaches. Aspirin didn't help at all, so the doctor sent out a prescription for him. Mostly, Papa shied away from any sort of pill, but one day when the headache was particularly severe, he was driven to take a couple of the tablets. The headache disappeared. The next day it returned and during the day he took the prescribed dosage to ease it. That evening when the pain had subsided, he called me into his bedroom.

"I know I'm seeing things," he said, "or I think I am, but it looks like water is running down that wall."

"No, Papa," I reassured him, "the wall is dry as a bone."

He felt well enough to get up and have dinner at the table,

but after dinner he went back to lie down again. He thumped his cane on the floor, a signal we'd devised without discussing it, and I went into the bedroom to see what he wanted.

"Am I still seeing things? There are millions of bugs crawling down the wall where the water was!" I went over to the wall and put my hands on it.

"No bugs, Papa. If you were a drinking man, I'd say you were getting a case of DT's. I think you'd better take another pill and get some sleep. Your headache is probably affecting your eyesight. You'll be all right tomorrow."

But tomorrow he was not all right. Tomorrow was a nightmare. It seems terribly sad to me that as dear as Papa was and as kind and loving, the many times he'd sung and rocked and played with my girls have gone from their memories. But they remember with great clarity the dramatic happenings that came after the bugs swarmed down the walls.

It began when he got dressed the next morning. He ate breakfast silently and then went and sat in the front room. I noticed that he was picking at his trousers and moving his hands as if he were winding yarn.

"What are you doing, Papa?"

"It's this damn wool. Some of Ma's skeins are tangled all over my legs!"

"There's nothing on your pants, Papa." He gave me a look of utter disdain—his "stupid woman" look. "Come out into the sunshine. It's a lovely day." I led him out and seated him in the rocking chair and went in to finish the breakfast dishes. When I looked out to check on him, he was halfway down the street, gesticulating frantically. I ran after him, with my dishtowel still in my hand.

"Papa, where are you going!"

"Those men that just passed. One of them dropped his arms on the sidewalk. I'm taking them to him!" There were no men, but it did no good to tell him so.

"I'll take them to the men. You come back in the house. It's too much for you to run like this." He came back docilely enough. I locked the screen and settled him on the couch with his Bible. I brought some sewing and sat with him. He read to me and seemed quite normal, though he read more loudly and rapidly than usual and would not lie down as I urged him to do.

Sally and Ann came home and I explained to them that I would need their help. Papa was not well and sometimes illness made old people act oddly. Sally was to tend Barbara and Ann was to watch Grandpa. If he wanted to go outside or began to act oddly, they were to call me. I went downstairs to put my delayed wash into the water, and then I heard them screaming for me, and there was a great thumping above my head. I dashed upstairs to find that Papa had grabbed the kettle of macaroni I was boiling for a supper casserole and had thrown it on the living room rug. He was stamping about in the mess. Sally was holding Barbara protectively on her lap, and all three were watching with great interest.

"He thinks the carpet's on fire," Ann explained.

"He grabbed the macaroni before we knew where he was going. We thought he was going to the bathroom."

"Here, Papa, you sit down. I'll put the fire out." He sat down while I cleaned the carpet. He was calm enough except for picking lint off his trousers all the while I cooked dinner.

At the table he picked at the food in front of him, which was rare. Papa usually ate heartily. After the meal, Papa seemed quite ready to go to bed. I tucked him in a little later than the children. Weary and worried, I called the doctor.

"Things like this happen," he said. "It comes along with old age. Often they get violent—does he show any signs of this?"

"No. It's just that he really thought the rug was on fire. He's fine when he reads or talks about religion or news or anything. It's just the hallucinations—and they make him so active!"

"Well, if he gets worse, call me, and I'll come out."

Papa was sleeping quietly when I went in to check on him before going to bed. His breath came puffing softly through his mustache. I looked at him with the same feeling that I had when I tucked in my sleeping children. I thought about the different kinds of love I'd had for him. It was a sort of maternal love now. I didn't think his love for me had changed at all; I would probably always be a child to him—and from time to time, he made it plain that he thought I was a recalcitrant one.

About midnight I heard his cane thump, and I hurried into his bedroom. It was dark and he was crouched in a corner.

"Where's the damn bathroom!" he was cross with me. "What's the use of building these dang newfangled bathrooms if a man can't find them?" I led him into the bathroom.

"Do you need some help, Papa?"

"When I can't go to the toilet by myself, then I'm better off dead!" He slammed the door, disgusted with my concern. I felt sorry for him; he was certainly not himself. But it had a funny side, and I stood outside the door waiting for him and chuckling a little.

Papa didn't go back to sleep. The minute I turned the light off, he reached for his cane and made a wide swipe above his bed, knocking the lamp off the night table.

"Get those damn birds out of here!" he yelled. We chased the birds out of the bedroom and I righted the lamp. I knew that I couldn't leave him alone, so I pulled the chair close to his bed and held his hand and patted it while he stared off into space or dozed a little. Fortunately, he went to sleep about six and slept soundly, long enough for me to get breakfast, bathe and feed Barbara, and do a few of the necessary chores.

When Papa woke up he was in an alien world. He seemed to know me when I demanded his attention, but he was in a talkative frenzy. He stayed in bed. He seemed bewildered by my attentions and refused breakfast, then his wildness increased.

He took the books from his bedside table and threw them at the bugs that were crawling down the walls again.

Sally and Ann helped me and we moved everything out of the room except his bed, the chest of drawers, and the rocking chair. I phoned the doctor again, and he came out to the house after dinner. Papa still refused to eat; he pushed the food from the tray and knocked my hand away when I tried to feed him, telling me that this was no time for such nonsense.

"There's only one thing you can do," the doctor told me. "You have to commit him."

"Commit Papa!"

"Evidently he's had some brain damage from his last stroke or from a subsequent one you haven't noticed. Maybe it happened during the night before this came on. I don't know how long it will last—maybe until he dies. But I do know that you can't handle this, not when you have a family and your baby. Don't worry about it. I'll make the arrangements."

"No," I said firmly. "No. You don't know how long this is going to last, so I'll take care of him. I promised him once that I'd never send him to a hospital. He has a horror of them."

"That's nonsense. You have your family. It's impossible."

"Well," I said, and my tone must have carried finality, "then I'll take care of him just as long as I can. It would kill him to come to himself in an asylum, and I won't have that. When I can't manage any longer, I'll call you."

That night, a terribly hot August night, Papa was restless and rambling. I opened the windows wide to allow a bit of a breeze to come into the bedroom, but Papa would raise his voice and start preaching and shouting, and I would have to lower the windows to keep from disturbing Les Galleon, who had called the police more than once for less disturbance.

I had moved a camp cot into the bedroom, and I was tired, so I lay down during the periods when Papa was quieter. After midnight, he became uncontrollable. He started shouting. Les

Galleon's light went on, but I could do no more than keep the windows shut and the blinds down.

Papa struggled to stand up in the middle of his bed. He held his hands out in front of him as if he were driving a team. He *was* driving a team! And then the words he was yelling began to be coherent.

At first I tried to get him to lie down again, but I could understand that you *can't* drive a team lying flat on your back, so I sat on my cot and watched him. His lean shanks were covered by the bagging bulges of two pairs of underwear. His striped shirt flapped loosely around his hips and his shirt cuffs were neatly buttoned and his bowtie in place. His white hair was awry and the old, blue-veined feet found difficult purchase on the shifting bedsprings, but it wasn't so frightening to watch him now because I knew what he was doing.

Somehow the team, Maud and Dick, had gotten stuck in a mudhole, while Papa was hauling a load of manure to some farmer. I didn't know until later just where we were, but I knew that we were stuck with Maud and Dick and the manure, so there was nothing to do but wait and let Papa try to get us out of the mud.

"Get up, you lazy son of a bitch," shouted Papa, smacking the reins on Dick's rump. At that, Les Galleon's lights went on again. I'd put up the window for a few moments for it was sweltering in the canyon. I pulled the window back down.

"Maud, you damned fool, get over there. If you don't get over there, I'm going to ram this pitchfork right up your rear end. GET OVER THERE!" Papa swayed back and forth on the wagon, slipping around, losing his footing. Once he fell and swore mightily at the horses. His language was a revelation to me. I'd never heard my grandfather swear in the house, but I'd heard him swear at the cows in the corral. It had been very effective with the cows, but this night Maud and Dick paid no attention to him.

I watched the old man teeter on the bed and listened to him swear and slid the window up and down for air. I wondered about my brave words to the doctor. How much of this violence would his aged body endure—and how much more could I stand? I started to cry and with the tears rolling down my face, I went over to the bed, reached up, and jerked his sleeve to pull his attention from the team.

"Papa, Papa!" I had to shout over the din he was making. "Papa," I screamed, "listen to me!" He let the reins go slack and looked down at me.

"What do *you* want, girl?"

"Oh, Papa," I said, sobbing, "I'm so tired and scared, and I haven't had any sleep for two nights. Please, please lie down and let me get some rest."

Papa looked down at me, plainly affronted at my interruption, but he saw the tears on my face.

"Don't cry, girl," he said comfortingly. Then with resigned disgust, "Get me a blanket to pull over me, and I'll lie right down here on this load of manure."

He sat down and smoothed out a place in the bed and then lay down, allowing me to cover him. He patted my hand as I tucked him in. I opened the windows and as the refreshing mountain air of pre-dawn Salt Lake City flowed into the room, I lay down on my cot and immediately went to sleep. When I awoke, hearing my husband and children coming upstairs from the cool basement bedrooms where we slept in summer, I saw Papa looking at me with a half-humorous, half-wondering look in his eyes. I went over to his bed and put my hand on his cheek.

"I had the dangdest dream last night," he said in his gentle, normal tones. "I dreamed I was hauling a load of manure down Provo Canyon and got stuck in the mud on that short, sharp curve above Vivien Park. The danged horses floundered around —it was an awful mess. Like to wore me plumb out."

"Yes," I said, "it like to wore me out, too!"

"Yeh. That's what I been wondering about. How come *you* were riding on top of that load of manure with me?"

Well, it was a wild ride, but I'm glad I went on it. For Papa was recovered when he woke up, and though the doctor thought such aberrations might occur again, they never did. I was thankful again and again that I hadn't allowed the doctor to take him to a hospital. And later the doctor told me that all of it might have been induced by the drugs he'd given Papa for his headaches. For one so unused to drugs, they could have had an untoward effect and stimulated instead of tranquilized.

That morning when I went out to get the milk and the paper, Les Galleon was waiting for me on her porch. She was already dressed for work in one of the expensive suits she always wore to the bank. She scudded across the damp grass.

"How is your grandfather?"

"He seems to be okay this morning. I'm sorry that we disturbed you. I simply couldn't keep him quiet." I was almost on the verge of tears again.

"Oh," she hurried, "that was fine—fine. I kept turning my light on to let you know that I was awake and that if you needed any help with the old man, I was there." She hit me on the shoulder what was meant to be a pat, I'm sure, and left, full sail ahead.

Papa seemed to recover completely. Since the death of my grandmother in 1941, Papa had spent summers in Heber and winters in California with Dora and Ann, his daughters. He continued his schedule for two more years, and during those years, Aunt Tressa—my husband's aunt by blood, but mine by choice and love—came to live with us while her son was away on a mission for the Church. I liked having Aunt Tressa. I learned a great many things from her. She showed me what herbs could do for food. She introduced me to bay leaves and basil, to rosemary and chives and savory. She was "Grandma"

to Barbara, the only one she would have for very long. As soon
as Barb could negotiate the steep stairs by crawling down
them backwards, she would come to "bisit."

"Have you anything to feed?" she would announce herself.
Aunt Tressa would give her tastes of cottage cheese and yogurt.
She introduced Barb to spinach and broccoli and a variety of
other foods that most children have to learn to enjoy by force.
I have always attributed my youngest's superb health partly to
Papa's christening "blessing" and partly to Aunt Tressa's vita-
min-loaded tidbits.

Mormonism produces some remarkably capable women, and
Aunt Tressa was one of them. Her husband had committed suicide in the early 1930's, leaving her with a mortgaged farm, a
large house, and two young sons, one of them an adopted
relative, the other just beginning school. She had been extraor-
dinarily resourceful, I thought. She leased her farm, rented
the big house, built a compact cinderbrick home for herself
and her two boys, and with the minimal income from her
leases and rents, she cared for and educated her two sons and
paid for her farm.

Once, when the money from the farm wouldn't stretch, she
went to the local banker and alternately bullied and shamed him
into lending her the money for the elder boy's college tuition.
(One of her boys is now a Ph.D. who teaches in an Idaho
university, while the other is a nuclear physicist.) When her
sons were educated, she sold the small house and gratefully
moved back to her big house, but she was there for only a short
while when young Ben was "called" on a mission. She again
rented the house, using this money to help him pay for his
mission, and moved from Idaho to Utah to live with us for the
two years that he would be gone.

Aunt Tressa seemed anything but self-sacrificing, and yet
now I know she was. I hope I made her feel welcome and
loved, for that's what she was. However, she was like all the

rest of my well-meaning relatives. Although she tried to be tactful, she could not help pointing out all of the marvelous opportunities I was missing by not going to Church—especially to the Relief Society meetings.

"Only come with me to Relief Society," she'd say. "You can learn so much. They quilt, they make things, they share wonderful recipes. You'd love the literature lessons."

"Not this time," I'd say, and she'd shake her head with regret at my resistance.

I was quite busy enough, I thought, with my three small daughters, sewing, books, music, friends and neighbors, and the great many visitors who still found it convenient to call on us and to incidentally ask me, "What are you doing in the Church now?"

The two years of her stay went by swiftly for everyone except Aunt Tressa. She went to Church every Sunday and took the older girls along. With planning, I managed to escape going at all. My husband golfed, so on the leisurely, lovely Sunday mornings, I had the house to myself, except for Barb who quietly entertained herself for hours. I bathed without someone in distress pounding on the bathroom door. I played solitaire, or most often, I stretched out on the couch with pillows at my back and read. Then Aunt Tressa came home, tied on an apron, and helped with dinner and the dishes. She would not break the Sabbath with knitting or crocheting, and her Mormon woman's hands, trained to be busy even when she relaxed, were restless. She fidgeted until the time to get ready for Sacrament Meeting. (Sacrament Meeting is the only meeting that Mormons are commanded to attend. You are only *required* to go to all the rest of them.) The house was quiet and peaceful. Barbara went to bed early and the girls played or worked on their lessons. It was truly a day of rest, and I'm glad that I was properly thankful for those days, for there were no more of them after Aunt Tressa left.

Ben came home and Aunt Tressa went back to Idaho and her big house. I moved Sally and Ann into the large room she had vacated, redecorated the small upstairs room with blue, flowered wallpaper and white ruffles for Barbara, and hoped that the single spare bedroom would deter the double-couple and family group visitors.

Chapter 2

IN THE PRESENCE
OF THE PRIESTHOOD

Two weeks after Aunt Tressa left, Papa had his
ninetieth birthday, and we knew that he was much too frail to
spend any more time by himself, or even to travel farther than
a Sunday afternoon ride.

He had to close up his beloved home in Heber City and spend
the rest of his time on earth with the three of his daughters who
lived in Salt Lake City: Zoa, Zola, and me. (I was a daughter
by legal adoption.)

Papa at ninety was a wonderful old man, sprightly and cheerful, clean as few really old men are clean. He was alert about
the past and the things of the present that interested him, such

as prize fights and politics, and he was learned and enthusiastic about everything that concerned the Church.

When Papa came I moved Barbara's small-girl furnishings into the yellow bedroom downstairs and put Papa in her dainty bedroom, furnished now with a single bed, a small chest of drawers (it is amazing how few clothes an old man needs), an ample bookcase, a table, and the rocking chair I used to rock Barbara in after my boarders had accustomed her to going to sleep that way. (Accustomed isn't quite the word. They *forced* her to allow them to rock her to sleep. At first, she had struggled, but finally she had succumbed to their desires to hold their own children, and then she loved it. It was fine while they were there, but they had left me with a baby who had been a marvelous seven-o'clock-turn-out-the-light-and-go-to-sleeper who refused to shut an eye unless it was rocked!)

I could not put Papa downstairs, not because of any difficulty he might have had going up and down the steps, but because he could not orient himself to my house. He had lived nearly seventy years in his home in Heber and he constantly tried to fit the floor plan of my house to his own, an obsession that was troublesome for both of us. It made it impossible for me to leave him alone, and my errands, or even the laundry, had to wait until Sally and Ann were home to take turns watching Grandpa.

Four-year-old Barbara would take his hand and walk with him around and around the block. They were both warned not to cross the street, and when his old feet would have confusedly wandered across the quiet, residential streets, she would adamantly stand on the curb.

"No, Grandpa! We have to go *this* way. Mama says not to cross the street, or she'll spank me!" He loved to walk, and she loved to go with him. They knew every neighbor and shrub and bush around the block, and they were quite willing to stop at the corner grocery for me. While Barbara gave the grocery list and the money to the clerk, Papa would visit with the butcher, a Catholic, who had lived among missionary Mormons so long that he parried Papa's obvious attempts to "talk religion" with amiable skill.

"Fine feller, that meat man," Papa would say. "Some day he'll see the light." He was not so sure about me.

"I just didn't have enough time with you when you were a child," he deplored, "but surely a woman of your intelligence could see the truth of things by now—if she was ever going to!" He seemed to be afraid that he'd never see me in the Celestial Kingdom with the rest of his family. But he loved me, despite my backsliding in his "marvelous work and wonder" of Mormonism.

It was a rare occasion that brought forth any verbal assurance of his love. Once, only three weeks before he died, something I did or said brought it to the surface, and I prize those words.

"You're a daughter to me," he said. "You're as much my own as the twins, or Dora or Ann, and I thank the Lord for every one of you. You've all been good daughters. Not one of you has ever lifted a lip to me. Not a cross word . . ."

"Why, Papa, we wouldn't dare!" I said, and laughed with him at my vehement response.

Papa died at nine o'clock on October 31st of his third year in Salt Lake City. The neighborhood children had been ringing the doorbell since seven for their Halloween treats. I could see the disappointment on their faces when they only received the treats, for they loved to come and perform for old Mr. Hicken, who delighted so much in what each child would do. Papa found a special talent in each small visitor and was always amazed at the originality of the costume of a three-foot ghost. His white mustache would bob and his violet-blue eyes would twinkle, and when the children were through, he passed out the treats with such zestful largesse that more than one child wondered.

"Are you sure you're not Santa Claus?" a four-year old once asked him.

"No, son, I'm afeared not."

"You sure do look like him, 'cept not so fat."

It was from Papa that I inherited my love for holidays and, except during the Plague years, for visitors. He had always enjoyed Halloween better than Christmas because he loved the children.

"You have to get old before you can understand how wonderful the children are," he told me again and again. And now that I'm past the halfway mark in life I know what he meant. I know what he meant about many other things, too, because it was only after he died that I finally comprehended most of the things he'd been saying to me since I was seven years old.

It was a long and difficult day. Papa, bored if he wasn't busy, had been making a cane for me. He had selected a sturdy tree branch with a crook at one end, a natural handgrip, and then he had pared and scraped and polished until it was as smooth as bone.

"You don't need it now, my girl," he'd said, "but the day'll come."

He'd made several canes for his friends and members of his family, and he always walked with his eye trained to see the likely twist of a handle in a branch whose cutting would not harm the tree. Mine was the last cane he made. That morning, he brought it from the porch, holding it carefully by the tip so as not to mar the final coat of varnish. I thought he looked weary, although it was not yet nine-thirty.

"Here," he said, "it's done. Put it away so the children won't scratch it up."

"Come on, Papa," I coaxed, "why don't you lie down until the girls come home for lunch. You've been up since six working on this."

"Beautiful morning. Everyone oughta get up early. Folks miss half their lives just lyin' in bed. You'd never know this was the 31st of October, girl. Seems like summer out."

I guided him into his bedroom because he seemed so frail, and knelt to unlace his high, black shoes.

"Beautiful," he said, looking out at the fall-flamed trees in the back yard. "Just beautiful."

Then he jerked and fell back on the bed, and I saw his face lose expression and his eyes become unseeing. He jerked and shuddered once or twice more and awkwardly toppled sideways across the bed.

After I graduated from high school, I had gone to nursing school, and now, as in other such emergencies, this training helped me. I knew he'd had a stroke—he'd had others, very mild ones, in the past five years.

I pulled him around straight on the bed, removed his coat and the carefully buttoned vest. It seemed to me that his bones must have shrunk, for the weak arms were once so strong that he could lift a heavy tree onto the wagon bed without help. I worked the bedclothes from under him and pulled off his trousers. As I did, I thought of Ham discovering Noah as the old man lay drunk and naked in his tent and of the curse that Noah put upon his son when he sobered. And amid the fearful anxiety that I was trying to control, I had to smile.

There was no fear of exposing Papa! Next to his body, he wore the long-legged, long-sleeved, high-necked, and round-collared garment of the Priesthood, the old-time style of the garment which is now only worn in death and in the Temple ceremonies, and by the last remnant of the aged and piously devout Latter-day Saints. Over these he wore a pair of knitted "drawers," woolen in winter, heavy cotton in summer. I did not remove his shirt or his bowtie, knowing that they hung loosely about his wrinkled neck. Besides, I'd never seen Papa without his shirt and tie, even in bed. (He had not removed them at night since his young manhood when he was called out at all hours to administer to the sick and had found that getting completely dressed took too much valuable time. Now he wore them as a matter of long-fixed habit.) I remembered once when I had been crying in the night with an earache and he came into my small bedroom, his bony, veined feet bare on the cold linoleum. He was in his seventies then.

"What are you cryin' for, girl?"

"I have an earache."

"Bad?"

"Oh, yes."

"Here, now," he said, "we'll fix that." He touched the top of my head with a drop of "consecrated" oil from the small bottle that he'd carried into the room with him, and placed his hands firmly on my head and closed his eyes. Standing there with the heavy drawers bagging down his skinny hips and legs, his bluestriped shirt-tail hanging loosely, his collar starched stiff enough to withstand sleeping in it, and the black, silk bowtie moving gently over his knobbed and wrinkled Adam's apple, he administered to me—blessed me, so that I would be free of pain. He'd closed his eyes as he talked confidently to his Lord, but I opened mine to watch him. I did not see anything at all ridiculous about his attire. The enveloping warmth of his voice and hands spread slowly down and through me. I was asleep before he left the room—at least I do not remember him leaving.

When he looked comfortable in the bed, his limbs straightened, his head supported by the pillow, I called the doctor. Papa's eyes were still glazed, but his breathing and pulse were good.

"Make him comfortable and keep him quiet," the doctor told me. "I'll be out as soon as I can." When I went back to the bedroom, Papa recognized me and tried to speak. There was apprehension in his eyes.

"Keep quiet, Papa," I said. "You've had a little spell. I've called the doctor, and now that you're all right again, I'm going to call Zoa and Zola. Do you want anything?"

He shook his head and looked around the bright bedroom.

"It's a damn shame," he said.

"What's a shame?"

"That I have to die here." And I knew what he meant, just as I knew it would be futile to try to comfort him with untruths. He meant that he wanted to die in his own home where he had lived with my grandmother for over sixty years. He wanted to die in his beautiful Heber Valley where his father had died and where he had been born, where Mama had died and where his sons, one of them my father, and daughters were laid down.

"Oh, Papa," I said, and I tried to put the comfort into tones that I could not put into words, "this isn't such a bad place."

I followed his eyes around the little room, papered with small, blue flowers, carpeted in soft blue, curtained with white criss-crossed, organdy ruffles.

"It isn't very masculine, I'll admit, but it's clean and sunny, and the bed is good." He looked at me from beneath eye sockets, suddenly sharp and protruding. "Well, it isn't Mama's feather tick, either, but you're comfortable, aren't you? You have your books . . ." I patted the stack on his bedside table. It really was his bedside table. Since his marriage it had stood at his side of the five-foot-high headboard of the bed that he and Mama had shared. Square-topped, spool-legged, and double-decked, it held many of his beloved Church books.

"Well, now," he said with resignation, "now, I'm going to find out." He looked at the books meaningfully.

"What?"

"If it's all true." His voice was faint. It was difficult for him to speak. So Papa had doubts, too. I never thought he had!

"Oh, Papa," I scolded him, "don't you get any funny ideas —you've had these spells before. You're not going to die—not yet." But as I said it, I knew that he was, maybe not this minute, but there were perhaps only hours left.

Then as I watched him, his body arched and his stiffening spine forced his head deep into the pillows. He was having another seizure and this one was obviously worse than the first. I held his hands until it was over. Afterward, he could no longer speak or control his bowels.

"I'll have to change your clothes, Papa. Now don't worry about it!" But his eyes were filled with mortification and his thoughts came to me clearly as I worked over him.

"Hell, this is *worse* than dyin'!"

BEFORE MAMA DIED, she had been bedfast for a year with a broken hip. Because of her age and physical condition, the doctor did not recommend surgical pinning of the hip, so we immobilized it with sandbags, and we rubbed and turned her for a year to avoid bedsores.

Mama's bed bath was an ordeal for her. Even though we used a bath blanket and a towel to greatest advantage, she complained of the indignities. It is hard to understand this unless you realize that Mama was the true Victorian-age Mormon. The only time she was completely unclothed was in the tub, and I have my doubts about that.

Toward the end of her year in bed, she became incontinent and it was at this time that Papa performed for her one of the most tender services of their more than sixty years of closely woven understanding.

I was glad that Mama was saved the mortification of knowing that she had to wear the large diapers that are specially made for the aged incontinent. For by this time her lucid flashes were few except when Papa sat with her; she seemed unaware, mostly, of the care that we gave her. But Papa knew that she wore diapers, and he would rise very early in the morning, knowing that she would be wet and soiled. He would remove the diaper, dispose of the big pads inside it, and place clean ones for her. Then he would wash the reusable diaper outside in a tub that he had set upon two sawhorses. This particularly unpleasant task was seldom required at any other time of the day.

We took turns taking care of Mama. In succession, Dora and Ann came from California for two months each. Bessie came down from Idaho, and I went up from Salt Lake City, taking Sally and Ann, not much more than babies, with me. Zoa and Zola went up, taking their turn together, and Helen Hicken, my Uncle Rodney's wife, who lived on Papa's block, took care of Mama between our stints.

I had been home a couple of days before I realized what Papa was doing.

"Papa," I said as soon as I knew, "I'll do that. I don't mind at all." I was doubly shocked because I was aware of Papa's fastidious modesty.

He raised his shaggy, white eyebrows and looked at me with his deepset violet-blue eyes.

"But Kate minds *your* doing it *for* her—or she would if she knew that you were. And I would rather do it than have you do it. There's little enough I can do for her any more, and it isn't like you think it is. She's part of me, like my own flesh." He looked at me pityingly. "If you can imagine sixty years of living with someone you love, then you'd know what I mean."

"I know, Papa, but still . . ."

"That's enough. We'll speak of it no more."

Now as i cleansed and changed his bed, I knew a little of what he meant. But as I thought over what little I really knew of their lives together, I thought that in all the many ways Papa had shown his love for Mama, it seemed to me that the last way he showed it was his greatest act of devotion.

My back was beginning to ache from the bending and lifting over the low bed, so I ran downstairs, got four large, empty coffee cans from the storeroom, and hurriedly filled them with sand from Barbara's sandpile. I'd used them before when Sally had had her appendix out. I put them under the four feet of Papa's bed. Now it was hospital height, and I could work more easily. The linen was clean, and Papa was wearing a fresh, striped shirt and a new, black bowtie when the doctor came.

"You've gone to a lot of work, young lady," he said noticing the coffee-can bedlifts, "but we're going to have to hospitalize him."

"Can they do anything for him there that I can't?"

"Probably not as much, but they can do it more easily. He's not going to get over *this*," he smiled at me, remembering the other time when he had told me that. "He may be ill for days, maybe weeks. He has a strong heart and a remarkable body for his age, but he'll be bedfast as long as he does live. Let me call an ambulance."

"Let's wait awhile. I'm sure that he knows what's going on. He blinks his eyes when I ask him to."

"Well," the doctor was doubtful, "if you change your mind, call me. This could be a long vigil."

It was not a long vigil. Papa died that night.

My twin aunts came soon after the doctor left, and while they sat with Papa, I called the rest of his children. The doctor had suggested that I should. My Uncle Ward in Heber said that he would be down, but it would be a few hours. My aunts in California said that they would take the next plane home, and that they would call the rest of the family.

It was Halloween and I did not want the children to connect

this skeleton rattling holiday with death. I called Mickey Aloia across the street and asked her if the children could stay there until I came for them.

"Of course," she said, "I'll watch for them when they come home from school. I'll give them dinner, and I'll come and get their costumes. There's no need for them to miss Halloween is there? I'll just tell them that Papa Hicken is ill and that it will be better for them to spend the evening with us. They can spend the night too . . . ?"

"No. Thanks, Mickey," I said. "I'll come for them when it's bedtime. I think I want them here."

My husband came home and I gave him dinner from the several dishes that the neighbors had sent in when the word about Papa got around, swiftly, as such news always does.

Toward evening my uncle came from Heber and went in to see Papa. The doorbell began to ring—the children, the Halloweeners.

And then Uncle Billy came—Aunt Zola's husband. I went with him into the bedroom. It had become very difficult for the twins to watch the convulsions that came on Papa more and more frequently as the day wore on. They were talking with Ward and my husband in the living room and serving the trick-or-treaters. Uncle Billy took Papa's hands in his.

"Now, what's all this?" he asked, his voice strong and cheering. Papa opened his eyes and looked at Uncle Bill, and I read his thoughts again.

"Billy holds the Priesthood. I will die in the presence of the Priesthood." And he died. The color washed from his high forehead, down his cheeks, over his chin and throat, and downward out of his hands, leaving his skin faintly yellow. In an instant it was over. And for that instant there was such a feeling of relief in the house that it was almost palpable.

Papa looked so much at peace that I was peaceful, too.

While the others wept and spoke their love for him into his unheeding ears, I didn't cry. I tidied the house, and listened to Ward call the undertaker in Heber.

I gathered my children from Mickey. Barbara was asleep, and I carried her, already in pajamas (bless Mickey Aloia), across the street without waking her.

"Is Papa dead?" Ann asked. I had dreaded this. I could not have borne their tears, for I had no comfort to offer anyone.

"Yes. I want you to be good girls and go right to bed." Sally was big-eyed, but like Ann, calm and tearless. I went in to kiss them goodnight, and they hugged me hard to comfort me wordlessly.

"Oh, dear," I said, letting my grief show, "I don't know how I'm going to tell Barbara. She loved Papa so. I don't know how to explain it . . ."

There was nothing more to do except to wait for the undertaker to come from Heber. My husband rose from his chair and said goodnight to my aunts and uncles.

"I have to work tomorrow. I'm going to bed now." I watched him leave the room. He had always hated clutter, and whenever possible he avoided it. He avoided it now.

I visited quietly with my relatives while we waited for the hearse to come down from Heber. We reminisced some, and even laughed a little—for you could hardly reminisce about Papa without laughing. I told them the stories that Elisha Hicken and Dee Broadbent had told me recently.

"Lishe said he was working with Papa on a road crew when he was a kid, and the men were profaning and telling dirty jokes. 'Uncle Dave came over to me and said, "C'mon, Lishe, you work over here with me a spell," and he took me up the road a piece and worked the heck out of me. You know Uncle Dave, he always went like a house afire.' Dee Broadbent heard Lishe telling me and he laughed harder at the story than I did. Then he explained why. 'Uncle Dave did the same thing with

me. It was when he was marshal of Heber. He was foreman of
a road crew then, too. I was about sixteen, my first job. One
day it rained so hard that the men had to quit work. They
went into the tent and were drinking coffee and talking about
things I'd never heard mentioned before. Very interesting
things, I thought. But Uncle Dave made me put on my coat
and go out with him. The two of us worked all day in the rain!
I was sore at him for years for making me work in the rain
while the others laid off. Then one day, when I had a son of
my own, I realized that Uncle Dave hadn't enjoyed working in
the rain any more than I had! ' "

It was a typical Dave Hicken story, and I sat there wondering
how many other young ears Papa had protected.

It wasn't until Bishop Olpin, the Heber undertaker, came to
take Papa out of my house that my loss suddenly tore me apart.
I hung onto the kitchen sink to keep from holding onto Papa
as they trundled him past me. And then Uncle Billy, whom I
had really not known well, held out his arms and pressed my
head against his shoulder with a hand that felt almost like Papa's.
I was surprised by the consolation it gave me, and I discovered
in my grief what millions of women know—there is nothing so
comforting to a woman as a strong, male shoulder.

"Thanks," I said after a while. I was a little embarrassed.
"What would I have done if I'd been alone!"

And yet, I knew that now I was.

When the children came upstairs the next morning, I found
that my additional burden of sōrrow for Barbara's loss was un-
necessary. Papa had prepared her.

"Ann told me that Grandpa died last night," she said
brightly. "Isn't that nice! Now he won't be lonesun any more.
Don't feel mad, Mama," she pleaded, and she quoted Papa, I
knew, "All of his friends were on the other side. It was awfully
lonesun for him here."

Papa's daughters arrived from California and Idaho, and we

opened up his house and brought him home to sleep in it for the last time.

I managed to get through the viewing and the funeral and the subsequent arrangements without breaking down into the spectacle of grief which so many people go to funerals to witness. But even after he was buried, when the "healing process" is supposed to start, I carried a load of bereavement that felt like a physical weight. Loved though he was by his family and friends, few of them could have understood my grief, for the time had come to let him go. He was an old man, frail, ill, and terribly restless after his eyes began to fail and he could not find enough things to do to fill the long days. It was a miserable sentence of boredom that he lived under. He had no contemporaries to talk to, and though once he had told me, "You're really not so bad to talk to for a woman," it was obvious that I was a poor substitute for the kind of conversation he craved. Occasionally, when I had seen old men walking alone down the sidewalk, I had inveigled them into coming up to the porch and "passing the time of day" with my grandfather. They were always quite obliging—I guess they felt the same needs he did—but there weren't many old men who walked down our street.

You have to live a word to understand it. Take the word "pregnant." No *man* could possibly understand that word—its heaviness, its discomfort, its misshapen fullness. There is as much fear in it as promise. Only a woman can know that word. I am sad that there are so many who will understand what I mean when I say that after Papa died, I lived "bereft."

The days after the funeral were terribly empty. Barbara was now in school all day. I had no drop-in company; all of them had been discouraged long ago. The neighbors came by, but their visits were brief although I coaxed them with coffee and cake to stay. I could not read, a chance Biblical phrasing in a paragraph would intensify the emptiness of the chair that Papa had sat in to read to me from his books while I ironed the end-less baskets of small girls' dresses. I had never realized how much religion permeates even atheistic books. It was hard for me to iron, for I missed the steady drone of his voice as he read passages that I knew by heart from hearing him read them over the years. I missed the arguments about religion, a continuation of arguments I'd had with him when I had lived with him.

" 'He that is tithed shall not be burned,' " he read.

"The Church has made a good thing out of that tithing bit," I said.

"It is only the Lord's just due for all that he gives you," Papa snapped the book shut, preparing for battle. "Why, if I hadn't paid tithing, I wouldn't have what I have today."

"You'd have 10 percent more. Over your period of life, it would be a tidy sum."

" 'Will a man rob God,' " Papa quoted, "yet ye have robbed me. But ye say, Wherein have we robbed thee? In tithes and offerings . . . Bring ye all the tithes into the store-house, that there may be meat in mine house and prove me now herewith, saith the Lord of hosts, if I will not open you the windows of heaven, and pour you out a blessing, that there shall not be room enough to receive it.' "

"Oh, Papa. When you take time to consider them, everyone has blessings. With Mormons, it's sort of an accounting. They pay out x many dollars, so they sit down and count up x many blessings. If they think the blessings are worth the money they've paid, well and good. If they can see that they are going in the hole, they still pay the tithing because they are afraid if they stop, they'll lose what little they have." He was impa-tient to interrupt me, but I raised my voice and kept the floor.

"I know people who've never paid a cent of tithing who have more of everything, health, wealth, and, apparently, happiness, than a lot of people I know that pay a full tithing—like the Church wants you to, before taxes, before expenses. They don't give you the benefit that the Internal Revenue people do—they want their 10 percent right off the top!"

" 'Your words have been stout against me,' " quoted Papa, with an aptness that always astonished me. " 'Ye have said, it is vain to serve God: and what profit is it that we have kept his ordinance, and that we have walked mournfully before the Lord of hosts? And now we call the proud happy; yea, they that work wickedness are set up; yea, they that tempt God are delivered.' "

"I'll admit that tithing may give the payer peace of mind, but it is a fragile peace, and it's all in their heads. And you can't deny that blessings to most Mormons means material things. It's in the hope of obtaining money, land, and goods that they're putting out their 10 percent. Mormons pay tithing as if they were paying on an insurance policy. It isn't that, it can't be. In this shaky world you can lose any of your blessings overnight!"

"Ah ha," said Papa, "but tithepayers don't."

"Oh yes they do. Look at the Ohlwiler family. Wendell went on a mission to the South Seas. He was gone an unconscionably long time. His mother only lived to see her son again, and he came home to find her in her coffin—dead of appendicitis. Now, he paid his tithing, she paid her tithing, the whole family paid a full tithing all of their lives, and on top of it, they'd just paid for their son's mission, besides his giving three years of his life to the Church. How do you account for all that?"

"Well," he was still grieved about Rhoda Ohlwiler, "she was as fine a woman as ever lived. I guess she was needed worse on the other side."

"Oh, Papa, who could possibly need Rhoda Ohlwiler worse than her husband, Johnny, with his poor, old broken back!"

"All this has nothing to do with tithing."

"But it has to do with blessings, and that's what the Church guarantees if you pay your tithing. Why, Papa, I've heard the Priesthood speakers guarantee blessings from the pulpit—absolutely—and I've also heard many a testimony bearer get up and say that when they can, they pay more than their 10 percent. In fact, in some Mormon communities, they vie to see who can pay the highest tithing, and it's not the ones who make the most money, either! I've seen the kids of some of those high tithepayers living pretty close to squalor, their folks didn't even have enough to afford the 10 percent without robbing their families!"

"Well, I've never believed in paying more than 10 percent. That's carrying things a little bit far—unless, of course, they don't have anything else to do with their money."

"Paying more than 10 percent is piggish, too. It seems selfish to buy more than your share of blessings, even if you can afford to, especially since it's obvious every day when you read the newspapers that there aren't enough blessings to go around!"

"You don't buy blessings," reproved Papa.

"That's what they're doing. If they thought they were going to be blessed anyway, how many of them would pay tithing at all, except that you have to pay it to get into the Temple. And if you can't get a Recommend to go to the Temple, you are automatically labeled: THIS MAN IS NOT A GOOD MAN!"

"You carry things too far, girl. There are many fine men who wouldn't be given a Temple Recommend."

"Because they drink liquor, or tea or coffee, and don't pay their tithing."

"Come, now. You know there are other things."

"Papa, you know in your heart that you think that smoking and drinking are sins. You think that in order to be a truly good man you must be tithed. These are the first priorities of the Church."

"Now, you know better than that."

"No Papa, I really don't know better than that. What other things are there that are preached about so much. Fornication? Adultery? Stealing? Lying? I know of girls, and so do you, who were married in the Temple who had normal babies in five and seven months. Not preemies, healthy babies, seven and eight pounders. Seems like the emphasis should be put on those things—and on the Golden Rule!"

"Things like fornication and adultery are hard to preach about. People get shocked when you preach about them. And I know that you've heard plenty of sermons about honesty and loving your neighbor, haven't you?"

"Some," I granted, reluctantly. "I haven't heard very many about honesty. I've heard a few about keeping oneself unspotted before the world and morally clean, and some came right out and said "chastity," but chastity needs defining for kids— not what it is but why it should be. Papa, do you know that I didn't realize that chastity meant not sleeping around until I was a grown girl, practically, and I wouldn't have learned that if I'd depended on the Church to tell me, even though it's supposed to be one of the most important commandments! Papa, have you heard what the men who were stationed out at Kearns said about Mormon girls?"

"No. I don't talk much to the men at Kearns."

"They say that Mormon girls won't smoke or drink or take the Lord's name in vain, but they sure know how to have fun!"

"That's a nasty thing to say, and it isn't true."

"I don't think so, either. Not for most of them, but it must be true for some of them, and if so it's because all they ever hear preached is the Word of Wisdom and the Law of Tithing. Out in the world, Papa, Mormons aren't known for their honesty or their clean living—they're known because they turn their coffee cups upside down when they attend a public banquet."

"I consider myself a good Mormon. Have you ever heard me tell a lie or be dishonest in any way?"

"Oh no, Papa. You're the best man I've ever known, and if all Mormons were like you, people would be flocking to join the Church in droves."

"I can name you a hundred that are better men than I am, and they are all Mormons."

"We're not talking about the good things in the Church today," I smiled at him, "we're talking about the bad. Papa, I truly think that all you really have to do to get a Temple Recommend is to be an accomplished liar. I know of one member of our family who drinks so much coffee she has a natural tan, and when she asked for a Recommend she got it without a bit of trouble. We all knew she drank it, and the Bishop knew she drank it, but she went. I was a little sick when Pete Isaacson took his wife through the Temple. And everybody else was so thrilled and pleased that they went. His aunt called me later, she was investigating the Church, you know. She was so mad. She said, and those were her words not mine, that if that son of a bitch could go through the Temple, it was no place she ever wanted to be!"

"Now, high judge, who are you to say that Pete didn't repent? I think that he did, and I was glad that he did, and glad for his little wife that their marriage could hold out some promise."

"Repent! Oh Papa, how do you repent of three illegitimate children by different mothers? How do you repent of seducing your brother's wife? How do you repent of stealing sheep from a widow? He was just what his aunt said he was."

"Now you stop right this minute, young woman," Papa would thunder. "Of course, there are the liars who go through the Temple, and the sin of the lie is on their heads, but there are thousands of fine, worthy people trying to live right, trying to do right. Eternal marriage in the Temple is the goal that

makes them what they are. The Church teachings aren't wrong
—it's the people who are!" By this time Papa would be pounding the floor with his cane to emphasize his points.

"YOU thump CAN'T thump JUDGE thump THE thump CHURCH
thump, thump BY thump THE thump, thump PEOPLE!" thump,
thump, thump.

"Then what can you judge it by? The people are the Church.
Without any members, it'd be a pile of useless script. It'd be
dead."

"It'll never be dead! The Church has been brought back to
the earth in this last dispensation through the authority of
Christ and the apostles, the true Church, the *only* true Church,"
and he would pound his cane and shake his bony finger at me.
"Woe unto the unbelievers . . ."

Our arguments always went like this and we argued every
phase and teaching of the Church from the Word of Wisdom
to not questioning or criticizing the actions of the Church
leaders. That last was always good for two or three hours of
shouting and arm swinging on Papa's part, and some good fast
ironing on mine.

"I don't believe in upholding the leaders of the Church
without question," I said.

"It is a commandment," Papa said.

"But I sometimes wonder about the interpretation of those
commandments. I have a friend who told me the other day that
she'd been asked to be president of the YWMIA* in her ward.
She asked her Bishop which man was going to be the Young
Men's Superintendent. And the Bishop told her.

" 'But I can't work with that man,' she said. 'You know,
Bishop, that he's a known philanderer. Besides that, he's lazy,
he never does his job well. He likes to take all the credit for

* Young Women's Mutual Improvement Association, also known as MIA or
Mutual.

things, but he won't carry his share of the load.' Do you know what the Bishop said, Papa?"

"How could I?"

"He said to her, 'Sister Anderson, how dare you say those things about Brother So and So. Don't you know that the blood of the Prophet flows in his veins!' Well, she wouldn't accept the position, but she said the Prophet's descendant became Superintendent and did just what she had known he would, and she felt the Bishop had known it, too."

"I don't believe if I'd been that Bishop that I would have taken that action."

"But he did, and according to him, Helma Anderson was the person in the wrong. I think that if the authorities are wrong, they should not be upheld or sustained. But even when the people know of wrongdoing, they're afraid to vote against them."

"You can disagree with them privately. It is just not your right to discuss it or publish it."

"Brigham Young said that you were *supposed* to question the authorities."

"Now just where did Brigham Young ever say that!"

"In his *Discourses*."

"I can't remember it."

I went into the bedroom to get the book. It took me a while to find the passage for I did not know exactly where to turn as Papa could so easily do.

"Here it is, page 135, Chapter XII. 'I am more afraid that this people have so much confidence in their leaders that they will not inquire for themselves of God whether they are led by Him. I am fearful they settle down in a state of blind self-security, trusting their eternal destiny in the hands of their leaders with a reckless confidence that in itself would thwart the purposes of God in their salvation . . .'"

"Yes, I've read that before. But that doesn't say that you can *criticize* the leaders of the Church."

"Well, it certainly does not mean that you should not question. And if you question and find them wanting, are you just supposed to keep your mouth shut? Papa, what if one day the Church leadership should fall into the hands of some very hard and egotistical men? These are powerful men and power is known to lead good men astray. And the prophecies say that in the last days 'even the very elect shall be deceived.' What if some of our leaders, the very elect, are deceived?"

"They won't be," Papa said positively. "The Lord has led us well and safely to this day. If, as you say, the leadership of the Church should falter in righteousness, then the Lord would depose them."

"How, Papa, when all the people vote the same way and they are so terribly afraid to criticize?"

"I don't know how, but I don't have to know. God will take care of his own! In the meantime, young woman, you leave matters that are God's to Him. You are treading a dangerous path when you criticize or disobey the authorities of the Church."

"And if I do? Then I'm on the way to apostasy, aren't I? It's a good way to eliminate all criticism, Papa. Apostate is the worst word in the Mormon dictionary, isn't it?"

"Hell, I don't know. I'm going to take a nap, woman." I followed him into his bedroom to see that he was properly covered against the sudden chills he sometimes had. I was contrite—perhaps I had been too harsh. But he arose from his nap ready and eager for another go 'round, armed with refutations from the Scriptures, girded up and eager for battle. Or, as he called it, to "talk religion."

Once a friend of mine called on me, walking unwarned into the fray. Her coming couldn't diminish the intensity of our battle for a few minutes, and then Papa got up and thumped his way into the bedroom.

"Oh, my dear," my friend said, aghast, "how *could* you talk to that dear old man that way? I thought you loved him!"

"I do love him," I laughed at her shock. "Papa's arguments about religion are his staff of life. I do it to keep him *alive!*"

"I don't see it."

And I guess it would be hard for anyone to understand unless one had lived with my grandfather as I had.

Chapter 3

PAPA AND
THE LIGHT

By the time I came to live with Papa and Mama as a child, my grandfather had already "filled" two missions for the Mormon Church and had taken upon himself a lifelong work of "bringing the light to those in darkness." Only, for Papa, it wasn't work. It was an exuberant joy—and such joyousness is almost impossible to withstand. To quote Papa, "The Devil has to stand right in front of a man all the time to keep him from the Faith, and even the Devil can't be everywhere at once." So if Papa met resistance in one quarter, he shifted his attack and focused on his original objective after he thought the Devil had moved on to tempt some other "poor soul" to waywardness.

Of course, there were a few who eluded him. There was my Uncle Harry, the husband of Zoa. After years of righteous confrontations, Uncle Harry put himself out of reach by joining the Masons. Papa took this blow with a headshake and a shrug. "Harry's a good man. The Prophet Joseph was once a Mason, and the Light came to him," he said hopefully; "it'll surely come to Harry." But Uncle Harry died fighting a fire in the Victory Theatre in Salt Lake City. The balcony collapsed suddenly, and he and two other firemen were burned to death in the cauldron of the fire hoses' steaming spray and the blazing timbers.

There was no viewing of his body, and that helped to dull the regret that Uncle Harry was not buried in Temple clothes. Aunt Zoa gave the undertaker his new brown suit and his shined shoes to lay in the casket with his body. I was a wondering child—suspicious is too strong a word for that time—and I wondered if the undertaker *did* put those clothes, that unworn suit, into the casket which had to be hermetically sealed before it could be brought into the chapel for services. But I guess thinking of the availability of the clothing to Uncle Harry's resurrected hand was a comfort to my modest aunt.

Anyway, after the Church's prescribed wait of a year, Zoa, to Papa's great satisfaction, had the Temple "work" (which included baptism for the dead, confirmation, ordination into the Priesthood, and Temple marriage) performed for her husband. And while Uncle Harry hadn't seen it here, Papa was positive that the Light was glowing for him in the next world. If it was, and Harry "accepted" the work, he would be entitled to wear the white robes of the "endowed," and then, I thought, it was surely a waste of a good, brown suit.

Papa's daughters were always active Church members, none of them giving him a minute's worry or trouble, but two of his sons-in-law were a challenge for a time. Uncle Billy finally stopped smoking, a habit he must have taken up after his Temple marriage to Zola (because this impurity would have stopped the issuance of his Temple Recommend) and he became "as fine a churchman as you'd want." For years Uncle Billy was ward clerk in his ward, and he compiled his family's genealogy so that their work could be done for them as it had been done for Uncle Harry. Papa was never personally interested in the keeping of records. His bent was to arm-swinging oratory. Nevertheless, he thought that Uncle Billy was doing the work of the Lord, for the Church teaches that "you cannot be saved without your dead."

My Aunt Dora's husband, Lloyd, of whom Papa was very fond, finally saw the Light as Papa had known he would, and overcame the weaknesses that conflicted with the teachings to become a pillar of the Church in California. The youngest daughter, Ann, didn't marry during his lifetime, thus depriving Papa of a possible target.

Papa's sons didn't give him the satisfaction that his daughters did. Two of them died in infancy "without mortal blemish," and two more of them died (one was my father) when they were very young men, thus placing their wives out of Papa's patriarchal jurisdiction. The remaining son, Ward, wandered around the world for twenty darkened years, returning just in time to bring pleasure to Papa's old age by marrying within the Church, producing a son to carry on the Hicken name, and, gradually, "embracing the gospel."

My grandfather, David William Hicken, was a regally proud man, but this pride was an eccentric one. The largest portion of it was "in having been born of *Mormon* parents in the beautiful Heber Valley situated high in the tops of the mountains of Zion," and of living his entire life in one place—most of it in one house. He was incredibly vain of his white, wavy pompadour, of reading without glasses, and at ninety, of still being able to stand on one leg while he shakily pushed the other one into his trousers.

"The mark of an old man," he told me scornfully, "is having to sit down to put his pants on."

Most of the people in Papa's beloved Heber City were active Mormons. There were a few who were backsliders or jack Mormons and even fewer nonmembers. Papa paid periodic calls on all of them. Strangely, active members, backsliders, and non-members welcomed his visits, for he enveloped them in a genial aura of love. He didn't love them as children of God or because all men were brothers; he possessed a singular, encompassing love for people: babies, boys, girls, the sick, the old, and the helpless, Saints, and gentiles. And although his visits were solidly rounded out with a good jolt of Mormon "Doctrine," he left them all feeling that they were people of worth and import.

I was seven when I came to live with Papa and Mama Hicken in their white, clapboard farmhouse. They were then in their late sixties, and they had already reared their own seven children and some extra ones besides: Bessie and Raymond Murdoch, Mama's niece and nephew, who were as much theirs as their own children, and another niece, Isabelle Hawkes. All three of them left Papa's home with enough of the Light to last their lifetimes, but Papa got them when they were babies. He had more difficulty with me. Once, he looked at me, the crease between his eyebrows so deep they almost met.

"Train up a child in the paths of righteousness until he is eight, and he will never depart therefrom," he said, more to himself than to me. "Well, we're a little late starting," he squeezed my shoulder briefly with his firm, hard hand. "Time isn't with us, but surely the Lord will be."

With his family grown and gone, his neighbors holding to the straight and narrow, and most of his traveling restricted to walking distances, Papa zeroed in on me. I was already going on eight, the age for baptism for Mormon children, and a lot of valuable time had been lost. He made an exception of the Biblical rule for me—he didn't stop at eight. He didn't stop ever.

Papa died in 1953, yet at intervals there is strange, personal evidence that Papa is still trying to get me to see the Light.

I was baptized in the cement font in the basement of the Seminary building which occupies the northeast corner of the high school block in Heber. I didn't feel any different after starting a clean page in my book of life, although my Sunday School teacher had assured me that I would. The baptismal font was about six by eight feet and held three feet of water. It had been sunk in a small, dark-walled room that smelled of warm mildew. A bare light bulb hung from a cord in the ceiling. It was a clear light bulb, but it had been there for a long time; the curling filaments inside it were dim.

I went first—no one demurred, the other children seemed more hesitant than I. I tested the water with my toe, found it pleasantly warm, and descended to my armpits in front of a young man, already standing in the water. His wet shirt somehow made him look miserable and embarrassed. I don't think that he really was, he shouldn't have been—he was a returned missionary.

I knew that if I didn't go under the water all the way the first time, they'd duck me again, so when he took my left hand in one of his and placed the other around my waist, I was watching for the moment to let myself go down. At the last, I grabbed my nose with my free hand, and came up with my wet hair in my eyes. There was an official observer by the font.

"It's good," he said, which meant that none of me had come out of the water when it shouldn't. I knew then what baptism by immersion meant, and I found it utterly devoid of beauty or dignity.

Nowadays, children wear little, white pajama suits or simple white clothing. When I was baptized I wore my old, brown bathing suit. I wondered about that suit. The other girls wore cotton dresses and underpants. The boys wore pants and shirts. None of them were white, just clean, and something the water wouldn't hurt. I wasn't embarrassed about wearing my bathing suit; it seemed eminently suitable, and I wondered why the other children hadn't worn them.

"What does it matter what you wear when you're baptized?" Papa asked me when I mentioned it to him. "John the Baptist wore the skin of an animal when he came in from the wilderness crying to Jesus for baptism."

"It doesn't show that in the picture in the Ward. It shows them both wearing long, white dresses, and a dove's about to light on their heads. Getting baptized isn't really that way at all." Papa didn't seem to notice my disappointment. He sounded puzzled when he spoke, and I thought maybe he hadn't paid much attention to the picture before this.

"Artists sometimes get carried away." Then cheerfully, "Anyway, you are now a member of the Church of Jesus Christ of Latter-day Saints, or you will be Sunday when you are confirmed. And you are entitled to life eternal in the Celestial Kingdom—that is," he qualified, "if you keep the commandments."

"What are these commandments I have to keep?"

"You've already complied with some of them. First there is Faith, Repentance, and Baptism. You have the Faith, haven't you?"

I knew I'd better have faith. In the Hicken household you were born with it. If you didn't have faith, whatever faith was, you were a doomed soul. But then there was repentance.

"Papa, repentance is being sorry for the things you've done, isn't it?"

"Yes. The Lord says, 'Repent and be baptized . . .' "

"I didn't."

"You didn't what?" I'd caught him just as he was beginning to get wound up.

"I didn't repent. I can't think of anything that I'm really sorry I've done. Not sorry enough to want to face the Lord and tell him I am, anyway. I'm not even sorry for sticking a pin in Miriam Hicken the other day. She deserved it."

Normally, Papa would have gone into the whys and where-fores of the pin-sticking, but that day my immortal soul seemed to be hanging on weightier things.

"You don't have to repent. As an eight-year-old child, you have just barely reached the age of accountability." Papa never explained the meaning of words, he just used them, expecting you to understand—and oddly, you did. "You can't have done anything bad enough, as the world knows sin, to need the kind of repentance that is meant. But you've reached that age now. From this time on, you'll be responsible for the evil you do."

I was relieved that Papa didn't know about all the bad things I'd done already, that, magically, I didn't even need to repent of, but the sudden, terrible weight of all the sins I could and would commit in my lifetime pressed down on me. It was a crushing load. Papa lightened it, or tried to.

"But if you are truly repentant, then you will be forgiven for those sins through the Atonement."

That heavy word "atonement" frightened me. I'd heard all about the poor Savior hanging on the cross and drinking vinegar.

"I have to go feed my cats, now," I said and slipped out into the bright sunshine. I cuddled the half-grown kittens that ran to me from under the woodpile when I whistled.

"Why don't cats have to be baptized?" I asked them. "Do cats sin? Killing is a sin, and you kill every mouse and bird you can catch." I thought about the barn cat that ate all of her kittens. Once she had thirteen and had eaten twelve of them and was chewing the front foot off the last when I caught her. Now, there was a real sinner! The baptism must have had some effect because I decided I didn't want to live in any Celestial Kingdom that didn't have cats in it, so I baptized them all.

Papa came out of the house just as I had thoroughly immersed the last one in the watering trough. He helped me dry the bony, shivering little wretches with towels he took from Mama's clothesline.

"Cats don't sin," he said, "they live by instinct. They don't hate. They kill for food. This is like baptizing a baby. When there is no sin, there's no need for baptism."

"But, Papa, you said that I hadn't sinned either, and you made me get baptized."

"I can see," he said, rinsing the towels in the watering trough, "that I'm going to have my work cut out with you." He hung the towels back on the line as neatly as Mama had hung them.

"Ma'll never know the difference," he grinned, "but don't do any more baptizing, young lady. That's a matter for the Priesthood."

My confirmation the next Sunday had more meaning for me. I had a rare, new dress of red taffeta with a white lace collar and cuffs, and silk, ankle socks, and new, black patent slippers with cut-outs at the toes. I had a ruffle on my white, cotton slip, and I wore my first silk undershirt and pants, pink ones. I rustled splendidly when I walked down the aisle to where my grandfather waited with two of the members of the Bishopric, behind a chair that had been placed for me.

Papa was not a tall man, but most people thought of him as tall. He had a back bent from more than sixty years of hard labor. His nose was blue-veined and prominent, with a suggestion of a rounded hump, and his deep-set eyes were a piercing purple blue. I don't know what his mouth looked like, for he wore a mustache, which had a distinctly red tinge in the brown. He dyed it very carefully with a toothbrush for important occasions until his hair turned white, and then he allowed his mustache to whiten too. His chin was firm and bony, and a little of his sinewy neck was visible above the stiff-starched collar of his white shirt. He stood behind my chair with his hands lifted to place upon my head, and I knew even then that he was a man whose dignity and character did not come with the donning of his dark, Sunday suit.

He may have thought I was nervous, for he lowered his head toward me so that I could see the twinkle in his eyes before I turned to place myself in the chair. And then he confirmed me. To him, I am sure it meant that I was taken into the fold. To me, the warm pressure of my grandfather's hands upon my head in loving blessing meant more. Papa didn't simply say, "Now, through the power of the Priesthood, you were made a member of the Church," as many men did. He gave a patriarch's blessing which protected me from the elements, illness, evil, and temptation. And this meant more to me than he was ever to know.

It was my link to love. My father was dead, my mother had "given me away," my grandmother was aging so fast that she was unaware of me some of the time, and when she knew I was there, she called me by the names of her absent daughters. But Papa, who loved so many people, loved me, too—in a very special way. He did not tell me so, in words, until he wrote it in a letter twenty-five years later. And he told me again that time just before he died, but he didn't need to tell me. I knew it that Confirmation Sunday.

Chapter 4

ALL CIRCLES
ARE CLOSED

I ALWAYS WENT TO Sunday School without urging, but it wasn't because I enjoyed it. I went for the pleasure of walking to and from Church with Papa and to hear him sing. (In the Mormon Church, Sunday School is as much for adults as for children; the small children, under eight, meet separately.) Papa always sang with the same fervor with which he preached, and I could hear his strong voice leading the congregation, although it was seldom that he held the song-leader's baton in his hand. Occasionally, when he did, we really sang! Then all the Church songs had a rousing march tempo.

I really went to Church for the walk. Papa knew everyone, and everyone in town knew him as Uncle Dave. We left home in time to stop for a brief visit with anyone we might meet along the way. And throughout the walk, he would point out the beauty of a tree, picking a leaf to trace its delicate skeleton, or we would pause for a moment to listen to the water as it sparkled along in the grassy-banked ditch.

"Sounds like it's talking . . . if you listen, you can almost make out what it's trying to say—just like old Granny Murray. She was a nice old lady, but she had all her teeth pulled out and never did get any store teeth. All the rest of her life, she sounded just like that ditch water." He worried about the Ohlwiler pine tree, too.

"That tree is going to be a beauty. One of the best in the country, if someone doesn't get a fool notion to cut it down." Papa was right about that tree. The pine tree towers above all the trees in the country, and only with some difficulty have the Ohlwiler descendants resisted the exigent pleas of officials looking for a pine to grace Salt Lake City's Main Street at Christmastime.

Many years later I felt an empathetic throb when my seven-year-old Barbara said with sad wonder: "You know that big maple down on the corner of Sixth East? It has never turned as red since Grandpa died."

No amount of urging would have sent me to Church for Primary on Tuesday afternoons with all the rest of the children. Most of them liked Primary. I disliked it intensely, and Papa knew this, but he didn't ask me why—and he didn't make me go. My reasons were personal and violent, and I think that if I had been ordered to attend, I would have disobeyed. Papa must have known that, too, so on Tuesday afternoons he usually arranged to read to me. All that scriptural reading might have been boring, but I don't remember being bored. Perhaps I was

awed by his Biblical bell-ringing or maybe I couldn't disappoint
him by showing a lack of interest in his marvelous and multi-
tudinous discoveries in the Word. He wouldn't have understood *that*.

But he probably did understand my reason for hating Primary. It was because of Sister Madison. Sister Madison had
five sons and one daughter, a girl only a few days older than I.
She was a nice girl, and I liked her, and I had often asked to
go visit her. My grandmother had a firm rule about children
going to play at other people's houses. I could go once a week
and I could stay for just one hour. On this "hate-Mrs.-Madison
day," I walked the six blocks to Donna's house eager for the
hour's play. Mrs. Madison met me at the door.

"What do *you* want?"

"I came to play with Donna."

"She can't play today," said Mrs. Madison sharply, and she
shut the door. I stood on the porch step shocked to tears. I
never knew why Donna couldn't play that day, but I never
attempted to visit her again. I avoided her if I could. Her
mother's cross and twisted face and the noise of that slamming
door always came between us.

Later, when Mrs. Madison was asked to be a Primary teacher,
she accepted only if she could teach her beloved Donna's class,
of which I was a member. I went once. When I saw her sitting
at the teacher's little table, I used the dirtiest utterable word
in my vocabulary.

·"Oh, pee!" I said, and I went home. I'm almost sure that
she told my grandfather, but maybe Papa understood Mrs.
Madison better than either she or I thought because he didn't
make me go back again. Sister Madison liked teaching her
daughter's class so well that as Donna progressed from the
Larks, to the Seagulls, to the Micanwee's (I never knew what
kind of bird that was or even if it was a bird, but it doesn't

matter—all the class names have been changed since then), and through graduation from Primary, up to the Beehive girls in Mutual, Mrs. Madison progressed, too.

Then they asked her to be president of the Primary, and this was an honor she couldn't turn down. That stopped her going into Mutual with Donna, so I went to the Mutual classes. I never recovered from the resentment I had because her mother cheated me out of my Saturday afternoon hour. Donna and I never became friends, although at times there were only five or six other girls in the class.

Through all those non-Primary years, Papa did not invade my privacy, which is a lot more than I can say for myself. Admittedly, I am a curious adult; I was a damnably snoopy child.

In our house almost everything was open and aboveboard. It was that way even though Papa and Mama *meant* to keep some of their discussions private, I am sure. They talked of these things after I had gone to bed at night or before I arose in the morning. Since neither of them had ever slept in my little room, which was sandwiched between their bedroom and the kitchen, they were unaware of how thin the walls were. I developed an uncanny sense of the times they were waiting for me to be gone so that they could speak frankly. At these times I obligingly went to bed early.

In this way, the happenings in the neighborhood, the town, and in our family were thoroughly explained to me without my ever having to ask a question—things like: how Polly Andrews could keep on having babies even though her husband had left her to marry another woman and moved to Idaho; or how we didn't need to worry about paying the light bill because Ann had sent five dollars in her last letter. There were drawbacks to this—I was never surprised. Mama always told Papa every single thing she bought me for Christmas, and I always knew when she had sent an order off to National Bellas Hess Catalog and what would be for me when it came.

There was one thing, however, that they were reticent to discuss even with one another, and that was Circle Meeting. There was a stock set of words they used:

"It's Circle tomorrow, Kate," Papa would say. This would be on a Saturday night. "I'll bathe in the morning."

"I'll get your clothes ready," Mama would answer. What clothes? Papa's Sunday clothes were always ready, pressed and brushed and neatly hung up the Monday after he'd worn them. Mama would rustle through my room and into hers, and she would rummage in the closet or a chest. Then she would return, and I'd hear the click of the handle as she fastened it to one of the two sad irons that always heated on the back of the stove. The next morning Papa arose extra early, bathed himself in the galvanized tub with water that was heated on the old Majestic stove, and was gone before I got out of bed. The kitchen would be steamy, smelling of Jap Rose soap and the acrid tinge of Papa's mustache dye. There was no smell of sausage or fried eggs, no oatmeal in the double boiler, no baking-powder biscuits in the warming oven. This would be Fast Sunday. (The first Sunday in every month.) On Fast Sundays we had our dinner before sundown the Saturday night before, and we skipped breakfast, giving the price of our skipped meals to the Church as Fast offerings to be used for the needy in the Ward. On Fast Sunday the Church meetings are changed around a bit to include Testimony Meeting. Sunday School is short-ened and Testimony Meeting is added—which drew out the meetings inordinately until the Bishops cut off some of the long-winded speakers so they could close the meetings at the specified time.

In this meeting, any lay member—man, woman, or child—can stand and bear his testimony to the truth of the gospel and the blessings of the Lord. Usually the same people get up every time and say the same things. In every ward I have ever known there has been one or two exceedingly tiresome and incoherent old men who never missed speaking on Fast Sundays. I have heard so many of these men so many times that I have reams of useless testimonies stored away, word perfect, in my head.

Occasionally, someone new would jump up and start talking fast enough to hold the floor. The new ones were always interesting, but sometimes someone would get up and tell about the sins they'd committed, and a couple of times, a weeping and repentant fornicator would arise and ask forgiveness. I was always embarrassed and terribly sorry for these unfortunates, and I decided then and there that if I ever had such confessions to make, it would be done between me and the Lord, and not in front of a congregation. Such things certainly added to the interest of what were usually dry and drawn-out meetings. It gave me the needed incentive to go to Church on Fast Sunday, and, though they'd deny it, I think it did and still does for a lot of other people, too.

There are some bishops who exhort their ward members to such public self-flagellation, but none of them urge it to the point it reached in one small-town congregation. A red-eyed and contrite woman arose to ask forgiveness for her daughter-in-law who was committing adultery with the local game warden. I think she was taking a little too much on herself—everyone should be able to reap the blessings for repenting of his own sins.

Every so often, Fast Sunday also included the mysterious Circle. On Circle days there was no walk to Church with Papa, so I usually didn't go. Instead, I'd do my homework on the breakfastless kitchen table, with the morning sun shining hot on my back as I sat in Papa's white captain's chair. But try as I did, for a long time I couldn't find out exactly what this Circle Meeting was. To this day I have found only one person

who knew anything about Circle who would discuss it with
me—for as Mama told me, "It is a function of the Priesthood
and women aren't supposed to meddle in it." I meddled.

Since no one would tell me about it, I listened and watched.
I discovered that Papa's Circle clothes were kept in the black,
cowhide valise that he'd carried in the mission field. It was
locked and kept inside the wardrobe. Then one Sunday I
found the bag on the bed in my grandparents' bedroom. It was
unlocked. Papa and Mama were relaxing, napping in their
kitchen chairs after dinner—Papa with his chin on his chest,
his Bible fallen onto his knees; Mama dozing in her high-backed
rocker. I knew that I would have time to explore the contents
of the bag.

Inside was Papa's Temple clothing. I'd seen it many times
when Mama carefully ironed and pleated the robes. Except for
the green, moire apron, all of it was white, including the soft-
soled shoes.

The nearest Temple was in Salt Lake City, and Papa seldom
went there. In fact, the only time I could remember a mention
of his going through the Temple was after my father's acci-
dental death, when he stood as proxy to be sealed to my mother
in eternal marriage. They had taken me along, too, a year-old
child, so I could also be sealed to my parents, as must be done
with children who are not originally "born under the Covenant." So where did Papa wear his Temple clothes?

I lifted out the carelessly folded clothing. Poor Mama. She'd
have to wash and iron all this stuff again. Among the clothing
was a damp, white towel. I removed that and hung it across the
wide footboard of the bed. Mama was so forgetful, she'd think
that she had done it, or that Papa had.

Later in the afternoon, I went back to their bedroom to
check through the bag again. Maybe there was a pamphlet or
a list of instructions or something that I had missed under the
clothing, for Papa kept things like that. But the bag was again

locked and in the wardrobe, the towel had been removed, and the dent in the feather bed where it had been was neatly smoothed away.

The next day I again asked Mama about Circle Meeting.

"Where do they hold the Circle Meeting?" I was very matter of fact. "In the Stakehouse?"

"Usually in the Ward."

"Where in the Ward?" I asked, amazed. "I've been all over that building."

"There's a special room. Don't be so nosy. Curiosity killed a cat," she said shortly.

There was no more information to be had from her, so when an opportunity arose for me to accompany the granddaughter of the Ward custodian on an errand to the Ward House, I went gladly and with intent, for he had sent her with his big ring of keys.

While my friend was downstairs in the storeroom doing whatever her grandfather had sent her to do, I went up through the chapel and into the only part of the building I hadn't explored thoroughly. I didn't think there could be rooms up in the wooden steeple, but there must be—had to be. I found a door at the end of the short, narrow flight of uncarpeted stairs and I was rattling the knob when my friend appeared with her grandfather's ring of keys dangling from her wrist.

I don't remember using any persuasion. She had unlocked the forbidden storeroom already, and we'd both visited the girls' room, which also had to be locked and unlocked, so without discussion we tried the keys until one fit.

"It's probably just another storeroom." And as the door swung open, "See . . . ," she said.

Very small and disappointingly square, it still had to be the Circle room. There was a low, velvet-covered pulpit pushed

* A stake is comparable to a Catholic diocese.

against one wall. I knew without being told that one was meant to kneel before such a low pulpit. There was nothing else in the room except some cupboards, which held old songbooks and dusty ledgers, and a washbasin. There were no chairs, only low, built-in benches that went around three sides of the room. It could not have seated more than ten or twelve people. The walls, benches, and cupboards were painted a very pale gray. There was a light bulb dangling from a wire in the ceiling, and the long slit of window was curtained in plain, gray percale. I was certain this was the Circle Room, but it gave little clue of its function.

Through observation, listening, and scripture reading, I think I now know what went on at Circle Meeting. The members of the High Priests' Quorum and perhaps some special Authority met there to discuss personal problems or problems in the Ward and to consecrate the oil used in administering to the sick (which was often done in the preliminaries of Fast Meeting, as were confirmations and blessings of babies). Perhaps they held prayer circles to pray for the afflicted, and, on the evidence of the New Testament, the damp towel and the washbasin were probably for performing the humble rites of washing the feet. (This would explain Papa's early Sunday bath, when it was his usual custom to bathe on Saturday nights—he wanted his feet to be as clean as possible before they were washed.) These things, or some of them, might ordinarily have been Temple rites, but these men could not get to the Temple easily, so no doubt it was a substitute arrangement, and that is why the robes were worn. Just recently, in looking at a plan of the Heber Stake Tabernacle, which has just been made a national historic site, I noted that there was a Circle Room. So they held Circle Meetings there, too—most likely for the members of the Stake High Council. I thought I'd been over every inch of *that* building also, but I'd missed the Circle Room.

I SPENT A GREAT DEAL of energy searching out the why of Circle Meeting. It would have been solved with a sentence if I had been a questioning *boy*. I do not believe that a loving God makes any difference in His regard of the sexes, so why should men be given keys to doors that remain forever locked to women? This assumption of male superiority has irritated me throughout most of my life, and it was the wellspring of some rousing arguments with Papa—arguments he always believed he had won, simply because he was a man.

Mama used to say, "Oh, let 'em enjoy their Priesthood, the poor things need it." But I never had her equanimity. The Church teachings of the "supremacy of the Priesthood" and of "unquestioning obedience to authority" made me continue debating Papa throughout his life. I'm afraid that he died with great uncertainty about my ever attaining a "state of perfection." But these were discussions that were reserved for my adult years. I would scarcely have dared dispute them while I was still in my teens and living under his roof. I plagued him enough as it was.

"Papa, if the plates of *The Book of Mormon* that Joseph Smith claimed to have found in the Hill Cumorah were of gold, as he said they were, he couldn't have lifted them."

Papa read the preface of *The Book of Mormon*.

"Perhaps they had the look of gold, maybe an alloy or covered with gold leaf."

"In Joseph Smith's vision, he said the angel told him they were gold."

"When I was a child, I was taught as a child," Papa answered with a rare bit of scorn. "It's what was written on them that is important, not whether they were gold or not."

"It matters if he could lift 'em or not—and there must have been a pile to get all the writing that is in *The Book of Mormon* on them."

"If God helped him find them and translate them, he could

also have helped him lift them." I supposed that was true, but somehow I couldn't see an angel of supernatural strength following Joseph Smith around just to lift those gold plates.

"You say you absolutely know that Joseph Smith was a prophet, and all the other presidents since him have been prophets, and that this is the only true Church of God. All the other churches say that, too, Papa, and most of them have a lot more people believing in them than this one does. How can you know? You can think it, maybe, but you can't really know it."

"Do you know there is a New York City?" This was an old and dirty argument.

"Of course."

"How do you know? You haven't seen it."

"I know people who have been there."

"Well, I know people who knew the Prophet. You know that New York City exists because you believe other people. I believe in the truth of the gospel for the same reason—and many others. It's a matter of faith."

I knew that this triumphant answer had no relevance to my question, but I could never find a rebuttal for his illogic. I was stuck with New York City and the truth of the Mormon Church all tied up into one of Papa's unmanageable packages.

Chapter 5

OF BEASTS
AND CHARIOTS

YOU ALWAYS LEARN important things about other
people when you learn important things about yourself. When
Papa died, I was surprised to find that it comforted me to talk
about him. Before that I'd always avoided the name of the
newly dead when I was with those in mourning. Of course,
there are people who do not want to talk, but most people do,
and as the words pour out it is as if an abscess is being drained.
And I learned, too, that next to time and talking, the balm for
sorrow is work.

No matter how sympathetic people are, there comes a time
when sympathy runs a little thin. (As with me and Poor

Cornelius.) I had grieved for Papa and talked about Papa until my friends didn't want to hear about him any more. Of course they didn't say so, but such things are easy to perceive, even before the listeners themselves are aware of them. So I quit talking.

I cleaned house. I papered and painted and made new drapes and curtains. I sewed for the girls. I canned fruit and jellies and pickles as my grandmother had done. I even planted flowers. Although I love them, the care of flowers had always been tedious and unpleasant for me.

Other women can dig in their yards wearing big hats and canvas gloves, looking like ads for flower-seed catalogues. (They have such fancy, feminine gloves to lure women into yardwork that I think the designers must be men.) I look terrible. The dirt gets under my fingernails—even through the gloves. My hair falls down into my eyes, my elbows and knees get muddy, and I grate with dirt as I move from one flower bed to another. But I planted petunias, roses, peonies, sweetpeas, and those long-stemmed, purply-blue delphiniums that hid one side of our garage and reminded me of Papa's eyes every time I looked out the kitchen window.

The only thing I didn't do was iron. I couldn't do that—it was too achingly lonely.

The girls were all in school then, all day; after school they were busy with their lessons and their friends. I had few callers. All the people who had visited me had long since gotten out of the habit. There was a congenial neighborhood coffee-klatch, but you can't spend all day, every day wandering from house to house drinking coffee—although for a time I tried hard. After seven years of not being able to see an end to the things I had to do, suddenly there was not enough to fill the hours.

I joined a couple of clubs which took up a few hours every two weeks. I led a Brownie troop. I volunteered for all the benefit drives, heart fund, cancer fund, community chest, and the Mother's March. I took some classes in creative writing at the University. I went to PTA meetings—the first I'd ever had time to attend. I did all the "lonely woman" things, yet I had many hours and much energy to spare.

The Relief Society visiting teachers called on me every month and urged me to come to Church. I rather enjoyed the sisters. It was a break in my day. Although they gave lessons that were sometimes too "sweet," and were always slanted toward living the gospel and obedience to the authorities, they were endurable because of the sincerity and warmth of the women who read them to me.

The Ward Teachers (these were men) came occasionally. Nonactive members do not bring out the best in their Priesthood visitors. More often, in lieu of a visit, I found a little slip in my mailbox saying that the brethren had called and left the month's message in printed form. I read the messages. They sounded like Papa watered down and strained through cheese-cloth.

Then one night, I had a dream. Papa came into my bedroom while I was sleeping and eased himself down on the foot of my bed, waking me as he did so. He still carried his cane, and he rubbed his thumb over the smooth handgrip as he talked, a habit I had never noticed. He told me that there was a message for me in one of the books that had been on his bedside table when he died. I was to find that message, and I would surely know it because it had to do with beasts and silver and gold, and chariots, and it would ring "familiar in my ears." When I found it, I was to send a copy to each of his children. Then he got up and thumped his way out of the room. I awoke as he went out the door, and I lay awake thinking how good it had been to see him, to hear his voice again, even in a dream.

I went back to sleep. And I dreamed the same dream again. By then, it seemed much more than a dream. I could hardly wait until I had pushed everyone out the door the next morning so I could go to the closet where I had hurriedly packed all the things that were Papa's to get them out of my sight.

On top of the box of books was Papa's hat. He always wore his hats as they came from the box: domed, uncreased. When he had bought this one, seven or eight years before, he'd said that he intended it to be his last. And it was. He'd been careful with it. It looked like new. Fallen down into the corner of the box was the black bowtie that I'd removed from his neck the day of his stroke. Papa's bowtie and hat undid me, and I wept as I unpacked the books.

There was a surprising lot of books, and I couldn't remember which ones had been on his bedside table. There was *The Holy Bible, The Book of Mormon, Pearl of Great Price* and the small, marked, and thumbed copy of the *Doctrine and Covenants* that he'd carried on his missions in his inside coat pocket. It was bent and rounded to the shape of his chest. I cried about that, too. But it was the last time I was to cry about Papa. I was too busy after that.

There was *Discourses of Brigham Young*, and several volumes of Joseph Smith's *The History of the Church, Mediation and Atonement* by John Taylor, *The Discourses of Wilford Woodruff*, James E. Talmage's *Articles of Faith*, Joseph F. Smith's *Gospel Doctrine*, Melvin J. Ballard's *Three Degrees of Glory*. There were volumes of Brigham H. Roberts' and a tattered paper copy of *The Last Days* compiled by Richard and Elizabeth Smith, and many more, most of them written by presidents or apostles of the Church.

Where to begin? Unless I found the message, it was likely that I'd have to read them all. The dream was so real, the command so positive, and the curiosity about the message, if there was a message, were all goading me. I could not believe that the dream had been only a device of my own mind to make my grandfather come alive again for a few moments.

The Bible seemed to be the logical place to start looking for the message. I had attended Seminary, which is a three-year course of study of the Bible, *The Book of Mormon,* and Church history taught in conjunction with high school classes in Mormon communities. Many parents think these classes are more important than the regular schoolwork, and the Seminary classes are always well attended. The classes are taught in a special building, the Seminary, which is located near the high school campus. I had done very well in Seminary, but I'd never read any of the books. Papa read and explained the assigned chapters to me as I did the dinner dishes. He didn't seem to mind doing it, and I thought it only fair because I took the classes at his insistence. I would much rather have taken zoology.

As I read the Bible, I discovered why it is an alltime bestseller. I understood why so many thousands of scholars spent their lives deeply absorbed in the study of this text. But I found it quite a different book from the one Papa read. His favorite passages were the fire and brimstone warnings or the promises of wrath or blessings that one could expect, depending on how one "walked" or "sowed."

I loved the Bible. I found myself touching it tenderly as I picked it up. Its poetry charmed and comforted me, and it clearly illustrated the difference between literature and pornography—a difference that is so often made a point of law.

There is no low or sinful act of man that the Bible does not deal with. But it does so with words so beautifully put together that even descriptions of things most vile do not dirty up the mind. I think that it is because it was written by true-bone poets, and that modern writers, in their desire to portray "truth," have not truly mastered their medium. Their truth so often becomes obscenity.

There's an example of this in chapter 34 of Genesis, and if you aren't familiar with it, let me tell you the story. It is a tale

of rape, deceit, prejudice, connivance, disobedience, atrocity
and murder—all these the acts of a heroic Biblical family: the
sons of Jacob. (Mormons and Jews claim the same forbears.)
Most Mormons claim to be the descendants of Ephraim, the
second son of Joseph, the son of Jacob. Jews are the descendants of Judah, one of the older sons of Jacob. I've often
wondered if that is the reason why Mormons seem to accept
Jews a little more readily than they accept members of other
faiths. But I find it amusing that in Mormon semantics, a Jew
must be considered a gentile.

In the Book of Genesis, Jacob is taking his family through
the land of the Hivites, when Shechem, a royal son of that land,
saw Dinah, Jacob's daughter, and ravished her. But Shechem,
aside from his lust, was an honorable man, and he wanted to
marry the girl to make things right. The father of Shechem met
with the patriarch Jacob to arrange the marriage, and also to
arrange for the intermarriage of their peoples and to offer the
travelers sanctuary in the land of the Hivites. His offer was
accepted on condition that all the Hivite men allow themselves
to be circumcised in accordance with the Hebrew Covenant
with God.

However, the sons of Jacob were furious that a gentile should
defile their sister. "We cannot do this thing," said Jacob's
sons, "to give our sister to one that is uncircumcised; for that
were a reproach unto us."

All the males of the country submitted docilely to circum-
cision, but "on the third day when they were sore" the Israelites
fell upon them, killed all the men, spoiled their city, stole their
sheep, oxen, and asses, took all their wealth, and their little
ones, and their wives, "and spoiled even all that was in the
houses."

Now Jacob did remonstrate with his sons, because he was
afraid that the surrounding nations would band together and
slay the Israelites, but nothing came of it. God told Jacob to

go to Bethel and everything turned out fine. (Of course, the Israelites got their comeuppance when those same sons of Jacob sold their brother Joseph into slavery, and as a roundabout result found themselves slaves of the Egyptians during one of the most amazing building programs in history.)

This is one of the many stories that never gets put into the Bible storybooks, yet it is so beautifully told that it would be hard for the prissiest reader to be shocked even though she's getting a quick, keen look at the ways of the world.

As I read, I discovered the Bible to be an ever-flowing fountain of material for the writer, as most of them have discovered before me. Hundreds, probably thousands of titles have been lifted from its pages: *My Son, My Son,* the terrible lament of David for his son, Absalom, *Exodus, East, of Eden, My Brother's Keeper, Giants in the Earth, The Way of all Flesh, Five Smooth Stones, The Strange Woman, The Sun Also Rises, Naked Came I, Days of Our Years,* and *A Daughter of Zion,* to name a few of them.

But I didn't find my message. So then I started on the standard works of the Church, which are the *Book of Mormon, Pearl of Great Price* (Joseph Smith's version of the Books of Moses and the disputed Book of Abraham), and the *Doctrine and Covenants,* which are either inspired translations or personal revelations of God to Joseph Smith. I found some interesting things in these books. I found that the Word of Wisdom, chiefly taken to mean abstinence from tea, coffee, liquor, and tobacco —the most often preached about and frowned upon sins—was not given "by way of commandment," although I'm told that Brigham Young made it a commandment later. It doesn't even mention tea and coffee, it says hot drinks. And it gives some instructions about the eating of meat that many Mormons take to mean abstinence from pork.

I found what might be considered justification for a fact that had always nagged at me: comparatively few people are "called" to the influential positions beyond the stake level* who are not descendants of The Blood—the first families of the Church. (The families who with Joseph Smith formed the nucleus of the Church: Smiths, Youngs, Kimballs, Richards, Taylors, Cannons, and a few others.)

Now, I was remorseful that I'd spent so much time arguing with Papa rather than learning from him. He could have answered so many of the questions that filled my mind as I read. I didn't know anyone else who could or would take the time to do it. These questions are discussed at length by the brethren in their Priesthood meetings (from which women are barred), but it is a rare man who will talk about doctrine in depth with a woman. (Why should he? What could *she* do about it?) It becomes insistently obvious to such an inquiring woman that her role is to support her husband in his Priesthood. She must raise up lots of children to follow the teachings of the Church, and make her home a place of love and refuge for her family. And she is to leave questions of doctrine strictly to the men who have been ordained to deal with them—by the authority of the Biblical Peter, James, and John, who came *in person* to bestow the Priesthood on Joseph Smith.

There is certainly a place for the woman in the Mormon Church, perhaps even more of a place than in any other religion, but it is as a doer, not a thinker. No matter the position to which she may be "called," it is always under the direction of a member of the Priesthood. She is raised to accept this—relatively few women ever think of questioning the dictums, and most of the sisters are shocked at the few who do question.

As I read, I knew that the only place I might find some answers and some help in my search for the message would be

---

* Although a ward bishop is highly respected, it is only at the stake level that obedience to authority begins to be a powerful pressure. The bishop of the ward as well as the ward members are under the guidance and dominion of the stake president.

in Church, but it was with great reluctance that I set my feet on the "narrow way that led to the strait gate."

The Lincoln Wardhouse, where I would spend a large portion of my time in the next few years, was a combination ward and stake meeting house, fronting on Ninth East Street. It was a busy, and, for Salt Lake City, a narrow thoroughfare. The members of our Ward, along with those of the other five Wards that made up Granite Stake, had combined money and effort to build it. Lincoln Ward had its own chapel, classrooms, and foyer. Mormon meeting houses always have large foyers. Mormons are such enthusiastic handshakers that they must provide a place to do it! From the foyer, doorways led into the Lincoln Ward chapel and out onto a patio where summer parties were held. At the south end of the foyer, stairs led down to the classrooms and activity rooms. Another set of steps led upward to the Granite Stake part of the building.

At the rear of the sprawling building were the Relief Society rooms, the kitchen, storerooms, and a large banquet hall. The second story of the building provided another foyer, the Granite Stake chapel, and a huge combination amusement hall. (They call them cultural halls now, and like a lot of these newfangled —Papa's word—names, the original one more clearly describes its function.) In this hall, dances were held, roadshows and plays were presented, wedding receptions were given, and the Young Men* played basketball.

The stage at the end of the hall was adequate for most of what it was used for, and stairways led down from it to rooms on the lower floor, where the noisy roadshow casts could be throttled until it was their turn to appear on the stage. A walk led from the front of the Church, around to the south side, and a wide stairway led up into the balconied chapel of the Stake house. The woodwork in the chapel was dark and solemn, the windows, high and arched, the draperies, heavy velvet. The

---

* Young Men's Mutual Improvement Association, known also as *YMMIA*.

motto so often seen in Latter-day Saint wards, THE GLORY OF
GOD IS INTELLIGENCE, was inscribed in ornate letters within a
golden circle, which was painted just below the balcony where
the whispering teenagers went to endure the Stake conferences.
(The same kind of circle had been painted above the rostrum
in the Third Ward in Heber. I'd read the words so many times
as I grew up that it was years before they had any meaning
for me.)

The facilities of the Church on Ninth East were adequate
for almost any need—although there were conflicts in the use
of the Stakehouse facilities, and in time, as new Wardhouses
were built in the other five Wards, they included their own
gymnasiums and banquet halls, until the members of the Lincoln
Ward had almost exclusive use of the entire building, except
the upper chapel.

All the Wards in the Stake met at Stake conferences, which
were held every three months. Even before the population
growth, the walls bulged and many people stood throughout
the conference sessions.

I had attended Church three times in all the years I'd lived
on Seventh East—each time with Papa and each time for a
specific reason. Once was when he "blessed" Barbara. The
other two times were when he confirmed Sally and Ann. Papa
had baptized Sally in the font under the Salt Lake Tabernacle,
the famed one on Temple Square. He obviously feared that I
wouldn't have it done, so he arranged, or made me arrange
things so that he could. It took more than a little doing, too,
because Sally lacked three days until her eighth birthday.

Papa was eighty-seven years old when he baptized Sally.
He had come down from Heber the week before to spend a
few days with us before he left to spend the winter in California. When he found that Sally was nearly eight, he decided
that he would baptize her before he left, and there was no
dissuading him. Baptisms are usually performed by young

priests—young men who have been ordained to the highest order of the Aaronic Priesthood—or by relatives of the child who are in good standing. I have never heard of a baptism performed by a man as old as Papa. Apparently neither had he, and I think that is partly why he did it. He was very proud of being old.

The baptismal ceremony was touching—very different from mine. As I watched it, I wondered why Papa hadn't baptized me. Perhaps because he was still too busy on his farm then. For sure, I wouldn't have worn my bathing suit if he had. Papa was always scandalized by bathing suits.

The font under the Tabernacle was quite a large one. It was painted white and the water was very blue and pleasantly warm. There were benches for observers in front and at the sides of the pool and dressing rooms conveniently close to it. There were tears in the eyes of many of the spectators during the ceremony.

Papa ascended and descended the steps into the pool from one side of it, Sally from the other—the very old, white-haired man with his patriarchal bearing, and the very small, golden-haired, trusting child. They met in the middle of the pool and she took his hand with a confidence that was plainly lacking in the other children who were baptized that day. He raised his arm to form "the square" and said the words of the baptismal rite with strength and clarity, although it had been over fifty years since he had performed a baptism. He laid her down under the water and brought her forth in a swift, strong motion.

I hurried Sally out of her wet, white pajamas, helped her dress, and worried about Papa, who, on the male side of the dressing rooms, had to shakily manage to get out of the flannel baptismal suit by himself. We waited for quite a while for him to dress, and I fretted about taking him out into the cold air of late October. That night was Halloween, too.

"Never wore a rig like this before," he said, as he handed me the sodden suit to take to the attendant. "Like to froze before I got it off me." Then his tone was jubilant. "Bet you never saw anything like that before, did you, girl?"

We went to Church the next Sunday so Papa "could finish the job." He was very pleased with himself. He confessed on the way to the plane that Monday morning that he had had a few doubts about the baptism, but he had "brushed them aside."

"Not many men can say they've baptized their great-grandchild when they were eighty-seven. It's a real fine thing. I never thought I'd be spry enough to do it," he said, chuckling with vast self-approbation. Papa is the only person I've ever known who could brag with modesty.

"No," I said, smiling at him, "I was very doubtful."

"No need to be. I'm not going to get old 'til I have to."

Papa only grew old after he had reached his ninetieth birthday. And when Ann turned eight, he admitted it. "I'm too old to baptize her, but I want to confirm her." That was my third visit to Church.

I would have taken Papa to Church in the years that he lived with us if he had wanted to go, but, strangely, he didn't. He was used to the love and respect that surrounded him in his Ward in Heber, and to "city folks" he was just another old man who gave an interminably long confirmation blessing. I think that must have been the real reason that Papa didn't want to go to Church at Lincoln Ward. He said the wooden seats hurt his bones and the meetings were too long, but when he went home in the summers, I noticed that he never missed a meeting and he walked all the way to Church, too. And the old Heber Third had the hardest wooden benches I've ever sat on.

THE FIRST TIME I went to Church after Papa died was memorable for me. I went with reluctance and trepidation because I was forced to go as much as if Papa were standing behind me in reality. He was, but I was the only one who was aware of him.

I was greeted perfunctorily by the Bishop and his councilors, who hurried me on through the press of people coming in the door to shake hands.

I wore a new gold-brown, watered silk suit, and gold-brown, high-heeled pumps and cream-colored gloves. I'd bought all this finery especially for my entrance into the Mormon Community. I wore a fair amount of my first bottle of Chanel #5 perfume, too. I felt elegant. I sat down on a bench near the rear of the Church, and I felt conspicuous although no one seemed to notice me.

I picked up the blue Sunday School song book and riffled the pages—most of the songs were familiar. I could feel Papa's presence beside me, nodding and approving. I thought that the people around me would no doubt get a whiff of my expensive fragrance when I moved. I was very pleased with myself.

An old man and his wife came in just as the Bishop stood up behind the pulpit and began to speak. The old man was plainly arthritic, and as he went past me in the aisle and sat in front of me, the essence of oil of wintergreen engulfed me. Poor old man. His hair was almost as white as Papa's had been.

When I sang the Sacrament song, it seemed that Papa was singing there beside me. They served the Sacrament bread and water, blessed in a ritual blessing by the young priests at the table at the front of the chapel, and served by the youngest of the Aaronic Priesthood members, the deacons. This was done in silence. You are supposed to think of the body and blood of Christ at this time. You are also supposed to be able to "accept the Sacrament" with a clean conscience. In the early days of the Church, even after the Word of Wisdom had been revealed, wine was served at the Sacrament, and there were vineyards and wineries for its production in Utah. But some of the brethren who were in charge of the Sacrament got drunk on the wine, so water was substituted instead, served individually in minute, sanitary cups. I'm told, too, that stills for the making of a whiskey called "Valley Tan" were once operated in Utah. Probably the product was made for sale to the gentiles. I cannot imagine many Church members buying it under the all-seeing eye of Brother Brigham. Although . . . somewhere along the line, Mormons picked up a taste for the stuff for the rate of alcoholism in Utah is just about as high as it is anywhere. Perhaps that is because drinking is frowned upon as being such a sinful thing, and the drinker has to keep on doing it in order to bear such baleful censure.

After the Sacrament, we had song practice. I knew the practice song very well from my childhood. Papa was singing, too, and the two of us forgot all about the rest of the congregation.

> *For the strength of the hills,*
> *We bless Thee, Our God, our fathers' God;*
> *Thou hast made Thy children mighty,*
> *By the touch of the mountain sod;*
> *Thou has led Thy chosen Israel,*
> *To freedom's last abode,*
> *For the strength of the Hills*
> *We bless Thee*
> *Our God, our fathers' God.*

This had always been one of Papa's and my favorites, but even as a child I wondered if we hadn't usurped a little from the Jews. The words came back easily, although I hadn't heard them in fifteen years. Wouldn't my good friends, the Kleins, be surprised if I told them that they weren't the Chosen People —we were.

Afterwards, I went to the Gospel Doctrine Class and listened attentively, but the teacher, who was certainly able, didn't answer any of the questions I had in my mind, and I was too shy at that point to ask any of them. The class members sat in intimate, little groups; I was left by myself in a corner of the room. No one, not even the teacher, spoke to me, but I didn't really mind. Sanctified, and self-approving, I was not going to be sensitive—they didn't know me yet, of course. I walked home, slightly euphoric at what I felt was a closeness to Papa.

"Oh, Mother, you smell terrible. What do you have on you?" Sally greeted me as I came in the door.

"Chanel #5. I can't smell terrible. I have to smell wonderful."

"You don't!"

"You smell like Grandpa's liniment," Ann said sniffing, "with your perfume, it's really awful."

As I changed my suit, I could smell the strong odor of oil of wintergreen, and I thought ruefully of Papa's warning, as I have often in my life: Pride goeth before a fall. I wondered what the people in the class had thought. And I had spent all that money for the Chanel. No wonder they had moved away from me. I'd thought it was because I was a stranger. Papa's favorite epithet came easily, "Oh, hell and damnation!"

I didn't go back to Church again until I thought everyone had forgotten my first appearance. They had—apparently as soon as I was out of sight. But I had to go back, because the questions from my reading were building up in my mind, and I hadn't yet found the message.

I finished the *Doctrine and Covenants* but as I read, I wondered more than once how the Lord could have been bothered with such trivialities as he obviously had allowed Himself to be. Then I read *The Book of Mormon*. Its title pages were given to proving the truth of the book through the testimony of twelve witnesses and of three witnesses who

claim to have seen and handled the gold plates from which
the book was translated. I read, too, the hypnotic PROMISE TO
BOOK OF MORMON READERS. It is found in Moroni, chapter 10,
verses 4 and 29. (In *The Book of Mormon*—not the Bible.) I
especially noted the words of that promise. It didn't say that
I'd know whether or *not* it was true. It implied that if I didn't
believe the book was true when I finished it, it was because I
hadn't read it with a sincere heart, with real intent and having
faith in Christ.

Nevertheless, I read it, and parts of it brought back the
brimstoned fears of my childhood, swaying like a Biblical
pendulum between threat and promise. In scriptural rhetoric,
it told a story of the origin and ancient history of the American
Indian. Joseph Smith swears that he transcribed it from the
golden plates he had been given by the Angel Moroni, with
the aid of a breast plate and the Urim and Thummim. Until I
started all this reading, I'd thought that the Urim and Thummim
were the gift of God to Joseph Smith solely to make this translation possible, but you'll find them being used in Exodus by
Moses when *he* talked to the Lord.

Briefly, *The Book of Mormon* tells the story of a remnant
of the house of Israel. Lehi, a Hebrew prophet descended
from the tribe of Manasseh, the elder son of the Joseph who
was sold into Egypt, under the direction of God, leads his
family and a couple of other families out of Jerusalem, through
the wilderness to the sea. Guided in their wanderings by a com-
pass-like instrument—a round ball of curious workmanship
called the Liahona, which worked through the faith and
diligence of the people—they built a ship of an unknown design
and traveled across the Indian Ocean and the Pacific Ocean
to land on the west coast of South America, said by Mormon
scholars to be near Chile.

I really wanted to know the truth, and I prayed about it. I
prayed and read with a sincere heart and very real intent, but

I could not stand up in Church, as I have seen and heard hundreds of people do, and state that this was the only true Church on the face of the earth today, that Joseph Smith and all the other presidents of the Church were prophets, seers, and revelators, and that I knew *The Book of Mormon* to be the work of God.

By this time, I'd prayed just as often and as hard as most of them did, and I'd read a great deal more. I asked a few of these people who were so certain some of the questions my reading brought up, and most of them didn't know, and, pointedly, didn't want to know what I was talking about. They just *believed*, like Papa, that if New York City could stand without his seeing it for himself, so could the truth of the gospel.

But the more I read, the more I realized that I needed some knowledgeable guidance if I was to find the message before I became an old woman. The only possible place I could find someone to help me would be in Church. Once I had decided that, my reluctance to go to Church left me. Suddenly, I could hardly wait for Sunday to come.

It is one of my assets and perhaps also one of my greatest faults that I either march ahead, full steam and whistles blowing, or I refuse to take a step. Now—I marched.

I went to Sunday School. I went to Relief Society. I went to Sacrament Meeting. I went to all the sessions of Ward and Stake and General conferences. I even went to Mutual. I can't remember exactly what I did there, because the Mutual Improvement Association is not geared to take care of members past the age of the young marrieds, but I went. I had to find someone to help me in my search. And I did. I found him in the person of Brother Clarence Gardiner. But like everything else in the Church, it took a lot of work to get what I wanted.

Chapter 6

SEEK AND FIND

MORMONS ARE INTENSE seekers after blessings, and the greatest blessings of all, they are taught, come from bringing even one lost soul into "the only true Church."

"Remember the worth of souls is great in the sight of God . . . and how great is His joy in the soul that repenteth! Wherefore, you are called to cry repentance unto this people. And if it so be that you should labor all your days in crying repentance unto this people and bring, save it be one soul unto me, how great shall be your joy with him in the kingdom of my Father! And now, if your joy will be great with one soul that you have brought unto me into the kingdom of my Father, how great will be your joy if you should bring many more souls unto me!"*

For seven years I had been urged to come to Relief Society by my sweet-faced visiting teachers, and on one of their monthly visits I said that I was planning to attend the next meeting.

"We'd be happy to come by for you, Sister Hunter." There was eagerness in the lady's voice. Her missionary zeal almost put me off.

"No, there's no need to do that. I'll be there unless something comes up."

The Relief Society room was located at the rear and in the basement of the Church building. There was always convenient parking next to the entrance, a boon because the women were constantly carrying armloads of things in and out: materials in, finished products out. The steps that led downward had strong rails to aid the many older women who make up the bulk of the ladies attending.

I entered a pleasant room. It was a very large one, stretching across the width of the Church. It was serviceably decorated in shades of cream and rose, carpeted and draped, and furnished with walnut tables, covered by crotcheted tablecloths, a piano, and sturdy folding chairs.

I had expected to feel like a newcomer as I had when I attended Church upstairs, but I was not allowed to. My visiting teachers were watching for me, and they came to meet me as I entered the door. They introduced me to Wilma Wetzel, who was the president, and she introduced me to her two councilors. Wilma was a well-groomed, delicately made woman with such a gift for gracious organization that few of us ever realized that we were being organized. While she was president, Wilma asked me to do some very difficult, demanding tasks, and she

* Quotation from the Latter-day Saint *Doctrine and Covenants*.

always made me feel that she was bestowing a special honor upon me by asking. This is a common attribute of all Church leaders. Along with the sharing of the Priesthood with every "worthy" man, it is part of the genius of the Mormon Church.

This first Relief Society meeting I attended was given to the theology lesson. That year the course of study was *The Book of Mormon*, taught by Lucinda Hamilton, wife of the Bishop. Sister Hamilton was a stately woman with white, beautifully waved hair. She moved and spoke with dignity, and I envied her years of study. She knew her Scriptures. I immediately felt that she would know where my message could be found, but I did not dare to ask her, and by the time I dared, I'd already met Brother Gardiner, who was a scriptural scholar and a natural-born teacher.

I'm sure that I would have faltered in my churchgoing if I had not been pushed by my dreams of Papa, for I dreamed of him again and again. Not the message dream, but dreams where he was exhorting me to some sort of action. I really was not interested in that first theology lesson. As I remember it was about King Benjamin and the city of Zarahemla which, according to *The Book of Mormon*, was destroyed along with other great cities during the terrible storms and earthquakes that occurred at the time of the Crucifixion. Zarahemla was the capital of the Nephite nation and was located in a country also called Zarahemla—*The Book of Mormon* name for South America. I was more interested in the Testimony Meeting which followed the lesson, for many of the ladies stood up and bore their testimonies—a thing that most of them would never do on Fast Sunday in front of the Priesthood. I noticed that of all the Relief Society meetings, the theology week was best attended, perhaps because it gave these ladies a chance to participate in the testimony-bearing after the lesson.

The next Tuesday, I went to Relief Society again. The class leader was Marge Brown who taught the social science lesson.

The course of study was the Bill of Rights and the Constitution of the United States. Marge taught it with all the ease of a political science major. Hers were exciting classes, and even after all these years, phrases from her lessons stay in my mind. After that first one I never missed a social science Tuesday.

I was eager for the third Tuesday and I wasn't disappointed. This was the literature lesson, and in school I'd loved this subject. We were studying nineteenth century writers.* I felt bad that many of the ladies obviously didn't share my love for them—the literature leader had a herculean task just keeping the ladies' eyes open and focused.

The fourth Tuesday was Work Day. Work Day began in the morning. You arrived at a time suited to your personal convenience. Luncheon was served, babysitters were provided, and the women could choose what they wished to do. Quilting was the choice of most of the older women and of those who had learned this skill. It was some time before I could bring myself to pick up a quilting needle, but when I did, I discovered a whole new world, as many women have before me.

In Relief Society on Work Day, the women make things. The amount of Work Day items are innumerable. I have abundantly scattered the works of my hands in my house and in the houses of my relatives and friends. I have also received dozens of these items. The best of them are beautiful and useful, the worst of them, such as the bouquets of Kleenex carnations and plastic, flower-trimmed scouring pads (to hold curler picks) are execrable, but funny. The Work Day was under the direction of the second councilor, who took charge of the

---

* The lesson policies of the Church have changed since I taught Relief Society. The 1971–72 *Relief Society Courses of Study* show that there are now virtually three theology lessons! The names of the lessons have also been changed. The theology lessons are titled "Spiritual Refinement Lessons"; the social science lessons are "Social Relations Lessons"; and the literature lessons are called "Cultural Refinement Lessons." Most of the sisters still refer to them by their old names.

quilts, arranging for the making of the quilt tops, marking the patterns to be quilted, planning how many quilts would be made for the members of the Ward (not as many any more, piecing quilts is a pioneer art rapidly being lost), and how many must be quilted for sale at the Relief Society bazaars.

The rest of the Work Day projects were under the direction of Gwen Lauritzen. I admire ward work leaders with an intensity that is almost reverence. They have provided hundreds of thousands of hands with fascinating activities, and in busying hands, they have healed sore hearts. I do not know where all the energy and the ideas come from. I do know that work leaders help other work leaders. An item popular in one ward can appear, like an epidemic, all through the other wards of the Church. Gwen kept upwards of thirty women constantly involved in one low-cost project after another. She never seemed to be rushed, she had time for individual help (and individual finishing for old hands gnarled by arthritis). She provided fabrics cut to measure, metals shaped for fitting or working on, holes already drilled in uncountable pieces of polished wood, already cut to size. Later I found that she did much of this work at home.

Relief Society women have made so many millions of things that it is a Mormon joke. One day a friend of mine was contemplating the plastic grapes we were making.

"You remember Mrs. McCloud, the visitor from New Zealand who we had during the holidays? Well, once she asked me if grapes had any significance in the Mormon religion." LuAnn waved her hand over the tables of grapes in various stages of preparation.

"Grapes!" I said. "How would she get that idea?"

"From these. She told me that every house I'd taken her into during her visit had grapes like mine—the ones I made here. She thought maybe they were something like the Crucifixes that you see in every Catholic home."

I could see why Mrs. McCloud wondered. Those grapes *were* in every house. I still have some, a cluster of beautiful purple ones that I first saw selling for twenty-four dollars in one of the local gift shops. Then some enterprising work director, with the help of Lee Ward's Catalogue—the work director's Bible—found how they could be made and the knowledge spread with amazing speed throughout the Church. That year, the merchants lost money on grapes, for every department store and gift shop stocked them. I heard at least one disgruntled clerk remarking about the "Mormon doodadding putting people out of business." But that is one of the enticements of Work Day. See something you like, too expensive to buy, and sooner or later it will turn up as a Work Day project.

But the joys of the work director's heart were things that could be made from nothing, like empty plastic bottles, used popsicle sticks, and old magazines. Plastic bottles turn into amazing toys, popsicle sticks into jewel boxes, and magazine illustrations backed with stiff cardboard or plywood are shellacked and tacked or crocheted together to make wastebaskets or yarn baskets. I've made clever four-poster doll beds from clothespins, empty spools, and, ah, *cigar* boxes.

On Work Days, too, I learned a great many sewing tricks. (The neat tailoring of a suit collar is nothing more than the way it is cut and clipped.) I learned how to make and dip chocolates, to paint on glass, to decorate cakes, to make hairpin lace. I learned to quilt, and while I would not want to make a quilt for money, I make them for the people I love. The hours of work cannot be counted, neither can the stitches, and I spill my blood onto each one (quilting makes the fingers raw, for it is necessary to feel the tip of the needle so that you are sure it has gone through the layers of fabric and batting), but I get an enormous sense of accomplishment from each quilt I make, and I know that it is a gift that cannot be purchased.

Quilting is also a companionable occupation, for few women

attempt to make one alone. If you are lucky enough to have friends who quilt, you call them and ask for help. And they always come, gladly, even if they are not close friends, because quilting is a recurrent disease which must every so often run its course. I've never put a quilt on the frames without hearing, "Call me when you get it on, I'd love to come and help." And they go away with a crick in their backs and their fingers pricked and sore, and feeling absolutely wonderful.

Quilting has brought me close to Mama, too. When I sit alone at a quilt, my grandmother comes to advise me: "Make the stitches smaller," or, "Be sure that your knots are firm and that you have pulled them inside the material here; rub the knot with your thimble, it will go into the material without leaving a hole." And I remember the many quilts that she had on the frames in our big living room. Once, when I was very small, I could not resist her patchwork trampoline. I jumped into the middle of it. I can remember the switching she gave me and I thought she was a mean old woman, but my viewpoint has changed. If any mean little kid jumped my quilt off the frames, she'd be hard put to sit down for a week. It surprises me how much I learned about my grandmother when I started to quilt.

Sometimes the materials are so pretty and the quilting so fascinating that I get carried away. I did that not long ago with some pieces of bright cotton satin. I simply could not waste any of the material and the quilt turned out to be king size. I have no king size bed, nor did anyone I knew, but my friend Veronica Bettinson, when I questioned her, admitted to *wanting* a king size bed. So I gave the quilt to her.

The last time I visited her, she led me into her bedroom. She was using the quilt as a coverlet on a new king size bed.

"I hope you aren't thinking of giving us another gift, soon," she said.

"Don't you like the quilt?"

"We love it. But we can't afford your gifts. This one cost us nearly four thousand dollars!" Veronica had to buy a new bedroom set so she could display the quilt, and she couldn't fit the bedroom set into any of her bedrooms, so her husband had to build an addition on the house to hold the king size bed!

I'd met Veronica in Lincoln Ward, where we'd worked together in Relief Society—and a lot of other things. We had become, as many Relief Society women do, closer than most sisters.

Through the Relief Society, courses were given or arranged to be given. Among others, I took a course in home nursing, in tailoring, in hot-packing a polio patient—before the Salk vaccine, when polio was a constant summer threat. There were lessons on every phase of homemaking and others that ranged from how to improve your personality to arranging a funeral. All the learning was so relaxed, without pressure, a group of women sharing what they knew. For at least one day a week, the emptiness in my heart went away.

A favorite song of the Relief Society in Lincoln Ward, and I imagine in wards everywhere, was one that went like this:

> *Have I done any good in the world today?*
> *Have I helped anyone in need?*
> *Have I cheered up the sad, or made someone feel glad?*
> *If not, I have failed, indeed.*
> *Has anyone's burden been lighter to bear*
> *Because I was willing to share,*
> *Have the sick and the weary been helped on their way?*
> *When they needed my help was I there?*
>
> *Then wake up and do something more*
> *Than dream of your mansions above,*
> *Doing good is a pleasure, a joy beyond measure*
> *A blessing of duty and love.*

The ladies of Lincoln Ward lived by this song. The Relief Society president and councilors called upon every member who became ill; they visited the aged and the lonely, and the members of the group were constantly urged to show their love for their neighbor.

One afternoon, Wilma was asking for ladies who could volunteer to sit in the hospital with members of the Ward who were ill. This was after World War II when the hospitals were still desperately short of help. I had the time, but I did not volunteer because I knew so few members of the Ward, and I didn't see how they could get much comfort from a stranger. However, I could offer nursing service. Before I thought what I might be letting myself in for, I impulsively went to Wilma after the meeting and offered.

"I've had some nurse's training, Sister Wetzel. If there is anyone in the Ward, old or chronically ill, who needs nursing care, I'd be happy to help them. I'm not much good at just sitting."

"There's no one that I can think of right now, but it's very kind of you, and if someone needs you, I'll let you know."

Brother Gardiner called about three days later. I could tell from his heavy, dry voice over the phone that he was an elderly man.

"Sister Hunter?"

"Yes . . ." I always pause when someone I do not know calls me Sister.

"I've been praying to the Lord for help," the voice said sincerely, "and you are the answer to my prayer."

"I am?"

"Sister Wetzel told me of your offer in Relief Society. I've been trying to find someone. I need help. My wife has just returned from the hospital. She's had an operation, and she also has diabetes. I can't manage her care by myself, and I haven't been able to find a nurse."

"I'll come to your house about ten in the morning, if that is all right. I hope that I can help."

"Thank you," he said after giving me his address, "and God bless you."

The Gardiners lived about four blocks away from us, and Mrs. Gardiner was truly in need of nursing care, but not a lot of it. Her husband did a great deal for her. He had retired from working in Zion's Savings and Loan, and could devote his full time to her. She was an advanced diabetic, and she was senile, like many old people, only recognizing her husband and her family. In the six months I went there before she died, she never knew exactly who I was. But that didn't matter.

Meeting Brother Gardiner mattered. He'd been a bishop twice, he had known most of the presidents of the Church since John Taylor. He knew most of the other leaders of the Church and he informed me that his "patriarchal blessing" had told him he was to be "defender of the Faith"—a charge he took seriously even though it led to small disagreements with some of the ranking authorities.

Brother Gardiner was a direct answer to my prayers, too, although I did not tell him that as readily as he had told me. I had been praying daily for guidance to find Papa's message, if there was one, and I had been praying to be led to someone who could answer my pyramid of questions. Brother Gardiner could and did.

Every morning, after I had bathed, changed, and cared for Mrs. Gardiner, he would sit down with me and answer questions. He searched his stacks of books and records and made charts and drew maps to give me the background of the answers to my questions. He did not resent my skepticism on some points. He acted as if my questioning was only flattering attention to the beliefs for which he and my grandfather, I am sure, would both have died.

I asked him a question one day which I would never have dared to ask Papa.

"What do you think about the Virgin Birth?"

"I think Jesus Christ was the Son of God."

"But my grandfather used to say, and you say, that everything happens according to natural law. If Jesus was conceived by a light coming upon a virgin, or by her 'being carried away in the spirit,' God would be breaking his own physical laws."

Brother Gardiner smiled. "In *The Book of Mormon* it says that Mary became the mother of Jesus 'after the manner of the flesh.' "

"You mean . . ."

"I mean that's what it says in 1 Nephi, chapter 11. And it is the Mormon belief that God has a physical body—that he has 'body parts and passions.' "

"Hmm," I said. "There have been virgin births recorded in medical history. In those cases the woman has been bisexual— snails reproduce that way—but in all those cases, the child is female. A male child has to be the product of male chromosomes." I could sense a reluctance in Brother Gardiner to discuss it further, so I changed the subject. Now, I wish I'd pursued it and clarified it as much as I could have, because in the years since, that conversation has given rise to some wayward thoughts.

In the Gardiner house were cupboards of books. The dining room and living room areas were divided by big bookcases, and these were filled with rare books. Most of them were religious books, and he generously loaned them to me. I read Flavius Josephus, who was nearly a contemporary of Christ. Josephus mentions Jesus, saying, "the so-called Christ," and it seemed odd to me that he did not consider the mission of Christ as divine, or even important. Although he was a Jew and writes of Judaism, he was a Roman citizen, protected by the Romans

and assigned to be a historian of his people—the Jews. I found
his *Wars of the Jews* and *Antiquities of the Jews* very readable
and most rewarding, explaining as they did many of the questions that I'd had about the Bible. I read some of Eusebius, but
it was heavy going, and I found that I would rather listen to
Brother Gardiner's quotes. He had one of the valued copies of
the "Inspired Version" of *The Holy Bible*. This is Joseph
Smith's version, the original of which is the property of the
Reorganized Church of Jesus Christ of Latter Day Saints—the
Reorganized Church appeared after Emma Smith, Joseph's
first wife, claimed that her son should be his father's spiritual
heir, and left the original Church when Brigham Young was
sustained as its second president.

Brother Gardiner's book shelves held the works of the leaders of the Church from the early volumes of Parley P. Pratt
and Orson Whitney to the ones just published. I read, and asked,
and we discussed. Then one day, Brother Gardiner was talking
about errors in the translation of the Scriptures—the meanings
of words in Aramaic, the original language of much of the
Scriptures, and the subsequent changes of meaning when they
were translated into Latin or Greek and later into English. "For
instance," he said, "in some places the word 'beast' has been
changed to 'idol' because many of the pagan idols were re-
productions of beasts."

Beast! It was my clue word! So I began reading the Bible
over again, looking for passages where such a transposition
might have occurred. Now I was reading passages looking for
the word "idol" with "treasures" and "chariots" and there were
many of them. I cannot understand why I did not use a Con-
cordance. Neither my Bible nor Papa's had one, but surely
Brother Gardiner had one that did. I did not even think of it—
I read the books all the way through.

I found my message in Isaiah 2:6, 7, 8. I had read it before, at
least twice, and missed it. The same Scripture can be found in

2 Nephi in *The Book of Mormon*—for many passages of *The Book of Mormon* are almost identical to those of the Bible. This one was.

I felt like a fool as I typed out the passage and sent it to all of Papa's descendants, but that had been a part of the instructions in my dream, so I did it. As religious as they are, they must have thought that I was slipping my cogs because not one of them ever acknowledged it. However, it did not mean to them what it did to me. After all, I'd spent nearly two years, praying and reading and going to Church trying to find that message.

After I found it, I couldn't understand why I'd had such a hard time. It was one of Papa's favorite passages and I'd heard him read it dozens of times. As he said in my dream, "You will know it positively, it will ring familiar in your ears." I should have been able to turn right to it. The passage read:

"Therefore, O Lord, thou has forsaken thy people, the house of Jacob, because they be replenished from the east and hearken unto soothsayers like the Philistines, and they please themselves in the children of strangers. Their land also is full of silver and gold, neither is there any end of their chariots. Their land is also full of idols, they worship the work of their own hands, that which their own fingers have made . . . O ye wicked ones, enter into the rock, and hide thee in the dust, for the fear of the Lord and the glory of his majesty shall smite thee." And this led me naturally to Papa's oft quoted passage from Matthew, chapter 6:

"Lay not up for yourselves treasures upon earth, where moth and rust doth corrupt, and where thieves break through and steal. . . . For where your treasure is, there will your heart be also." Read the rest of it for yourself, it ends up with some of the best words to live by that have ever been written.

It was no doubt just a dream, I thought, when I had mailed the messages. I'd followed a circuitous route to find the message, but I felt the peace that Papa had promised, and my grief for him was gone. Now I could remember only the laughter and love in my relationship with him. And one of the first things that I laughed about was, what if in truth the dream was no more than just the wandering of a sleeping, grieving mind—it had led me into active involvement in the Church in ways he could not possibly have forced me to when he was living. I was now deeply enmeshed in the web of the Ward—I was ACTIVE. And as I laughed at myself, I thought perhaps Papa was laughing delightedly there beside me—soundlessly, as he always laughed.

Chapter 7

THE NETS OF THE FISHERMEN

SHORTLY AFTER I started regularly attending Church in Lincoln Ward, the Bishopric was released and a new bishop was "sustained." It used to be that Bishops, like the higher Church authorities, once put into office stayed there interminably. Now they usually stay for five years, and all but a few of them consider that quite long enough.

Just before Bishop Hamilton was released, he gave a talk that I will always remember.

"Sisters," he said with grave sincerity, "I want to express my appreciation for all of the work you have done while I have been Bishop. Like most other bishops, I realize that without you good women and what you do for the Ward, we would have no Ward, or at least only a part of one. But I want to give you a warning.

"Some of you have small children, and I know that there are those of you who neglect your children to do the things that are asked by some of us who do not know all of your problems. You push aside the things of your homes to do the work of the Lord. Well, I want you to carefully consider when you do this. First, in the sight of the Lord, comes your duty as mothers and wives. Your family is to come first. If you neglect your family to work in the Church, do not expect the Lord to take care of your family—because He will not. This is your first responsibility. It is *not* the responsibility of your eldest daughter to be mother in your home while you attend to Church duties. Do not force your daughters to hate the Church because you spend so much of your time in it, leaving your home duties to them.

"If you have time, or can arrange your time so that you can do your Church work without loss to your families, how gratefully the Bishopric will accept your efforts."

Perhaps this stayed with me over the years because it was unusual advice—I'd always heard that God and Church came first—and it seems to in so many Mormon homes and especially with men. Only a week or so later, Bishop Hamilton's talk was emphasized forcefully.

I was in Relief Society meeting. It was Work Day, and I had taken Barbara with me, as I usually did when she was not in school. Lunch was served and she loved to play with the other children who came. Sally and Ann had a choice on such days. They could come up to the Church for lunch or they could have a picnic lunch in the back yard at home. In the summers they usually chose the picnic lunch, but in the winters, women who had school-age children were invited to bring them to the Ward from the school across the street for the delicious hot meal that was served.

While we were chattering and quilting and working on the trays that many of the women were making, we heard fire engines go by. I went outside, looked and listened, but though the sirens seemed close, I thought they were about four blocks away. I couldn't see any smoke, so I went back inside and busied myself with my work.

About four o'clock, I finished, and Barbara and I went home to find our yard in a shambles. Sally and Ann were out in back gathering up debris and raking the yard. Next door, Les Galleon's barn, a big relic of the early 1900's, had burned down. The flames had scorched all of her back yard and garden. They had traveled to our fence and shot up, burning the half of our beautiful big trees that hung over the fence.

"What on earth happened!"

"Oh," Sally said, "the firemen said they thought it had been set by some kid playing with matches."

"Why didn't you call me?" I scolded. "I've told you that in any emergency, any trouble, big or little, one of you is to run up to the Church and get me. I ought to whale the tar out of you."

"Well, Mom," Ann said reasonably, as she always did, "someone called the fire department right away, and as soon as it looked like it was coming over our way, we got out the hose, and I watered down our roof and the fence and the trees. We only have one hose and what could you have done more than I was doing? Besides, we thought you'd get too upset and excited. We just didn't see any reason to disturb your day."

"One of the firemen said Ann was sure doing okay," said Sally, backing Ann up, as *she* always did.

"I think you did a very good job, too," I said. "I'm amazed how well you've done—but next time, anything, anything even *different* happens, you come for me. First, you remember," I quoted Bishop Hamilton's thought, "I'm your mother. Next comes the work in the Church."

Part of my deep involvement in the work of the Ward came about because my children had outgrown many of their needs for me, and part of it was because of them. I found that when they went to Mutual I was closer to their interests and activities because I was part of the Mutual, too. It was the same in Sunday School—all of us went. For the most part, they were not involved in Relief Society, which is carried on during school hours, but they occasionally helped me out there, too.

WITH ALL THE INTEREST in who will be the next Bishop, it is a wonder that his identity can be kept a secret. Nevertheless, few people ever know who it is to be until his name is announced in Ward conference by the Stake president.

That Sunday, the president of the Stake rose and looked over the congregation. The Church was crowded. It always is at times like that.

"We are here to sustain a new Bishop of Lincoln Ward," he said. "We wish to thank Brother Hamilton and his councilors for their years of good and unselfish service. Will all those who wish to thank Brother Hamilton and who are willing to release him from this position as he has requested, please raise your right hands." Every hand was raised.

"It has been the decision of the Stake High Council and the Stake presidency to present as the next Bishop of Lincoln Ward Walter J. Trauffer." At the announcement of Walter Trauffer's name, a visible tremor ran over the congregation. For Brother Trauffer had been for some time the custodian of the Lincoln Ward and Granite Stake building. From janitor to Bishop!

"All of you who can sustain Brother Trauffer in this calling will signify by the raising of the right hand." Every hand rose again.

"All opposed, please signify in the same manner." There were no opposers. Opposition is so rare in such situations as to be virtually nonexistent, for Church authorities must be unanimously sustained, and one opposing vote theoretically can stop such appointments until the opposition has been heard and has been asked to explain his reasons for dissent and prove any charges for unfitness. Most Mormons simply do not have the ability to oppose Church authority—this kind of dissent has been trained out of them since infancy.

In the huge General Conference gatherings, or in any other assembly where authorities are sustained year after year, there is always a unanimous aye vote—never a nay. I have known many people who would like to vote nay, myself for one, but we satisfy our consciences with abstention from voting. No one notices that.

The tall, new Bishop lacked the social ease and commanding presence of Bishop Hamilton. He rose to address us, and I, like many others who did not know him well, wondered that he had been chosen. I did not wonder long. Walt Trauffer quickly and truly became the "Father of the Ward," although he and his wife, Hermione, had come to "Zion" from Switzerland and they still spoke English with pronounced accents. His chief interests seemed to be the young people of the Ward—probably because he had teenage daughters of his own—and flowers. Wherever Bishop Trauffer went, the flowers grew. I found him a vastly kind and charitable man with an unusual gift for understanding people—their hidden motives, their real feelings. He discovered and used their capabilities and when he had chosen someone for some work, he trusted them to do it. This trust could be a heavy burden. I do not know about many of Bishop Trauffer's relationships, but I have a feeling that few people ever told him no.

The enormous respect accorded the bishop of a ward must be difficult for a non-Mormon to understand. Overnight, this chosen man becomes lawyer, doctor, minister, water master, psychologist, arbitrator, and marriage counselor. He grants privileges, comforts the sick and bereaved, approves and is the initial source of Church welfare to the needy. He is the center of remarkable power in his ward community. In at least one ward that I know of, the members seriously discussed the possibility that the bishop would judge his flock come Judgment Day.

Allegiance from one bishop to another is transferred with the raising of the right hand. It is literally a vote to "sustain" him. I grew to love and respect Bishop Trauffer. I enjoyed hearing him talk; even though once in a while his phraseology slipped, his meaning was always very clear. Whenever he asked me to take some job or do some task to help in the work of the Ward, I could never turn him down, even when it was a personal sacrifice. It was something about the way he asked. He did not demand, he did not expect, he left you free to refuse without excuse—perhaps that is why so few of us could refuse. Many bishops demand and it has become easy for me to refuse such demands.

I was approached once by a Bishop who asked me to teach a Sunday School class. I refused saying that I thought I perhaps had some writing ability and I needed my spare time to develop it. My caller pushed aside my excuse with a contemptuous snort.

"I'm your Bishop," he thundered. "You are supposed to do as I say." But I did not *feel* that he was my Bishop, although he led the Ward in which I lived. Bishop Trauffer would have applauded my decision, I think. Once he called me into his office to explain to me why I was *not* being asked to take a certain position in the Ward, the only instance of this kind I've ever known—but then he was an unusual Bishop.

If a man is faithful, pays his tithing, attends his meetings, keeps the Word of Wisdom, pays his Church assessments, and attends to his various Priesthood duties, he is bound to be given a position of authority within his ward or stake. In a small town, he is almost certain to become a bishop or a member of the Bishopric. I have seen men, whose meager abilities made them nearly invisible, brought into the limelight of the Bishopric and I have watched them struggle to be what was asked of them until they actually met those requirements. I have also seen the status of Church office and authority turn men into mindless bigots and domineering fools. That this has always been true is shown by the oft repeated warning:

"We have learned by sad experience that it is the nature and disposition of almost all men as soon as they get a little authority, as they suppose, they will immediately begin to exercise unrighteous dominion" (*Doctrine and Covenants*).

I have seen several examples of this, though it seems to be evidenced more in stake presidents and higher authorities than in bishops. Inconceivably, this attitude is accepted, even expected among many members of the Church, for any refusal to uphold the leadership is a sign that you are slipping onto the road to perdition. And in Zion that road is a damnably rough one. There's no garden path to hell in Mormon communities. If you go down it, it'll be a grinding struggle all the way.

For councilors, Bishop Trauffer had chosen Roland Parkinson, a congenial little man everyone called Parky, and Clarence Walker, whose wife Beverly was an ardent Church and civic worker. Brother Walker was red-haired, and, I think, fiery-tempered. He once told me with finality:

"Some women take too much upon themselves. If all the Priesthood members were doing as they should, all the auxiliary organizations would be manned by men. Woman's place is in the Relief Society." I can't remember the cause of this outburst, but no doubt it was meant for me—at least I took it that way.

Brother Walker is now Bishop of Lincoln Ward. Gray has lightened his hair and wisdom has given him grace and tact.

When I last talked to him, he was kind and understanding, and I knew from our conversation that he would be a great comfort to the members of his Ward.

"What are you doing in the Church, now?" he asked me.

"Nothing." And such is my conditioning that I was embarrassed to say it. I told him that in the last Ward I had lived in I had offered to teach a Mutual class, knowing that a teacher was needed at the time. I had called the Bishop's wife and volunteered, after a long time away from such activity.

"If you need a teacher," I had said, "I've taught this age group before and loved teaching them. I have some time now and I think I could do a good job."

"I'll pass on your offer to the Bishop when he comes in," she said with the graciousness usual to bishops' wives.

"But, I'd better tell you—I drink coffee."

"Oh," and the graciousness receded, "in that case, we won't need you." She said goodbye and hung up, and I sat there feeling as if I'd been slapped. I've never offered my services to anyone in any ward since.

"Well, she shouldn't have done that," Brother Walker sympathized, "but I guess she hasn't yet learned that the Church is for sinners. Those of us who are perfect really don't need it at all."

And I thought: Clarence, I'll bet you've turned out to be a dandy Bishop.

LINCOLN WARD WAS SITUATED in the midst of a growing business district. As businesses came in, people moved out, except for the older residents who had lived most of their lives in the modest but solid homes of the Sugarhouse District. Before newcomers could be assimilated into the Ward Family, they had moved out again. So our Ward had a great number of older people, and while there seemed to be an abundance of children and teenagers, the work of the Ward had to be distributed among comparatively few workers.

It was a constant problem for the Bishopric to keep an officer in each position and a teacher in each class. There were about four hundred members of the Ward, but this included everyone who had been baptized into the Church who lived in the area the Ward covered. Many of them never came to Church except on Mother's Day and Easter. At least a third of the members were inactive, and with so many members past sixty, every willing worker had more than one job. (In an average ward there are about one hundred and twenty positions to be filled, not counting Relief Society visiting teachers and home —Priesthood—teachers.)

The Stake drew from our Ward members too, because there were about the same number of positions to be filled on the Stake level. Often, a Stake worker had to resign his Ward positions because the demands of both were too great. This is one of the keys to the continuance and growth of the Church. Each worker is made to feel a great sense of achievement and importance. Every one can be a big frog in a little puddle, and there are millions of puddles in the Church. Whenever they run out of puddles, they divide the wards and stakes and start all over again with a new supply of puddles to fit every size of frog. I splashed around in quite a few of them.

In less than six months after I had been going to Church regularly, I was a visiting teacher, literary leader in Relief Society, and leader of the (Mia Maids) fifteen- and sixteen-year-old girls in Mutual. I taught a class in Sunday School and had been secretary of the Primary. As soon as I could gracefully ask for a release, I got out of the Primary. Perhaps my old dislike of Primary was still with me, or maybe it was just that I dislike being secretary of anything.

In the Church everything is done by competitive quotas and percents. Like many other willing workers, I got pretty sick of quotas. There was a quota to reach and surpass in selling the Church magazines, quotas for cannery workers, quotas for building funds. If you are a good Mormon and if you move around a lot in the newer residential areas, the building fund can keep you poor.

The wards grow and are divided, and while I lived in one house in one area, we were members of four different wards and three different stakes. If the ward is old, it has been paid for, but if it is new, there is a Church house to build. The Church donates a percentage for the building, the rest of the money must be raised by the members of the ward. And the building must be entirely paid for before it is allowed to be dedicated. There is, understandably, a great reluctance to hold Church meetings in undedicated buildings.

The Churches get fancier and fancier and the family assessments for building get higher and higher. According to a statement in a recent Church magazine, the Church is building one new wardhouse every day, 365 a year!

In the area where our house belonged to so many wards and stakes, we paid the building assessment for the first Wardhouse that was built after we moved there. After that, I balked. Paying to build more than one Church in the same area was too much for me. But I am not typical of Latter-day Saints, since all those buildings were built and paid for.

The Bishoprics of these new wards desperately strive to raise money before the time set for dedication. In one Ward, lacking eight thousand dollars to meet its building quota, they held an auction. All the tools used to build the Ward were auctioned. And in the fire of dedicating enthusiasm, one shovel was auctioned for four hundred dollars, and a wheel barrow for a thousand. The money was raised in one night and the Church was dedicated on schedule. I thought that Bishop must have done a lot of hard praying.

Many Mormons take so seriously the Temple Recommend oath of giving their worldly goods to the building up of the Church that they deprive themselves. One widow, who lived near us, willed a large and valuable suburban property to the Church as the building ground for a wardhouse, keeping only enough of it for a modest yard to surround her even more modest dwelling. At that time the land was in a prime residential area where acres sold for five to ten thousand dollars. The odd thing was that her children, active Church workers themselves, and of equally modest means, agreed happily to this donation of their inheritance. There are more like her than one would think.

Being secretary of the Primary meant keeping records of all the quotas: how many children attended, how many teachers were there, how many officers attended, who conducted the meetings, who led the songs and what songs were sung, what lessons were given, how many baptisms were performed for the dead by how many girls and boys, how many copies of the *Children's Friend* were sold this year in comparison to last, how much money in birthday pennies was turned in for the benefit of the Primary Children's Hospital in Salt Lake City. (From earliest childhood, a child is made to feel that it is a special privilege each year to give a penny for every birthday to the Children's Hospital. On the child's birthday there is a special ceremony, and the child marches up to the stand to deposit the pennies in a special golden birthday bank, while the other Primary children chant the count. And yearly, there is a concerted drive to gather a penny for each year of the age of every member—now it's two—inflation has even affected birthday pennies.)

When I got through with all the record-keeping, all the percentages and all the quotas, what did I have to show for my hours of work? Nothing but a ledger book to be stacked away on shelves like those of the old Circle Room. Maybe I didn't like Primary because of what my energetic grandmother used to term my "sloth." She would shake her head in dismay and scold me.

"You don't get it from your father's side of the family. There never was a lazy Hicken." I grew up with the taint of laziness hanging about me, but now I know it was just that I could not bear to work and see nothing for my efforts.

During my childhood, for instance, I loved the summer's tiring canning days. My grandmother would compliment me with wonder in her voice.

"You deserve a white mark on the wall for this day's work," she would say. "Sometimes you seem like a different girl."

Even then, when I worked I liked to see a product: rows of canned peaches, their lids pinging as they seal, a cake swirled in frosting, standing on the cake rack, a stack of ironed linens, a full cookie jar, or a table of brown-crusted bread, hot from the oven. I do not really like to sew, but I like to see little girls' dresses, embroidered and appliqued, pressed and waiting to be worn for the first time. It satisfies something deep inside me to see a pile of books, already read, and waiting to go back to the library. I liked to help harvest Papa's garden, but I hated the planting. There was such a long time to wait before it produced.

I dislike ordinary household chores. It seems to me that a woman who has kept a spotless house for fifty years only to have it need cleaning the day after her funeral has wasted her life. But I've come along Mama's well-swept path far enough to know that certain of these monotonous chores must be done each day, and certain standards of order must be maintained to live with any degree of comfort—and I love comfort. But I try to keep those demands to a minimum.

EVEN THOUGH I WAS DOING more in the Church, I still went to the Gardiners'. The morning walk to their house was a lovely one. Salt Lake City in spring and summer is beautiful. It is a city whose streets are lined with trees and all the yards I passed were filled with flowers. I chose different routes, as Papa would have done, and I learned as I passed the houses where the various members of the Ward lived. I spent each morning except Sundays at the Gardiners, helping a little, being helped a lot.

There are many things in the Church that are accepted with the equanimity that comes with always having lived with them. But they must seem a little odd to non-Mormons—they seem a little odd to a lot of Mormons, too, if they take time out to think.

I've been told since childhood that one day the Saints would live the United Order. I knew it had been tried in the early days of the Church. Orderville, Utah was a town named for the experiment which went sour there as well as in several other places. I'd also been told that the reason for the failures of the United Order was because the people weren't ready—weren't good enough to live it. But I really didn't think about it much until the first time I mentioned the Order to a non-Mormon. I was shaken by his comment.

"Hell, that's Communism."

"It is not," I denied indignantly. "The Church is almost as opposed to Communism as they are to cigarettes."

Brother Gardiner and I talked about the United Order as we talked about anything else that puzzled me.

"It seems to me that my friend is almost right," I said. "In the Order we would have to pool our resources, work from there, and distribute the product of that work 'according to each man's needs,' doesn't it say? If this has been predicted, then why are there so many Mormons that are John Birchers and rabid anti-Communists? You'd think that they'd be against the principle of the United Order, too, but the ones I've talked to haven't been. It doesn't make sense."

"Well, there is one basic difference," Brother Gardiner pointed out. "Communism is under the direction of the State. It is political. The United Order would be lived under the Church—guided by God."

"In theory, Brother Gardiner. It's all very beautiful in theory —both the Order and Communism—but either way it doesn't work."

"Now," he was not disposed to argue the point, "we won't be living it for a while, anyway, even though I have heard it preached that the United Order is part of God's plan for the perfection of the Saints." He smiled gently at me and his eyes twinkled. "I grant the fact that we don't seem to be any more perfect than we were in the days of Brother Brigham."

"There's always the man," I said, "who only plants one row, but who takes the crops from ten—according to his needs! And there is the one who is quite willing and happy to lean on his shovel and chat while another man hoes and weeds and waters all day. I don't think it will ever work in God's world. It would be no different now than it was in Orderville. When the lesser lights of the Ward went to the storehouse, everything was picked over by the wives of the Bishops and Stake presidents and high councilmen. I'm told that's how it was in Orderville— after the tithes, the best of it had been sent in to the Church."

"Whoa now, Sister Hunter, don't make judgments. We could live it, *in God's world*, if we become finer, less greedy human beings."

"Nope," I shook my head, "that'll never be. Human nature is against it, unless force is used."

"Don't be so positive, young lady. You may find yourself living the United Order yet, and maybe polygamy, too. You know, there's the prophecy that seven women shall hang to one man's coat-tail."

"I thought they'd already done their best to fulfill that one! But if it is yet to come, it won't come to me. I'm one of those that'll never be good enough."

"You might have to learn to be . . ."

"Brother Gardiner, about being good enough—what do you know about Second Endowments?"

"About as much as most people do about First Endowments before they get them when they go through the Temple. They are apparently given to those people who have proved through their worthiness in this life that they are entitled to special blessings in the next one. They are reserved for only the very elect."

"The higher authorities and their wives and families?"

"I would suppose. But the Second Endowment is very secret, sacred, and rarely given, so of course no one knows very much about it. In fact, they may not do it at *all*, any more."

"Yes, I think they must," I said, "because I heard that Sister ——————— was being given hers this week. She is a Temple worker in the washing and anointing rooms, and the wife of a former Stake president." Brother Gardiner looked thoughtful. "I know them. Brother ——————— will be getting his then."

"Her daughter-in-law mentioned it to me. I was surprised because I hadn't heard anything about Second Endowments for years, but I don't think that Margaret would have any reason to mislead me. I think she told me because she was so pleased. I knew what she was talking about because I'd heard Papa mention them a few times. I always thought that if anyone should have received Second Endowments, he should have."

"I don't know how the choices are made or who makes them. It is something that I'd rather not talk about since I know so little about it."

"Like one of the *mysteries* that we're not supposed to delve into?"

"Something like that, yes."

"I've always thought that hands-off, or rather, minds-off-the-mysteries attitude was an effective throttle to any questioner."

"Perhaps," he admitted, "but there are some questions that are foolish to ask."

"Like who made God?"

Brother Gardiner shook his head wearily at me. "That's one that will drive you mad if you dwell on it. And there is no need to dwell on such things. But Mormons are a funny group. We spend half our lives arguing about things that literally have no importance to us at all. In this stage of our existence we do not have the enlightenment to understand the answers even if we had them."

"Maybe some people do. Maybe these things are like Einstein's theory—only a half dozen people in the world have the capacity to understand it." I paused, "Brother Gardiner, do you think that the President and the Apostles know all the answers? Papa was convinced that they did, or he seemed to be."

"Well," he said judiciously, "the ones I've known didn't seem to know it all," and then he added with irreverence not common to most bishops, "but a few of them thought that they did!"

THEN ONE MORNING, Brother Gardiner called to tell me that Sister Gardiner wouldn't need me any more; she had died in her sleep the night before. I sang with a Relief Society group and helped with the flowers for her funeral.

In Relief Society, I had almost immediately been drafted into service as a visiting teacher, and although I was very careful not to try to convert anyone, I went with my partner around our district every month. My grandmother used to call it "beat" or "block teaching," which meant, as it does now, that the district is usually about one block, or perhaps both sides of the street for two blocks. It was through his block teachers that Brother Gardiner's need had been discovered.

When a funeral occurs on your beat—I mean district—you are expected to offer your services to the family. The visiting teachers prepare or assign for preparation the vast amounts of food served after the funeral to the mourners and to out-of-town guests. Depending on the degree of help the family needs, it is one of the duties of the visiting teachers to offer. This even extends to scrubbing, cleaning, and preparing the home of the deceased for the funeral and for visitors, although I've often heard women instruct, and I've given these same instructions myself, "If I should die, don't you dare allow the Relief Society Sisters in to clean!" This is another bit of Mormon humor— with teeth in it. Fear of what the Sisters might find has forced many a woman into being a passable housekeeper.

A funeral in a Mormon ward is always an event. Often, programs are printed and passed out to those who attend the services. It is usually a very pleasant affair for all except those few who are deeply grieved. And the cheerful gathering is most likely the best therapy for the mourners. Always under the direction of the Bishopric, most of the women in the ward help where they can. I went to all of the funerals in Lincoln Ward, along with the rest of the good Sisters. I was a member of the Singing Mothers, a Relief Society singing group, much in demand for funerals. Also, it was the duty of the Relief Society officers, of which I was now one, being literary leader, to take care of the profusion of flowers. "Take care of" meant receiving and arranging them behind and around the casket, removing the cards to give to the family, transporting and arranging the flowers again at graveside.

As soon as the casket was wheeled from its place in front of the pulpit, the ladies hustled out with the flower baskets and awkward wreaths to the waiting cars. By the time the slow-moving cortege reached the burial grounds, the flowers were already banked around the grave, hiding the mounds of freshly dug earth.

Emotion makes people hungry, and after a funeral they seem to me to be the hungriest of all. Looking back over all the luncheons, parties, dinners, and banquets I've attended, I have concluded that no better food is served anywhere at any time than after a Mormon funeral. The women send their specialties, the abundance is staggering, the quality superb. And having been on the receiving end of this largesse several times, I find no fault with it, for when I'm feeling bad about something, I have no heart to cook.

The food is a service given and gratefully received. Last summer, when one of my aunts died, she was to be buried in the Heber City Cemetery, and after the burial one of the ac-companying Relief Society ladies from my aunt's Ward in Salt Lake City told us that there were several cars waiting, packed with food, paper plates, napkins, gallons of punch, and cups. The entire funeral party went down to the city park and spread the repast on the plank tables and had a picnic. If there is black humor in a funeral picnic, we did not see it. We were tired and hungry and grateful for the refreshment.

There is no such thing as a poorly attended funeral for an active Mormon. But I have wondered at times, being the wonderer that I am, if the knowledge of such hospitality does not swell the attendance. And after it is over, you always hear, "Wasn't that a lovely funeral?" Or, "It was one of the nicest funerals I've ever been to." (Mormons do not believe in the permanence of death. They believe that it is only a parting and that in time they'll join all their family again on the other side —*provided* they've been married in the Temple, or sealed to one another in Temple rites.)

Again, I am out of step with my Mormon community. I do not like to go to funerals. I went to them in Lincoln Ward because I felt it was my duty, but now I avoid all those I can. It is not that I am afraid of death; too many of those I love, like Papa, are on the other side for me to dread it. I am reluctant to think of people whom I have known in the cold state of death. I have felt this way ever since I was ten years old and I went to see Mr. McKnight.

Mr. McKnight lived at the top of our street. He was a nice old man who visited with my grandfather occasionally, and my grandmother was the McKnight's visiting teacher. When he died my grandmother sent me up to their house.

"Take this pan of fried chicken up to the McKnights for me," Mama said, "and don't sneak a piece of it on the way, either. And put on a clean apron before you go." I had no aprons, it was her term for a fresh dress. "And don't stay."

I would probably have eaten a piece of chicken if she hadn't warned me. Knowing my grandmother's frugality, she'd never kill two chickens on a week day unless we were expecting company. So if she sent the McKnights the chicken, we'd have fried pork side meat for supper, which I didn't much like.

I changed my dress and took the pan from the stove without complaining about the fairly long walk to the McKnight house, because I intended to see Brother McKnight stretched out in his coffin if I could manage it.

Mrs. McKnight accepted the chicken, thanked me for bringing it and asked me to come in, though I don't think she expected me to. I did, though, and stood in the hall waiting.

"Just a minute," she said, "I'll return your grandma's pan so it won't get lost." I looked at Mrs. McKnight closely. She'd been crying, but she seemed cheerful enough now. "She'll probably be all right," I thought, "until somebody comes to see her and then everybody will cry again."

"Mr. McKnight is in the front room. Would you like to go see him while I wash this pan?" She waved me toward a partly opened door. I went in quickly. There was no one in the room with him, although I could hear women talking somewhere in the house. Mr. McKnight's coffin was covered in gray plush, and he lay in it sort of crowded, I thought, with his shoulders touching the silk-lined sides, and his head upon a fluffy silk pillow.

He wore Temple clothes, and he had his hands, which looked dry and stiff, folded over the band of his green silk, embroidered apron. His robes were "done up" beautifully, lying in pleated perfection over his left shoulder. They partially covered his white shirt. He wore no coat but he had a white cap on his head.* It had a tassel on it which came down over one ear. It covered most of his head which had been quite bald and freckled. Dressed as he was, he didn't look like anyone I'd ever known. I'd seen my baby cousin, Florence, after she was dead. She had been lying on a pillow and she looked as if she were sleeping. Mr. McKnight didn't look relaxed as Florence had, he looked rather uncomfortable. I went very close to the coffin and watched his chest to see if maybe they had made a mistake and he wasn't dead at all. Did it move? I wasn't sure. I reached out with a forefinger and placed it in the center of his forehead.

He was dead all right. His forehead was stiff and hard. The skin didn't feel like skin at all. It had a solid coldness shocking on such a hot summer day. I heard Mrs. McKnight coming in with the pan, so I stepped back from the casket and tried to keep my face expressionless as she came in.

"Looks real good, doesn't he? Brother Winterrose does a fine job. I'm surprised he looks so good seeing that he was ill so long and looked so bad before."

---

* The cap, or veil for the women, is usually not worn until the casket is ready for closing. Then the eldest son puts the cap in place, or if the deceased is the mother, it is done by the eldest daughter, providing that the son or daughter has been through the Temple. Only the intimate members of the family are allowed in the room for this last service for the dead, and perhaps this is the most moving part of the Mormon funeral rites. I do not know why Mr. McKnight wore his cap.

She really wasn't paying any attention to me—not even talking to me, just talking to herself in front of me, and she didn't require an answer. I went out into the sunshine. The heat was nice. My finger felt queer, though, and I was a little frightened at what I had done. The coldness from Mr. McKnight's forehead had gone halfway up it.

"What did she say?" my grandmother asked. She always wanted to know every word. If people didn't say enough to satisfy her, I made some up.

"She said thank you very much. She had lots of cakes and pies and salad and stuff, but no one had sent in any meat. She said she appreciated that."

I poured hot water from the tea kettle into the basin on the washstand. I put my finger in it and let it stay in the hot water as long as I could bear it.

"What on earth are you doing?"

"Washing my hands. Must have gotten some grease on them from the pan." And I washed both hands thoroughly, soaped them a couple of times, and dried them briskly on the roller towel that hung on the kitchen door. But as I recall, my finger didn't warm up for quite a while.

It was a long time before I visited the dead again, and I go only when it is expected of me, and sometimes not even then. I try to avoid the popular "viewings" that are commonly held the night and the hour before the funeral. When it is required because the dead one is family or a close friend, I stand as briefly as possible at the side of the casket. I would much rather remember people as they lived and breathed and walked. And I never touch them. I don't want any more cold fingers.

Chapter 8

MAGNIFIED
CALLINGS

THE SUNDAY SCHOOL CLASS I taught was hardly a job at all since I went to Sunday School anyway. The lessons were repetitions of all the hundreds of Sunday School and Seminary lessons I had heard. In these classes one talked of Church history, the lives of the Prophets (Mormon Presidents), the Bible, *The Book of Mormon*, the Mormon settling of the west, and the lives and treks of the pioneers. These were *Mormon* pioneers. So far as a Mormon boy or girl is concerned there are no *other* pioneers. Except for the courageous and fruitless trek of the

Mormon Battalion, there was not much interest in this work for me.

Primary began right after school adjourned on Tuesdays and lasted until about five o'clock. With Relief Society beginning at one o'clock on three Tuesdays of the month and running for a full day on the fourth Tuesday, Primary from 3:30 until 5:00, and MIA again at 7:00, Tuesdays as well as Sundays are almost entirely Church days.

The other days of the week are not neglected by the Church. The Latter-day Saint passion for meetings to plan meetings to plan meetings is one that is moaned about throughout Mormondom. And those who should attend each meeting are mightily exhorted to be there so the 100 percent attendance quota can be met. I dislike meeting quotas for the sake of the quota. I dislike attending a meeting just to be marked as a digit in an attendance record, but I went to the meetings along with the others because I liked basking in the warm sun of approval, and was reluctant to be one of the backsliders who brought down the percentage. It *was* humiliating to stand up with the mere thirty of Lincoln's Ward attending officers and teachers and be put to shame by seventy of Fairmont Ward's bench-filling attenders when we were counted by the Stake clerk at the monthly Officers and Teachers Meeting.

For each class I taught or for each organization to which I belonged, I attended four to six meetings every month. Before Relief Society, Primary, and MIA there was prayer meeting for the officers and teachers. The officers often had prayer meetings of their own. There were preparation meetings for each class where you were given helps for teaching, or if you were an officer, advice in solving problems or planning programs. And there were fireside meetings after Church on Sunday nights. There were also private planning meetings you had to attend because you had been assigned to the food, entertainment, or decorating committees for various auxiliary functions.

The meetings are so many and varied that the Church has declared one night a week for parents to stay home with their families. This is Home Night and if it weren't for that, some active Mormon parents would meet their children only at mealtimes, if then. It is a common saying that the bishop's son or the stake president's son is the worst boy in the ward, and I wonder if it is because he is expected to be the best, or if it is because his father is so busy with the affairs of the ward that there is no time left for his home.

There is one great advantage to all of these meetings. It ties the individuals from the wards into the Mormon Stake Family. I grew to know most of the names and of all of the faces of people, not only of those in our Ward, but of active members in all of Granite Stake. In many cases I learned to know the people behind the names and the faces, and I found myself being drawn tightly and warmly into the vast, striving Mormon Clan.

Shortly after you have accepted a position in any level of the Church organization, you are called one evening to be "set apart." This intimate and impressive little ceremony usually occurs in the Bishop's office. The Bishopric, which includes the ward clerk or clerks, is there as well as the other people who are assuming new positions.

In turn, a member of the Bishopric places his hands upon your head and you are set apart for the work you have been asked to do. The blessings of guidance, inspiration, health, and energy are asked for you. Usually you are "given" various "gifts." Once when I was being set apart, I was given the gifts of discernment and perception—so I would be able to see into the hearts of other people, know their unspoken wishes, desires, and meanings, and would have the capacity to understand. Perhaps, it is the power of suggestion, but I have seen people blessed with such gifts develop them to an astonishing degree.

You are also told to "magnify your calling." This means to

work hard at your job, to use whatever means you have to make it a good work, and if you did this, you would be blessed in many ways. I don't think I did much magnifying in Primary and Sunday School because I thought of Primary as an affliction and taught Sunday School only as a favor to the Bishop—but I loved working in Relief Society and Mutual.

THE GROUP OF fifteen- and sixteen-year-olds in YWMIA were called Mia Maids. This was a class that up to this point had been run by the girls. And they counted coup on any number of teachers whom they had driven from the class by their inattentive rudeness. My daughter Sally was a member of this class.

"What do you mean, they try to see how many teachers they can get to quit? I hope that you are not acting up in that class."

"Oh, it's sort of a game, Mom. You know, some of the lessons are dull, and you *have* to go to get your 100 percent award."

"If I get any reports of you being rude, it will be a sad day for you." But teachers of Church classes are not prone to report unruliness, and I heard nothing more. Then I was asked to teach the class.

"It's rather a difficult age group," the MIA president told me, "but we thought perhaps you might take it because you have girls that age." She indicated my duty clearly.

So I took the class and for the first two weeks found teaching an impossibility. Just being heard was impossible. The girls were shrill, inattentive, and pointedly uninterested in me or anything I might have to say to them. One night, I'd had enough. I slapped my lesson book down on the table.

"I am not going to waste my time preparing lessons to which you do not listen," I said angrily. "I don't give a damn"—they gasped—"for your 100 percent certificate. If you can't behave, you won't be allowed in this class, and I'm willing, no, I'm

eager to tell your parents why. Tonight I came to the class-
room early and waited for you. I am appalled at the din you
made coming down through these halls. You've been taught
that this is the House of the Lord. If you think that it is, treat
it with the respect it deserves. If you don't think it is, you'd
be better off spending your time somewhere else."

Someone started to answer back about being made to go to
Church, and the interruption, justified or not, infuriated me.

"After this, in this class, you will wait until you are given
permission to speak. You will wait until I am through. It's a
good thing that the Lord loves you a lot more than I do, and
that He has a lot more patience than I do, too, because if I were
the Lord and you raced and screamed in my house as I've seen
you do in this one for the past two weeks," I paused dramati-
cally, "I'd strike you all dead!"

It hadn't come out just as I thought it would. I groaned
inwardly at my angry melodramatics, and waited for the girls
to titter.

But they didn't. The room was quiet. And in the quiet, I
picked up the book and went on with the lesson. I had no more
discipline problems. My girls were responsive and cooperative,
and there is nothing so delightful as an interested, expressive
teenage girl.

Every month, we had a surprise Tuesday, but the girls did
not know which night it would be. On these nights, we cele-
brated the birthdays of the girls who had been born in that
month with birthday cakes and gifts. I did not encourage 100
percent attendance, but they all came.

Non-Mormon girls came, too. I remember one especially. She
was the daughter of a Fundamentalist. (An offshoot group of
the Church that still practices polygamy.) I felt such great
pity for this girl, who wore high-necked, long-sleeved, un-
fashionable dresses. I didn't think she would be allowed to come
often, and she was not. I guessed that her father, who was

reported to have four wives, was afraid that she would be turned against the "principle" if she attended our classes.

The girls told me with greedy honesty that they came every time because they didn't know what would happen, what treat there would be, and they didn't want to miss anything.

Because so many Mormon girls marry in their late teens, the Gleaner class had only one lonely member, Sara Curtis. My class combined both the First and Second year Mia Maids, usually taught in separate classes, so the Bishop asked me if I would like to have Sara as an assistant.

"It would solve two problems, Sister Hunter. Sara would be drawn closer to the other girls, a badly needed teacher would be freed for another class, and you can probably use help with your big class."

I was pleased to have her and my pleasure increased as time went on. She didn't give the lessons; she was shy about taking charge, but she was close to the other girls in age and filled with suggestions about things that would interest them. She tirelessly worked on favors, parties, and refreshments. She ran errands and kept a beautiful class history book bound in pale blue silk. The book later won high praise from the MIA General Board. When I left the class for the Mutual presidency, I was given the book. I took it out of its box just the other day to refresh my memory for this chapter.

We had guest speakers: young beauty operators to show them how to pluck their eyebrows, the ways to roll their hair, and how to apply makeup; women whom they admired from our Ward and other Wards talked to them of grooming, of the necessity to use deodorants no matter how often they bathed, and of homemaking, flower-arranging, and etiquette. A friend of mine who was a registered nurse spoke to them of personal hygiene. When our lessons were on chastity, instead of skipping around with "keeping oneself pure" and the "sins of the flesh" they'd heard about innumerable times before, our family doctor came and talked to the girls. He didn't hedge. He told them of the results of promiscuity and venereal disease. He put the subject on an individual and very personal level. He was a handsome young man, and he impressed them. He told them that "sex was too little to *hold* a boy for long and too much to *give* him," and he explained why.

I expected some repercussions from a parent or two, but there were none. Girls that age are intensely interested in sex and very shy about revealing their interest, but it was obvious that they thought that was the best class they had ever attended. "Ooh, I sure would have hated to miss that!"

After that evening, if they had questions, they asked them. We set aside a portion of every class for questions. Sometimes I was both shocked at their lack of knowledge and at their directness in revealing it—and themselves. I thought it sad that they could talk with me so freely, and not with their own mothers. But at that age, mothers and daughters are worlds apart. I felt I was closer to mine than most, but I suspected that it was because in the MIA classes I was teacher and friend, rather than mother—though it did not escape me that my girls asked few questions and instead listened attentively to the answers to questions the other girls asked.

There was one girl in my Mutual class who had become a great worry to her parents. The Bishop was worried about her, too. I cannot describe the situation in detail without infringing on her privacy, but she was physically precocious, and she had certain social problems of which her parents were aware, but were helpless to do anything about. Carmella did foolish things which it was plain to see would lead her into some painful situations. I worried about her, but of all the girls in my class, I could talk to her least.

There is one thing in which everyone has a universal interest, and in which teenage girls are avidly excited: what the future will bring. I doubted that Carmella was any different than any other teenage girl, so we had a party for the girls at my house, and during the evening I read all of their futures—in their palms.

I know nothing about palmistry, but I didn't have to. What I wanted to tell these girls couldn't be seen in their palms by the most accomplished mystic. It was an exhausting evening for me, I suppose because it was such a hard stretch for my imagination. I read fourteen or fifteen palms that night just to be able to talk to Carmella privately and give her some truths about life that I could not tell her in any other way.

"Your hand shows a passionate and loving nature," I said. "Look! Here and here, crosses that show disaster. These are warnings," and I went on to give her the warnings without mincing words. It worked. She took the advice I "saw" in her hand, and she changed. The change was noticeable in her home and certainly in her relationships with other girls—in that long, palm-reading session, we discussed all of her problems. Carmella was one of those girls who had come to Church with reluctance and because of force. Now I could sense her eager interest in the classes, and I was further rewarded when Bishop Trauffer called me in one day to talk to me in the quiet, appreciative way he had.

"Sister Hunter, I thought I should thank you for what you've done for Carmella. What has worked the change? We've all tried with her. Her mother and father—you know what fine people they are. All of us in the Bishopric—it was to no avail. We think you've worked a small miracle. How did you do it?"

I thought it better not to answer that. I hum-hawed and tried to think of something. "The girls," I said, which was very true, "the girls have all helped. They've included her. They've asked her advice. They've gone out of their way to be sweet and friendly."

"Well, whatever it was, the Bishopric and her parents want to thank you."

I left his office feeling guilty and wondering what he'd have said if I told him I'd used a form of witchcraft. Or perhaps, I eased my conscience, it had been simple psychology. And then I eased it further. Wasn't there something in the Scriptures about using whatever was at hand, questionable though it might be, for the greater good? I thought and thought, but all I could come up with was: "It is better that one man perish than a nation dwindle in unbelief."

As I remembered, that was Nephi's justification for killing his uncle Laban when Nephi went back to Jerusalem to get the records that he had been instructed to take with him to Zarahemla. (Remember that first Relief Society theology lesson?) This was when they'd come across the ocean in a wooden ship that brought a group of Jews to South America several hundred years prior to the birth of Christ. As explained by *The Book of Mormon*, some of their skins were darkened for evil-doing after they had landed and they became the forbears of the American Indian.

ONE OF THE BIGGEST PROBLEMS my Mia Maids had was their lack of spending money. There was little work obtainable, and there were far more girls in our Ward than there were babysitting jobs available. Not all the girls were given allowances, and those that were found them inadequate. Sally and Ann came to us with lists of their needs and expenditures and complained that they just couldn't "live on" their allowances, and I knew that we were more generous than most.

I thought we could expand the babysitting outside the limits of the Ward if we had some sort of reliable service available. So on free Tuesdays (for which no lesson was required), I gave a course in babysitting. The girls who did not have small brothers and sisters, and even some who did, learned how to change a baby, how to prepare formula, how to take a rectal temperature, and how to set up a steam tent and use a steam kettle.

I'd had some terrible babysitters, and my experiences served as text material for the class. Once I had asked a seventeen-year-old girl to sit with Sally and Ann while my husband and I went out. It was two or three days before Christmas, and I had all the children's gifts hidden away. The babysitter searched our shelves and closets, took out the toys and entertained the girls wonderfully for the evening. I was aghast when four-year-old Sally asked me if the rocking chair in the closet was really for her. That was the end of that babysitter.

In the same neighborhood, I found another babysitter. She was an older girl from an impoverished family. She was thin, so in addition to paying her double the going rate, I made sure that the refrigerator was well stocked every time I had her in.

"Eat all you want," I urged. And I was always amazed at how much that girl could eat, for no matter how much I left, the food was almost demolished. I really felt sorry for her then. I thought she must be starving until I realized that no one could eat that much. And when all that was left of a six-pound roast that I'd left in the oven to finish cooking was the grease and a few scraps that had stuck to the bottom of the roaster, I questioned her.

"You didn't *eat* all that roast," I said, shaking my head.

"You said to eat as much as I wanted, you know."

"Yes, I did say that, but you didn't eat all of this roast by yourself?"

"The kids ate some of it."

"Sally and Ann. They don't eat enough meat to put in your eye. I have to *make* them eat it to get dessert!"

It was embarrassing for both of us, but finally the girl admitted that she'd been bringing in her brothers and sisters to feed them.

Not being able to find a reliable sitter was hard on me. After the roast incident I had to give up bridge and movies and stay at home with my children until Aunt Tressa came and Mickey Aloia offered to trade sitting time.

I knew our service would be appreciated. It was. I had so many calls for the babysitters that I had to install a private line. We had some rules for the people who hired the girls, too. We asked that if the sitter could not easily walk the distance, she be picked up by car. And she was to be taken home after dark even if it was a short way.

We talked about babysitting ethics: no boyfriends were to visit while they were sitting; no girlfriends, either, unless permission had been asked for and granted; no snooping; no snacking, unless they took goodies with them or unless they were specifically told that something had been prepared for them. We made up information sheets to be filled out by the parents: where the parent could be reached, the telephone numbers of doctors, police, and fire departments. On the slip, we had printed the fee charged per hour and also a line saying that the charge was for babysitting only—the girls did not clean the house or do dishes unless a special arrangement was made with the sitter. (However, we had stressed that it didn't hurt anyone to straighten up a front room or a kitchen if the children were sleeping and required no attention. There was such a thing as "earning" your money.)

I didn't advertise our service in the paper. It wasn't necessary. The news of it traveled, and in no time at all, any girl who wished to earn money had an opportunity to do so. When they called us, people could always get a sitter. If one was busy, the next girl in line was available.

I never had a complaint about a girl. They were so satisfactory and dependable that many of them were asked to stay for several days while parents took summer vacations. At these times, the girls knew that they could call me or their mothers if they had difficulties, but I can't remember that any of them called.

One evening at Officers and Teachers Meeting, the Bishop showed me the Church attendance record sheet for the Mutual Improvement Association. Our class was listed at the top of it. Shortly after that, Claire Middlemiss, private secretary for David O. McKay, phoned me and invited me to drop in for a brief visit with the President of the Church in his office, if I should care to do so. I never knew why I had been invited, but I didn't go. I was afraid that he might look through me as President Grant had once, and know that I told fortunes.

Chapter 9

MUTUAL IMPROVEMENT AND OTHER PEOPLE'S MIRACLES

I MAGNIFIED MY CALLING so much teaching the Mia Maids that I was asked to be second councilor in the YWMIA. The president was Minnie Garff, a long-time member of our Ward. I didn't know her well, for she had just returned from the mission field. I was surprised to be chosen as a councilor by Miss Garff. I supposed that she had heard of me through her sister, Thelma, who was active in the Relief Society.

For first councilor, Minnie had chosen Veronica Bettinson. Veronica and I worked together in PTA, and I respected her. She had as little regard for red tape and the endless petty discussions of endless petty procedural topics as I had. Between us, we connived to propose, second, and carry motions in the briefest PTA meetings on record. Veronica had also replaced Marge Brown as the Relief Society social science leader since Marge was moving out of the Ward.

Three more different women than Minnie, Veronica, and I would be hard to find. Our backgrounds were disimilar and there was a wide difference in our ages. We thought differently, reacted differently, and worked differently.

Minnie was the eldest of nine children in a devout Mormon family. She had been born in Hawaii when her father and mother were serving on a mission there. She was reared according to strict Latter-day Saint standards and ideals, which she adhered to as closely as her parents had. When their father died, Minnie and Thelma, both school teachers as their parents had been, chose to help their mother with the responsibilities of the growing family. When the other children were grown and had gone from the big, brown-frame, house, the two older girls stayed at home to care for and cherish their aging mother.

Veronica was an English woman who had married an American soldier and come to this country. They had met in a London branch of the Church during World War II. She was the daughter of a former Labor member of Parliament and she spoke with the accent of a grand dame and moved in a way reminiscent of the manner of the Queen Mother. This manner and accent served to make her occasional bursts of temper quite devastating. Veronica had lived through a psychologically destructive war and the terrible London blitz. I thought it was because of this that her English calm had a fragile shell which sometimes cracked.

Minnie was tall and slender with soft brown hair. She dressed in tailored suits and simple dresses. She spoke softly, but clearly, and I never saw her lose her temper, although I have known that she was angry. Veronica was small boned and blond with a fair English complexion. She was subject to the sudden onset of migraine headaches, to which she would publicly admit only after she had fainted from the effects of them. The first time I ever saw her was when she fainted and fell off the piano bench while she was playing for Primary one afternoon. Her remarkable poise returned with consciousness, and she gave me the impression that if I showed concern it would be bad form. I saw her husband Neil pick her up and carry her out of the Church another time, and he did it with such aplomb that it was as if he expected you to think it was part of the Church service.

The first councilor's duties were to look after the spiritual side of the MIA program—the classes, the attendance records, and so on. If a teacher was absent, Veronica must be prepared to take over the class on a minute's notice. My job as activity councilor was to direct the social side of the girl's program. MIA is mostly a social outlet for teenagers and young adults. There was supposed to be a young marrieds' class, but it never amounted to much because the young marrieds who could attend such a class were pressed into service as teachers and directors of the sports, drama, speech, music, and dancing parts of the program, and the others were tied to their homes with young children.

Minnie was the coordinator and had the deciding vote in any discussion. She was also the protective go-between for the Young Women and the Young Men (as the officers and teachers of the women's and men's organizations are commonly called).

She could accept the dictums of the Church hierarchy and pay the respect that Mormons are taught is due the Priesthood, yet she could be logically firm in any position she chose to support.

Surprisingly, we got along beautifully. In the three years that we were in the presidency, we met several times a month to solve problems and make plans. Often we took opposing views into our meetings, but we always left them with a feeling of solidarity. We were three women with one goal—to make of the Lincoln Ward YWMIA one of the finest in all Mormondom.

There is always a running stream of gossip in every ward. There are undercurrents and cliques. The activities of the people are so enmeshed that everything is everyone else's affair, and they talk about all of it. When Minnie was appointed president, there were those who thought a younger woman should have had the position. Minnie had worked in the MIA years before —I think she had been president then, too. The little words flew about. Perhaps it was these words that drew Veronica and me so close to her. She mentioned them diffidently one day.

"Maybe they are right. Maybe I'm too school teacherish, too stiff, maybe just a little too old. I don't feel that I am, but . . ." We would listen to no more. We were determined that Minnie should be the best YWMIA president in the history of Lincoln Ward, and I do not disparage any of the fine women who preceded or followed her, when I say that I believe she was.

Although the girls' sports program was supposedly under my direction, I was not at all interested in the softball, basketball, or volleyball teams. Minnie and Veronica took complete charge of these. Our music was handled by the Ward organist, Emma Tadje, and the Ward chorister, Ida Whitely—both competent and imaginative women. Although that, too, was supposed to be one of my worries, anything musical—songs to be learned, music for programs, song practices—all of it was taken

care of so well by these two that I never gave that vital part
of the program a second thought after the first month.

Not long ago, Veronica said to me, "I didn't appreciate
what you and Minnie and I had together when we worked in
the MIA presidency. It was my first experience, and I thought
all presidencies got along like that, but it's not so. I've been
in several in both ward and stake since then, and it has never
been the same. What we had was very rare."

As in every other organization, the Young Women's presidency worked under the direction of the Priesthood, in this
case, the Young Men's Superintendency. Our responsibility
was for the girls of the ward. Classes and sports programs outlined by the YWMIA General Board were conducted independently from those of the young men. Long ago, the
Church had incorporated the Boy Scout program into the
Young Men's Mutual Improvement Association. Scouting took
care of most of the classes for the boys. The sports program,
too, was scheduled. "M-men" basketball was an all-Church
sport. There were inter-ward, inter-stake, and inter-state Church
tournaments. This program brought a great number of young
men into participation. Anyone eighteen to thirty, Mormon or
non-Mormon could play, so long as he kept the Word of
Wisdom and attended the required Church meetings. However,
no more than two nonmembers could be on the floor at one
time during a game. (This activity seems to have a powerful
missionary pull. My friends, the Burton family, staunch Presbyterians, joined the Church via this route. The three boys, starting early in their teens, went to play basketball in the Ward
with their Mormon friends, became members of the M-Men
teams, were all Brigham Young University stars, married Mormon girls, and converted their parents and grandparents.)

The heavy social schedule of the MIA integrated both boys
and girls. I have heard criticism of the fact that boys and
girls mingle so freely in the MIA programs, and it is true that

Mormon girls marry young. Mormon boys are urged to marry immediately upon returning from their missions.* They heed the advice. My daughters wouldn't go out with a missionary until he'd been at home at least six months. "They aren't dates," they complained, "they are wrestling matches." While, of course, there are "have to" marriages in every ward, I have never personally known of such a marriage brought about by MIA social activities.

I've explained some of the problems of Lincoln Ward, but one of the most difficult for MIA leaders to work with occurs when the girls of a ward greatly outnumber the boys, as they did in our Ward. We had dances scheduled month after month, but there weren't enough boys to partner all the girls. These dances were held during Mutual time and for the most part they were not date dances. The boys who came stood grinning and jeering in one corner and wouldn't dance. I damned them frequently, to Minnie's raised eyebrows and Veronica's unspoken ladylike agreement.

We tried Grand Rights and Lefts, circle dances, square dances, Virginia reels, prize games (where in order to get the prize you had to dance with the person whose name was pasted on it). We had girls' choice dances sprinkled liberally through the programs—girls are far less reticent than boys in this age group.

Our dances were agonies of sideline confusion, loud music, and empty dance floors. We did not encourage girls to dance with girls. This rubbed like sandpaper on Minnie's and

---

* "I will give each of the young men in Israel, who have arrived at an age to marry (over eighteen) a mission to go straightway and get married to a good sister, fence a city lot, lay out a garden and orchard and make a home.

"There are multitudes of pure and holy spirits waiting to take tabernacles [bodies], now what is our duty? To prepare tabernacles for them; to take a course that will not tend to drive those spirits into the families of the wicked, where they will be trained in wickedness, debauchery, and every species of crime. It is the duty of every righteous woman to prepare tabernacles for all the spirits they can" (from *Discourses of Brigham Young*).

Veronica's sense of what was proper, but I have noticed that girls who do dance together and make it look like fun are the first girls that the boys ask to dance—when they do ask.

We always served refreshments at the very end—because as soon as they were served, the boys went home. It was discouraging.

All three of the Bishopric were always on hand for the dances. They did their jovial best, their conciliatory best, their forceful best, to get those boys to dance. The two or three couples who were going steady danced with their partners—and no one else.

We set up a jukebox atmosphere, with lowered lights (and we heard about that!). We gave colored slips for every dance the boys danced, which they could redeem for extra doughnuts and hot chocolate. This worked better than anything else, but we found that only a few boys ate all the doughnuts. We allowed the kids to bring their own records and Minnie brought an expensive record player to play them on. We used live music, on occasion, but that was even worse. The kids clustered around and watched the orchestra,

Most of our private officers' meetings were discussions on how to get the boys to "participate." These were boys who held the Priesthood, but whatever they were told in Priesthood meetings, it wasn't about courtesy to women or social responsibility.

It was the same with the roadshows. The roadshow is a specific type of torture designed to teach modern Mormons what the trek across the plains taught the pioneers—perseverance and endurance. It is also supposed to encourage creative talent and ingenuity. It will do all this and also turn the director into a frenzied harridan. I have known of at least one nervous breakdown which resulted from such pressures.

The roadshow is an annual stage production which must be originally written to a specific theme. It must be kept to a time limit, usually twelve minutes, adhere to Church standards, and be so flexible that it can be presented on stages that vary from fifteen to fifty feet, by a cast that can dwindle or expand from twenty to a hundred. You must provide costumes, makeup, stage props, scenery, and transportation for all of it on a budget of TWENTY-FIVE DOLLARS.

This is supposed to be the responsibility of the drama director with help from the activity councilors—except that most of the time the drama director was involved with other projects and the Young Men's activity councilor was never around. That left me.

There are those who, when reading this book, will shake their heads at the slight that I do the Young Men, but others who have worked in Mutual will know the truth of my descriptions. I've made a sporadic twenty-year survey on the efficiency of the Young Men's Superintendency—and to a woman, I get almost the same answer to my question:

"Have you ever worked with a good Young Men's Super-intendency?" The answer comes with an indignant snort.

"I've worked in the MIA for years, and most of them don't do much but take their turn presiding at opening exercises."

The best MIA Superintendent we ever had was a woman. Her name was Martha Lee Moser. Martha Lee should have been a man, and had she been, she would have been a power in the Church. She had married an easy-going, pudgy sort of man who she was trying to push up the rungs of the Priesthood, no doubt to increase her own glory in the Celestial Kingdom, but also with an eye to elevating herself to the General Board, I think. Nevertheless, during Martha Lee's reign, we had lots of help from the Superintendency, for she possessed an abundance of "positively great" ideas and she was not loathe to present them in loud detail in our meetings. Martha Lee was born to take over. She appointed herself leader in Superintendent El-

ray's name, quoting him at every turn, but Elray seemed as surprised at his quotes and overcome by his decisions as we were.

If Minnie had been capable of it, she would have disliked
Martha Lee. Veronica and I loathed her. But this feeling of
animosity toward Martha certainly unified us. An even more
powerful adhesive in our relationship was our prayer meetings.
We had prayer meetings about everything. We prayed about
the subject of the roadshow, and that I might write it well.
We prayed for Ron Speirs who resisted discipline like a thorny
thicket. We prayed for strength to bear Martha Lee.

All three of us were busy, our days full. Veronica and I had
our families, other demanding Church work, and the PTA,
Minnie was in school all day long, so we tried to sandwich our
prayer meetings into the times we were going to and from
other meetings. We took turns picking one another up, and in
the car we would have the prayer meeting about the particular
problem of the moment.

After Minnie returned from her mission, she splurged, and
bought a modest, Minnie-like car, a dark, compact one that
ran well. And she learned, belatedly, how to drive. Veronica
was so nervous about Minnie's driving that when it was her
turn to pray, she always prayed first that we would not have
an accident while she had her eyes closed, and her prayers
were always swift and to the point so that she could get back
to helping Minnie with her driving. She had a way of saying,
"Minnie, dear, do drive a little more to the right, please. It
gives me claustrophobia when I feel the cars in the next lane
going past so close to us." Minnie would obligingly steer to the
right. Minnie's driving didn't bother me. I never thought for
a moment that the good Lord would allow us to get smashed up
while we were so dutifully carrying on His work, and Minnie
had the confidence of the unknowing innocent.

Poor dear Minnie. I wonder if she ever knew that Veronica

and I both called her that when we spoke of her. I'm afraid she took the brunt of the heavy work in the presidency. During her tenure of office, the Church asked for a census of all the girls in the Church. This meant a visit to the home of every girl in the ward by a member of the MIA presidency. Veronica and I went on some of these visits, but comparatively few, while Minnie went every night for months to visit one or two girls— except on those evenings when she was obliged to go to MIA or PTA or to the Church meetings which were required because she worked in the Mutual or taught a Sunday School class. It was a task and a trial. I cannot help but believe that Lincoln Ward was covered more thoroughly than any Ward in the Church, for I doubt that there are many Minnies in ward MIA presidencies.

When I think back on the months of work and the number of questions that were required to be asked of every girl in every ward in every stake all over the Church, I wonder to what purpose those answers were put, and was the purpose important enough to have cost Minnie Garff all her hours of patient trudging.

Although I can't remember that many of the Young Men were much more than figureheads, I should not complain about them too much. Even though different Superintendencies came and went so often that I cannot remember the name of one councilor, the Bishopric remained steadfast and they were always on hand to help us.

Clarence Walker ran the lights for every roadshow we gave. The Bishop helped us strive for order in the chaos and took charge of building the sets, and Parky ran around encouraging everyone, telling us that the worse the roadshow looked in dress rehearsal, the better show we usually had.

The first year that I worked in MIA we were lucky enough to have Ida Whiteley, an old roadshow hand, write and direct it for us. She did an amazing job. Her costumes were original and colorful (she made them all herself), and her dances were sprightly. She presented a moon-shot fantasy that predated any public talk of the real ones by many years. I didn't help much that year, but I watched Ida and Emma Tadje work with the young people. I learned a lot.

Ida Whiteley earned a living for herself and her young daughter, Kay, as a designer seamstress. She led the Sunday and Tuesday night music, taught a Sunday School class, and held a weekly fireside meeting for young people in her home. After that one strenuous roadshow when she had to sew all night, night after night, to make up for the time she spent with cast and costumes, we did not have the nerve to ask her to do it again. It was a good thing I had watched her at work.

The next year our drama director was in the midst of presenting a three-act play, and she had a sick husband, so Minnie, Veronica and I decided that we'd have to take over.

I wrote the show, but I couldn't find any music that would fit my lyrics so I wrote the score, too. I know nothing at all about music and I can play a little by ear. But I played the melodies with one finger for Emma Tadje and sang the songs the way they were supposed to go. She sat for hours with me putting the melodies down on paper. Getting the time right was the difficult part, for I seldom played the songs exactly the same way twice in a row.

Ronald Speirs, whom I have mentioned before as a subject for prayer, was one of the leading troublemakers in our Ward. He was the ringleader of the nondancers and the noisiest of the party shouters. He could bring pandemonium in seconds to a group of Boy Scouts who had been sitting quietly in their section of the Church. Ron was really the Young Men's problem, but I thought maybe they didn't hold prayer meetings, or if they did they weren't getting through. There wasn't much we could do except watch him with a jaundiced eye.

Ron was fun to watch because he had an odd, elfin face

and though he was rude, he was witty. I heard him fiddling around with the piano one evening when I was early for Church, so I went up to the front and sat down on the bench by the piano. He began slamming and banging at the piano, more out of self-consciousness than anything else, I thought.

"Don't do that, Ron. I heard you playing when I came in. I didn't know you could play like that. It was marvelous. Since we're both early, why don't you play something else for me before someone comes. I'd like it very much."

And without any clowning or face-pulling, he sat down again and played a Chopin étude. He played it well. I truly enjoyed it and my face showed that I had. Before I could ask him to play more, the room began filling and Ron turned himself into the devil's disciple again. But I had gotten an idea.

I talked to Emma Tadje about it first. I told her that I thought Ron Speirs might like to play for the roadshow, and if we could get him to participate, maybe it would give the other boys some interest in it, too.

"If you can get him to play, that's wonderful. I can surely use my free time." I called Ron and asked him to meet me at the Church an hour before Mutual the next week.

"I don't know if I can make it or not," he said evasively.

"But you will try?"

"If I feel like it then, I will." I wished he were my son, I'd break a broom over his head. But I said gently, "Do try, Ron."

Tuesday evening he was at the piano when I went into the Church. I gave him the pieces that Emma had written out on the music pad. He played them easily, filling in the base chords and making an arrangement as he went. Then I asked him to play for the roadshow. He was so pleased, he didn't even try to hide his pleasure.

Ronald Speirs, I am convinced, was a genius. Even his pranks were originally evil. I think his bent was toward mathematics, but it was also to music, and he did marvelous things with my little one-finger melodies. He transposed one piece into a wailing minor key that made the show. Ronald did as much to control the gangling, teenage boys as we did. "All right, you guys," he'd bellow up to the stage, and his riotous pals would settle down to rehearsal.

Veronica and Minnie were in charge of makeup. And Ida designed and made most of the costumes, though she stayed up nights again to do it. The Bishopric built the scenery, with some help, I think, from the Young Men. The scene changed from a forest to a fairyland, so in an instant's dimming of the lights our trees and shrubs turned on swivels to show dark green on one side, and pinks, blues, and lavenders sprinkled with sparkles on the other.

Everyone wanted to be in the show, but no one wanted to rehearse. We made rules about attendance at rehearsals. If someone missed three of them, he was out of the show. We kept to the rules, but we had repercussions from the parents—in the form of complaints to Bishop Trauffer. (Repercussions always come in the form of complaints to the Bishop.)

Dance directors seem to be another sore spot in the wards. It is rare that you can find one, and rarer still to keep one. That year we didn't have a dance director, so the choreography of the roadshow was also my task. Since I don't dance, it was hard to teach someone else, but between the three of us, we managed. Another difficulty was that all of our dances had to be designed for girls. The few active boys were pressed into the lead parts. We had all-girl choruses and practically all-girl casts. Our roadshows had to be mainly written about female characters, because in Mormon gatherings, women posing as men are usually objects of ridicule.

You *learn* as you produce roadshows. Boys and girls of Mutual age have a misty quality—you can never depend on them to be where they are supposed to be, or where they were a moment ago. You learn that taped music or records are subject to power failures, operational failures, and being lost. Everything is subject to being lost. You have to arrange transportation, usually in trucks, for all of your people and helpers and equipment: lights, programs, makeup, scenery. I have never known of a roadshow troupe that didn't lose something. Sometimes it is the leading man's wig that transforms him from a youth into an octogenarian, or it is Cinderella's glass slipper. Sometimes it is the truckload of scenery—and one time it was the cast. Once I ran after scenery which was running either ahead or behind me from ward to ward all night. I found that you can do without scenery if you must, but there's nothing you can do without a cast except lead the audience in community singing until it arrives.

It is a night of calamity and catastrophe.

There is always the big, tall kid in the back who noisily crunches his gum, like a horse, and his twin sister in the front row who makes the muscles of her jaw ripple while she chews hers. (Minnie stood at every stage door with her hand outstretched to gather up the wads of gum in the napkin she held, but some scene stealer slipped by every time.)

Every ward has at least one girl who has been told a hundred times or more about Church standards in dress, yet who appears just before the curtain goes up in a strapless formal—and not enough in front to hold it up. For these, if you are experienced, you are prepared with a white net scarf.

The can-can is a very popular dance in road shows, and Mormon can-can costumes are modestly equipped with ruffled bloomers or pantalettes. But there's always the girl who forgets and leaves hers home.

But true to Parky's prediction, production night amazes you. It may not be good, but it is perfection compared to any of the rehearsals you've dragged yourself through. The kids really try. They chew gum and they show their underpants, but they remember their lines and they sing so that the audience can understand the words.

Afterward, we had a supper for our cast and everyone was jubilant whether we had won or not. (No one really loses— they are just given a lower rating: superior, excellent, good.) In retrospect the roadshow is such fun. But once we mourned righteously. We thought we had performed a miracle on our twenty-five dollars, and so we had. Our show moved, it had change of pace, it was beautifully costumed, well lighted, and it was on time in every ward for both entrance and exit. (Points were lost for lateness and running overtime.) Our entire show was original which should have given us extra points. We had obeyed every rule to the letter and we lost.

The show that beat us had broken just about every rule and won. That is what hurt so bad. We griped about the judges' choice—Bishopric, leaders, kids, all wailed bitterly together. The winner had been almost thirty minutes late starting. It was an abbreviation of *Teahouse of the August Moon*, complete with knockdown teahouse, Okinawan philosopher, props, and costumes. The boy who had played one of the leads in a Brigham Young University production a while before had arranged for the whole thing to be borrowed and transported to his home Ward. And the act went a half-hour overtime, backing up all the other roadshow companies. The point penalties for that alone should have wiped them out.

We granted that it had the best costumes, best scenery, best lines and best music—all of-them lifted. We granted, too, that it was the most entertaining act of all, but rules had been broken for its presentation and the show should have been thrown out, we thought. I could not understand how it had won, but I did later.

The judges were not familiar with *Teahouse*. They didn't know the lift when they saw it and they thought the entertainment value outweighed the time lapses. This lack of knowledge seems to mark many Mormons with a surprising degree of provincialism. Sometimes it is infuriating.

Later, I wrote several roadshows, most of them for other wards. One of them was absolutely ruined because the drama director wanted a smash ending and added a finale full of stars and stripes and Latter-day Saints which had nothing at all to do with the rest of the show. I'd written this for a friend who had pleaded with me to do it. After it was over she approached me.

"The show was certainly loused up," she apologized.

"Yes, it was. Why did you let them do it? I thought you were directing it?"

"I was, but I couldn't help it. The activity director wanted the changes and everyone went along, I was outvoted."

"I can't imagine why."

"Maybe because her father is such a high official they like to agree with her, but then everyone says she's so talented."

"She's talented. She has a marvelously developed talent for mediocrity. I think that's something we seem to *strive* for in this Church, anyway." I said. "If I ever have the occasion, I'll tell her so."

"Oh, you wouldn't," my friend gasped.

And no, I wouldn't, or I didn't, for it is an unspoken law in the Mormon wards to let sleeping dogs lie. As a result, we have more damn sleeping dogs lying around than you can shake a stick at. When I judge roadshows, I mark them down considerably if they end with the raising of the flag, the Statue of Liberty, or the pioneers coming over the crest of Emigration Canyon exclaiming, "This is the place." It is not that I do not esteem these things. It is that I esteem them too highly to want to see them fouled by an unprofessional song and dance routine while Brother Brigham chews gum as he gesticulates.

The last roadshow I wrote put me out of the roadshow

business. I thought it was the best piece of writing I had done so far and I was proud of it.

The Bishop of the Ward had come to my house to ask me to write it. (This was not Lincoln Ward.) I didn't want to do it, but he said that the Mutual officers had been trying for weeks, and they were desperate. They had asked me earlier and I had refused. Finally, they'd asked him to use his influence. He put his case very well, managed to make me feel very uncooperative and lacking in my duty as a member of the Ward, and so I eventually agreed to do it. I was working then, and my time was limited, but I sacrificed some things that I *wanted* to do and wrote the roadshow.

The shows for that year had to be written around a published nursery rhyme. I chose "The Little Man Who Wasn't There." I wrote the music for this one, too, and spent several hours with a musician getting the score down on paper. Then I turned the script and score over to the Bishop. I hadn't been asked to direct it, for the Ward had a drama director. I heard no more about it. No one called me to question anything in the script or about the music. I thought things were sailing along, and I was more than a little interested in how it would turn out.

One evening after work, I went to the Ward to pay our budget.* As I left the building, I heard the roadshow cast rehearsing, but the music I heard hadn't come from the show I had written. I turned back to ask the Bishop about it, but he had already invited someone else into his office. I walked home wondering what was going on and then called my sister-in-law, who was very active in the Ward.

"What about the roadshow?" I asked. "I heard them rehearsing and they weren't rehearsing the show I had written."

"Well, I'm glad that you finally found out," she said to my

* Every family in the ward is assessed according to their income so that the expenses of ward and stake can be paid. Our budget for that year was 250 dollars.

astonishment. "It's been the talk of the Ward, and it has been embarrassing."

"What do you mean?"

"That you cheated. You know the rules. I can't understand why you did it. They had to throw out the show you wrote, and they've had a terrible time getting someone else to write it in the little time you left them."

"Why didn't you tell me about this before?"

"I didn't want to have any trouble with you over it. It wasn't any of my affair." Bewildered, I called the Bishop.

"Bishop, I'm told you couldn't use my show because of something that I did that wasn't according to the rules. Is that so?"

"Yes, it is, Sister Hunter. You had to use a published nursery rhyme—that was written in the rules you were given. Apparently, you made up your own."

"No, I didn't. I used a *published* nursery rhyme."

"The Stake leader who approved the scripts said that you hadn't. She told us that we couldn't use it."

"Why didn't you come and ask me where I'd found the verse?"

"Because I didn't want to embarrass you. I'm sorry," he said simply. "As it turned out, we found someone else to write a new show," his tone was conciliatory.

"You *should* have asked me, Bishop. You know that I didn't want to write that show, but after I did write it, I feel bad that you aren't using it. I feel worse that you accepted an accusation against me without ever asking me about it."

"It seems that we should have, Sister Hunter. I'm really sorry." I heard him talking to someone else in the room.

"I suppose there's nothing you can do about it now, so I'll let you go," I said. He said goodbye with evident relief.

I was still amazed and hurt, and suddenly I seethed with anger. I called the MIA president and asked her the same question. Why hadn't they come and asked me where I got the verse?

"We took the Stake leader's word. She was positive that there was no such nursery rhyme. And in *her* position, she should know more than you do." I could tell that she still didn't believe me.

"I think that it is inexcusable," I told her. "You didn't even bother to check. I have the book here. I can show you the verse. I did not cheat and I am not a liar."

"Really, we didn't mean to hurt your feelings," she apologized.

"Well, you have." I snapped and hung up. My fury had risen with the answers I had gotten. I called the Stake leader.

"Mrs. Goring," I was not going to call *her* Sister, "I understand that you threw my roadshow script out for infraction of the rules."

"Well, I had to," she chided gently. "You know the rules, or you should. They told me you'd written roadshows before. It is only fair to the other wards that we make certain that no one breaks them. It was a good show," she said patronizingly, "and I was really sorry that I couldn't allow it to be produced. But you know how it is, we can't let anyone break the rules."

"What makes you so sure that I did?" She didn't seem to notice the ice water dripping out of her earpiece.

"I have a degree in children's literature from Brigham Young University," she told me with great assurance. "I've never heard of the poem you used."

"Mrs. Goring, there are probably thousands of nursery rhymes that you haven't heard of, but it reflects on your degree that you haven't heard of this one. It's been around for a century or more, and it's been printed dozens, maybe hundreds of times. You can find it if you are interested." I gave her the number of the page and the name of the book that I held in my hand as I talked to her. "If you can't find it, drop by, and I'll show it to you in this book and in three others that I have."

"Well, I have never *heard* of it."

"Then," I asked her, as I had asked all the rest of them, "why didn't you make it very simple for everyone, and ask *me* for my reference book?" There was silence on the phone.

"Mrs. Goring, you may have a degree in children's literature, but you are not God, and you do not know everything about anything. It simply appalls me that you thought you did. And Mrs. Goring, if I were in your position, my conscience would force me to resign."

I waited for her to say something, but there was silence, so I hung up. I did not feel even a twinge of regret when I heard soon after that Mrs. Goring had resigned.

Looking back, I can see that it was the proverbial tempest in a teapot. But such petty teapots boil and bubble in every ward, in every stake, all over the Church. Unlike mine, most of them do not boil over.

BESIDES DANCES AND ROADSHOWS and three-act plays, each year the wards hold a speech contest. The winner of the ward contest goes to the stake finals, and that winner gets an award, and the opportunity to give his speech in Stake Conference—a special honor.

My daughter Ann entered a few times and she won every time that she entered except the first one. I asked her if she needed any help with her speech and she said she didn't think so. I was busy, so I left her to write and learn it. I must have been very busy, because I never heard that speech until the night of the contest.

Even at that age, Ann was a freethinker. Her talk was about prayer and the answers to prayer. I thought she'd chosen a good topic and she developed and delivered it well. But where Ann had found her material, I do not know. Certainly none of it came from Mormon writings. She had powerful examples of Presbyterians, Catholics, Jews, and Lutherans praying and getting miraculous answers. There was not one Mormon example.

Veronica and I were sitting in front of the judges, strangers from wards outside the Stake. Veronica looked at me with a glint of laughter in her eyes.

"You have just seen your daughter lose the speech contest."

"I know. Poor little thing."

"You should be proud of her. She did very well."

"I am proud. I think she's wonderful." Later I told Ann how pleased I had been with her speech. Though you could not tell it from her reaction, I thought she might be disappointed.

"You couldn't have won with that speech, honey. Not if it had been the best speech in the world."

"Why not?"

"Because this is a *Mormon* speech contest. You should have used Mormon miracles."

"What difference does that make? All the miracles don't happen in *this* Church, do they?"

"I am sure they don't. It's just that the judges seem to be sure that they do."

"Surely, Mom, you don't think that only Mormons are going to get into heaven."

"No. But then I'm not an authority, dear. Just about any authority will tell you that only Latter-day Saints will get into the Celestial Kingdom, and only a few of them. There is a scriptural figure of 144,000 to be exact."

"Only 144,000 people will be good enough to go to heaven." Ann gasped.

"That's what I've heard preached." I didn't have the heart to tell her that the Jehovah's Witnesses had already claimed every single seat.

Chapter 10

OF SEEDS
AND SHOVELS

AFTER THE AGE OF FIFTEEN, or thereabouts, a Mormon
youngster can obtain a Patriarchal Blessing. These Blessings are
patterned after those of the Biblical Isaac and Jacob, and usually
given by the Stake Patriarch, who holds his position for life.
(There is also a Church Patriarch, and this office is the only
one that has been handed down from father to son. The first
Patriarch of the Church was Joseph Smith, Sr., the father of the
Prophet. After the elder Smith's death, Hyrum Smith, the
Prophet's brother, became Patriarch and the position has been
passed down through the Smith family.)

The Blessing tells the recipient of his lineage. I used to be puzzled about how the Patriarch would know this, but I have since found that is quite simple. Most Mormons are told that they are of the "seed of Ephraim," the son of Joseph who was sold into slavery in Egypt. Ephraim's posterity supposedly have the ability to recognize truth—meaning the gospel. Some few are of the seed of Joseph, himself, and the American Indian is said to be the seed of Manasseh, Ephraim's older brother. Allowance is made for those of obviously gentile blood, for instance the Chinese, who join the Church. In these cases, the gentile blood is said to be purged, and they are *grafted* into the House of Israel. It is my *strictly* private opinion that Joseph Smith made the wrong choice of a seed scatterer. In Revelations, where the 144,000 are mentioned as the ones to be "saved," it lists their progenitors. Joseph is listed and Manasseh, but there is not one person chosen from the seed of Ephraim!

When you go for your Patriarchal Blessing, the Patriarch lays his hands on your head and, calling on God for inspiration, tells you some of what you may expect from your life, providing you live the commandments of God and the teachings of the Church.

Usually the Blessings are not of a spectacular sort any more, though they used to be. Sometimes the person is told that his work will be in the temples—that it is his mission to seek out the names of his ancestors and see that they are endowed so that they may inherit the blessings of the Covenant. Occasionally, still, someone is told that he will work on the long-prophesied Temple to be built in Jackson County, Missouri. Many people in my grandfather's and father's generations have been told this and nearly all of them have died before ever lifting up a single stone.

I asked Brother Gardiner about this and he said that some of the earlier Patriarchs had been "carried away," although he had heard it said that these people would work on the Temple as resurrected beings.

I have one friend whose Blessing says that she would live to welcome back the Ten Tribes from the north. These are ten tribes, descendants of the sons of Jacob, who are supposed to have mysteriously disappeared during the reign of the Biblical King Zedekiah, and who are supposed to return just prior to the Second Coming. The whereabouts of these tribes has always been a popular subject of speculation among Mormons. I've heard some Priesthood speakers say that the Ten Tribes were taken up like the city of Enoch, others who think they may be living on the star Kolob, and still others who think, like my friend's Patriarch, that they are hidden somewhere beyond the north polar cap.

In *The Young Woman's Journal*, Volume III, published by the Church in 1892, I find the following fascinating paragraphs in an article by O. B. Huntington:

Nearly all the great discoveries of men in the last half century have, in one way or another, either directly or indirectly, contributed to prove Joseph Smith to be a Prophet.

As far back as 1837, I know that he said the moon was inhabited by men and women the same as this earth, and that they lived to a greater age than we do—that they live generally to near the age of a 1000 years.

He described the men as averaging near six feet in height, and dressing quite uniformly in something near the Quaker style.

In my Patriarchal blessing, given by the father of Joseph the Prophet, in Kirkland 1837 [this was Joseph Smith, Sr., the first Patriarch of the Church], I was told that I should preach the gospel before I was 21 years of age; that I should preach the gospel to the inhabitants upon the islands of the sea, and—to the inhabitants of the moon, even the planet you can now behold with your eyes.

The first two promises have been fulfilled, and the latter may be verified.

From the verification of two promises we may reasonably expect the third to be fulfilled also.

In the same article are references to the Ten Tribes and the Patriarchal blessing of my friend: "One truth after another men are finding out by the wisdom and inspiration given of God to them.

"The inspiration of God caused men to hunt for a new continent until Columbus discovered it. Men have lost millions of dollars and hundreds of lives to find a country beyond the north pole; and they will yet find that country—a warm, fruitful country, inhabited by the ten tribes of Israel, a country divided by a river, on one side of which lives the half tribe of Manasseh, which is more numberous than all the others. So said the Prophet."

Blessings such as these are now rare.

I was fifteen when I received my Patriarchal Blessing. Our Stake Patriarch lived in Charleston, a little town about five miles from Heber. Most of Charleston is now under the waters of the Deer Creek Reservoir.

A dozen or so girls were taken over to Brother Daybell's by some of the MIA leaders. I was the youngest of the lot, and so I was the last to be blessed. The other girls sat in a circle, like ladies, and listened to the lengthy promises given to their friends, but I spent the day wandering over the hills that lay behind Patriarch Daybell's house.

The Patriarch was an old man, and he was tired when he got to me late in the afternoon. My Blessing covers only about half a page. (The Blessings were taken down in shorthand and sent to us later.) Most of my Blessing was general stuff about keeping the commandments and resisting evil and temptation. But a few lines of it stayed in my mind: a heavy admonition that I "live a life full of good deeds so that you might come forth in the First Resurrection, and might stand clean and unspotted from the world, and receive that crown of glory which is only for the faithful, and stand before our Father in Heaven as a good and faithful servant, a beloved Daughter of Zion."

Every so often, something brings me up short, and I am forced to the realization that my good deeds have not been adding up to much, so I start baking cakes for the elderly, trying to cheer the sad, or in some way adding a little more to weigh the scale in my favor. As I envision it, though I am not quite the type who would ever wear a crown of glory with any ease, I would very much like to receive a loving pat on the head.

I SUPPOSE THAT MY PATRIARCHAL BLESSING, given at the time when I was very susceptible to suggestion, has been the motivating factor behind many of the things I've done, but I don't think it had much to do with helping Leone Curley. I hope not.

Across the street from me on Seventh East, lived the Curley family. Bill Curley was a bus driver for the Salt Lake City Lines. His wife, Leone, was a swift-moving, quick-talking, competent, little person. She had red-gold hair, a beautiful, clear complexion, green-blue eyes, and a trim figure. They had three girls. My daughter Ann and Leone's Nancy were in the same grade.

I had frequently chatted with Leone. She'd lived in the neighborhood since her marriage, and when we moved there she introduced me around. But the times I spent with Leone were brief, for she was always moving, always busy. Her house was spotless, her porches gleamed with fresh paint, her windows shone, and her children were always scrubbed and starched. She asked no baby-sitting favors. Although our girls played together, she did not trade children as Mickey Aloia and I did when we wanted to shop or visit. Leone always took her three bonneted and white-gloved little girls along with her wherever she went.

Leone hadn't planned on a fourth baby, and when she became pregnant she was very unhappy about it. But that summer she seemed to have a little more time for visiting, and once in a while, she would join us in the neighborhood coffee klatches. Independently. She always brought her share of freshly baked rolls or cookies.

Her baby was a boy, Mike, and Bill's joy in having a son made up in part for the unwanted pregnancy. But after the baby was born we hardly saw her. Her passion for cleanliness and order and the work of the new baby kept her too busy for klatching.

Then in that horrible summer when polio was such a constant threat that the public pools were closed, and the hospitals were crowded with Sister Kenney's tubs of woolen hot packs and iron lungs, Leone contracted polio, too.

It was a day when the clouds lay low and pressed the heat down upon us. None of us knew that Leone was ill until the ambulance came. But then we knew whatever it was, it was bad, and we gathered on her dustless porch and watched the attendants carry her, moaning, down the step. Mickey Aloia, Selma Kendall and I all watched in wordless, tearful shock.

Bill's sister took the children for a while, and then Bill brought the two oldest ones home to stay with him, for it was a long time before Leone got out of the hospital. For more than five months she was in an iron lung, clinging to life, choking for air. She had both bulbar and lumbar polio, and she was completely paralyzed.

I went to see her as soon as she was out of the lung and could have visitors other than her husband and parents. The first time I went was almost more than I could bear.

"How are my children?" she asked.

"They're fine. Bill is doing wonderfully well—you'd be surprised." I floundered for things to say. I chattered about the neighborhood news. I'd gone down to St. Anne's to see Katy Aloia's First Communion. I told her not to worry about Easter dresses for her girls. I was already making them. I tried to be cheerful, but there were tears in her eyes as there were in mine. I held her hand which hung limp when I lifted it.

"I'm trying," she said. "I'm supposed to squeeze these little red balls, but I can't. Oh, I can't do it. I'd wish I were dead but there's little Mike. I have to try for Mike."

And she tried for Mike. She tried so hard that, after almost a year, she was allowed to come home in a wheelchair. I went to see her when I saw that no other cars were there and that Bill had gone to work.

She was sitting in the wheelchair, and the twisting effects of the disease were already becoming evident.

"What can I do to help you, Leone?"

"Not much. You've already done a lot. Thank you for making the Easter dresses. They are darling. I didn't see them before. I couldn't see the kids much in the hospital—only when they could wheel me to a window to look down at them."

"I'd like to help some, I really would."

"Marilyn and Nancy wait on me. Even little Betty helps. Bill is very good. You can see he's cleaned and painted the house. He bought this new kitchen set. He's doing everything. The kids had a wonderful Christmas, and Bill did all the shopping for them—decorated the tree—it's the first time he ever has. He cooks. He cleans. He even washes. He's taking care of things quite well. I'm surprised, as you said I'd be. All I *need* is people to talk to, so sit down. Can you make us a cup of coffee?"

"Sure," and I busied myself at her stove.

"I think there are some sweet rolls in the breadbox. Oh, you don't know how I hate not being able to do for myself."

"You'll be able to in a while, you'll see."

"I don't like being by myself too much. It's hard to keep from thinking. But I'm having lots of visitors, and Mama is here all that she can be. She comes down and does my ironing."

Leone talked rapidly as if words would improve things. "She and Dad have been wonderful. One of them visited me every day in the hospital. It was so far away. And they had to ride on the bus, Dad doesn't see well enough to drive any more. This has been so hard on them, they're so old and tired. I've been worried that they'd break down and if they did, I couldn't help them at all."

"Well, they have stayed well. It will be a while, but eventually you'll be able to get around and do for them," I said comfortingly. And when I said that she cried.

"Oh, look at me. All I can move is my head and this. . . ." She worked her right index finger across the table. "I can move this finger forward. See. And then I can pull my arm back. That's all I have. I can't even turn over in bed at night. The doctors as good as told Bill, I'd be nothing but a talking vegetable for the rest of my life." And she cried, and I cried. What else was there to do?

But we couldn't cry long, for tiny and frail Mrs. Sands, Leone's mother, came in with the shopping bag she always carried. The skin of her delicate face was finely wrinkled, and the years had bent her back, but she was sweet and cheerful and she smelled of violet scent and herbs.

"I brought you some t'ings you like," she said, and she placed on the table containers of fruit pudding, *lutefiske* (a type of boiled fish concoction that Leone had eaten and enjoyed since childhood), and a box of lacy cookies that she had baked that morning. Last, Mrs. Sands brought out a small bottle of olive oil. It was, I knew, a bottle of consecrated oil used for administering to the sick.

"How did you get here, Mama?"

"On ta boose." Mrs. Sands was Norwegian. At sixteen she had left home, with only what belongings she could carry. She had been forced to leave because she had joined the Mormon Church. She had worked her way to this country and married

Leone's father, Marius, whom she had known in Norway. His English was heavy with Norwegian, as was that of Mrs. Sands.

"I'm coom to gif you a blessing," Mrs. Sands said, and then she did something that I've never seen any other woman do. She preempted the prerogative of the Priesthood, opened the tiny bottle carefully, poured a few drops onto Leone's head, and then laying both hands on the top of her daughter's head, she "administered" to her. She blessed her that "health would return to her navel and marrow to her bones." It seemed to revive Leone's spirits immediately.

"The Elders haf coom to bless her, but tay do not lof her as I do, and surely when tere is much lof, ta Lord hears more plain." The brethren might not agree, but it seemed reasonable enough to me.

"If prayers will do any good, I ought to get better," Leone said laughing. "Father McGuire came in to see me (Bill was Catholic, Leone, Mormon) and he asked if I wanted him to pray for me. I said I sure did. I'm glad for all the candles that burn and all the prayers anyone wants to offer up. I need them all."

Most mornings after that, after Bill had gone to work, some of the neighbors called on Leone. But there were hours and days that she was left alone in her house, sitting in her wheelchair, squeezing the little red balls she had brought home with her from the hospital, and improving hardly at all. She couldn't have her baby with her for she could neither hold him nor take care of him. And it hurt her terribly to have him come for a visit and then be taken away again.

I often thought of her, once so quick and young and energetic, chained to that wheelchair. I prayed about her, and I asked that I might find some way to comfort her.

One morning after the kids had gone to school, I went over to Leone's and found her sobbing in her wheelchair. She tried to stop when I came in, but she couldn't.

"Mama does so much for me, and I don't want her to do it. She'll have another heart attack. I want Mike, and I can't have him. I'm trying to get better so that I can, but I'm afraid that he'll grow up hardly knowing me. I lie there and try to move my muscles when the therapist comes. I try until I think something inside me is going to burst, and nothing happens. My God! Nothing happens. It would have been better if I'd died in the hospital. It would have all been over. Now, I'm just a burden to Bill and the kids, to my parents, to my neighbors, to everyone."

"You're not a burden," I said, "but you are being terribly impatient and overemotional." I had decided that crying with her might relieve my sorrow, but it sure wasn't going to help her. And sometimes when Leone cried, she had a hard time getting her breath coming regularly again. I frantically cast about for something to change the subject, and then saw a deck of cards that the kids had been playing with the night before. If Leone had been well, they would have been neatly put away.

I picked them up and pushed her chair close to the table.

"Do you like to have your fortune told?"

"I've always just loved it. *You* can't tell fortunes?" I couldn't, but I'd been blessed with a good imagination. I thought if I could read palms, I could tell cards, so I laid them out as I'd seen my Aunt Helen do when I was a girl, and I told her fortune.

I told her that she'd have unexpected company that afternoon, that she would talk to someone she loved that evening whom she hadn't seen for a long time, and that she was going to get a wonderful surprise before the week was out. I thought I could *make* that much happen. I could call up some of the neighbors farther down the street who hadn't been there for a while, and I could have some flowers or something sent in. But as it happened, I didn't need to do anything at all.

One of Leone's old schoolmates just happened to drop by

after I left, her sister called from California that night, and that
week Bill came home with a new television set, their first. They
were happy coincidences, which I recognized but Leone didn't
seem to. She really thought I had a gift, and so did her mother.

After that, whenever I went over to Leone's I read the
cards for her. I foretold simple things, generally possible things,
and of course they happened. If I saw that she felt despondent,
I said that there were some black days close, but that bright
days were coming. At first, I was rather hesitant about saying
that she was going to get her wishes, because I knew very well
what she was wishing. But one day as I spread the cards out,
the wish card was very clear next to her face card and surrounded by all the warm, red hearts in the deck. I said positively
she would get her wish. She had wished that SHE WOULD BE ABLE
TO WALK.

That was the thing she wanted to hear so terribly, desperately, and in my equally desperate wish to comfort, I began
telling her that she *would* walk. I knew that I shouldn't, but I
couldn't seem to help it. She was growing a little stronger. She
could use her hands awkwardly and stiffly. As soon as two
fingers would flex, she washed dishes, resting her helpless, upper
arms on the sink. She manipulated her wheelchair better now,
and somehow she dusted, straightened and pushed the iron.
She made her beds slowly, using small, innumerable twitches
until she pulled the bedding straight. She was as independent
as she had always been, and when we offered help she always
refused it, saying, "Oh, no, the exercise is good for my muscles.
I can manage."

Her therapist, provided by the Polio foundation, came daily,
and no matter how painful the exercises were, she wanted to do
more. Her determination was pitiful to see. I prayed for her,
and I told her fortune, minimizing the black cards, emphasizing
the bright ones. It was uncanny how much of what I told her
came true. Now, as I read them, I spoke without conscious

thought. I told them as they fell. I'd picked up a fluency with them by that time, but it was odd how much of what I saw came to be. The wish card turned up more and more often surrounded by bright cards.

I went home more than once with some heavy wonder roiling inside me. Prayer and cards! The Church said they didn't go together, but I comforted myself. Lucifer was a fallen angel, but he'd been the other contender for Christ's role on earth, so even he couldn't be all bad. I'd been told all my life that cards were of the Devil. Well, I thought, even Lucifer would take pity on Leone Curley. Right or wrong, the fortune-telling made her happy and that was enough for me.

One night I had a realistic dream. It wasn't about Papa this time. I dreamed that an old man named Brother Bartholomew was leading me up a trail, and we stopped on a plateau and looked up at a huge mountain which blocked our way.

"When you have reached that point in your life when you can hold out your hand with its tiny seed (the mustard seed of faith) and command the mountain to move," Bartholomew told me in his dry, rasping voice, "then prepare to take your shovel in hand."

I thought a lot about that dream. I thought it was philosophically sound, but I didn't realize that I was actually taking Brother Bartholomew's advice when I announced to Leone that morning that while the cards said she was going to walk, and her mother promised her with the holy oil that she was going to walk, she never would walk if she didn't start doing something about it except listening to us.

"What can I do?" she wailed.

"We'll walk you," I said without thinking. "Here, I'll hoist you up out of your chair. I'll brace you with my body."

"What if I fall?"

"What if you do? I'll hang on so you go down easy, or you'll fall on top of me, and that should be plenty soft. Okay now, here we are. Walk." I had given her the crutches, which up to then had only stood against the wall for encouragement, but she had squeezed enough red rubber balls to be able to hold onto them. I put my arms under hers and locked my hands around her. I held her close, putting my knees and legs behind hers which were encased in heavy braces.

We took two steps and fell down. Perhaps it was good that we fell right at first, because she wasn't hurt as she had been so afraid that she might be. She wasn't discouraged, and we laughed as we untangled ourselves. I pulled her up and we took another couple of steps. Then I read the cards and told her something wonderful was going to happen. It has to, sooner or later.

Selma Kendall, Leone's best friend and closest neighbor, taught school all day, but before she changed her clothes and started dinner, she always came to Leone's for a cup of coffee and a brief chat. Leone told her about the walking that morning, and Selma must have thought if once a day was good, twice a day would be better, for she walked Leone that night. We never discussed it, for I rarely saw Selma, but we coordinated our "shoveling." For two years, I went over to Leone's every morning, sometimes only for ten minutes, just long enough to walk behind her, gradually taking a few more steps until we could go across the living room. Every night Selma Kendall took the same steps with her. Somehow, between prayers, cards, and shoveling, Leone garnered enough strength to stand on her crutches alone, although when she tried to walk with just the crutches, she fell.

With each bit of returning muscle strength, she assumed new tasks. As soon as she could stand, she put her dishes away, one at a time, shuffling them into place. Standing a few minutes at a time, she could tidy her cabinets, dust and wipe the finger-marks off the woodwork.

About a year after the walking began, we were invited to

visit a neighbor who had moved into a new house. I don't know just how we managed to get her into and out of the car, but there were several of us and we lifted her wheelchair down the porch steps and maneuvered until we managed. But when we arrived at the new house, we had problems.

"I can't go up that flight of steps," Leone said hopelessly. "You'll have to let me sit in the car and wait for you, or take me home again."

"After all this trouble," I was indignant, "I'm certainly not going to take you home. And, of course, you can do it," I said with assurance. I got behind her as we did in the walking sessions and tried to allay her terrible fear of falling.

"Really, they are too steep, and there's too many."

"They're steep, but at every step, I'll brace myself. If you have to fall, then fall, you'll only fall on top of me, and you've done that before."

We managed the stairs. The next day, Leone went to the hospital for a muscle check, and the doctors would not believe that she had gone up a flight of steps.

"You couldn't do that," they said. "You don't have enough muscles to hold you up. You can't even stand." But she had.

Then one day, when the cards didn't seem to be saying enough to please her, I pulled her hand toward me and read her palm.

"From your palm, Leone, I can see that you have broken lines that grow together here. Do you know what I really see?"

"What? What do you see? Now tell me the truth."

"I see that in a while, maybe a year, maybe two years, you will walk by yourself. You will do all the things you want to do. You will go on trips, and you will walk."

"Alone?"

I hedged, I didn't quite see that.

"You'll walk, maybe as far as two blocks. You won't walk without help of some sort, but you'll walk. And some day, you'll be able to go to the stores and do your *own* Christmas shopping."

We kept up the morning and evening walking and when she could negotiate the steps with the aid of the railing Bill had installed, an elbow crutch, and a helpful arm, we went swimming. Twice or three times a week, Florine Evans, who lived down the street, and I took her to Wasatch Springs. Wasatch was a municipal pool that had small, hot mineral pools, and we used these and gradually went out into the big pool.

And then one morning she walked her two blocks! She wore elbow crutches on each arm and Mickey and I walked close to her, but she went all the way down to Florine's house for a neighborhood get-together. It was slow, and she was exhausted when we arrived, but that day there was a celebration on Seventh East.

For my part, it had been mustard seeds and shoveling. Leone's part had taken suffering and courage, unbelievable perseverance and persistence. She had lain unconscious from a fall down the basement steps when she slipped. She could gradually work herself down the steps, moving like a baby does, on his bottom, and pulling herself upright again when she reached the last one with the aid of the wall and her crutches. Bruised from the falls, she went back down again the next Monday to do her washing.

She took wonderful care of her family. She managed little Mike, who was walking when she finally got him home. Mike has always been an exceptional boy with his mother.

"And to think I didn't want him!" She said over and over again. He had given her the will to live and then the determination to walk. He was unfailingly gentle with her. He willingly ran errands that most little boys would have complained about, and he has always been her joy and her strong support.

Leone's father and mother died, and she had no other help than what her family could give her, but she kept a spotless house. She sewed and mended, washed and ironed, cooked and baked. There was always something special prepared for her numerous unexpected callers.

Once, I remonstrated: "You don't have to bake for everyone, Leone. People don't expect it. They come just to see you."

"My friends are my life," she said. "My family is first, but I won't tie them down. Without the friends I've had, I couldn't have lived. Before the polio I didn't have the time, I didn't know how much I'd been missing. Now I have all the time I want, and the little baking is all I can do for my friends in return for what they do for me."

After we had started the fortunes and the walking, I never saw Leone cry but once again. That once was quite unexpected. I knocked one afternoon, just running in for a moment after a shopping trip uptown. I found her standing in front of her bedroom mirror, the wheelchair locked behind her in case she suddenly collapsed.

Her face was swollen and wet with tears and she looked at me with revulsion and horror in her eyes.

"This is the first time I've ever stood up to see myself," she said. "Look at me! My spine—it's crooked. Look at my stomach. I have no muscles to hold it in. My legs are crooked. Oh . . ." she wailed, "I'm so ugly."

"You're no such thing. Everyone looks bad to themselves if they search for their faults. I don't enjoy looking in the mirror, and I haven't had polio."

She sagged into her chair and sat with her head in her hands and the sobs wracked her. There was a heartbreak and hope-lessness about her that I had never seen before—even in the hospital—even when the only muscle she could move was the one in her right index finger.

"Oh, Leone, you've come so far. You can get around. You can do for your family. You have Mike at home. Don't give up now. It's a miracle, really, when you think how bad you were. You know it is." But there was a black despondency about her that terrified me. I thought she might be thinking of suicide.

"I know all that," she said wearily, "but is it worth it to try so hard, and look so horrible? Bill and I were invited out to-night—the first time, the first party since I got sick," she started to shake again with sobs. "I came in here to see which dress I could wear, and none of them fit. I'm so terrible to look at that I don't want anyone to see me. Bill was always so pleased with how I looked and now . . ."

Suddenly, I was Leone. I knew exactly how she felt. She had been such a shapely, trim, pretty little woman. Her arms and hands were well shaped and softly rounded, her legs were the kind men whistled at when she stepped on a bus. She'd been straight-backed and firmbosomed and flat-stomached. And now . . . she was right. She twisted and sagged.

She couldn't see the courage that showed in every plane of her body as she stood. The fingers that splayed themselves to perform the chores they didn't have enough muscles to do, the legs at awkward angles, knees locked by pure force of will to keep her standing. She couldn't see the sweetness, the look of patience, that had come into her face. She didn't see that her hair was still red-gold and lovely or that her complexion was without blemish. She saw only the jaw muscles that were slack, the back that swayed inward, and the rocking lurch of her body as she forced herself to walk.

I felt my heart swell, and I knew that I would soon sob, too, but I ran from the room saying I would be right back. I dashed across the street and grabbed the dress box I'd just brought home. Inside was a blue wool dress. I'd gotten it on sale at an exclusive shop. It had a flared skirt with plaid inserts to make it swirl from the hips. The bodice was cut so that deep darts shaped the waist and the bust most becomingly. It had a high neck, and a detachable cape that was cut to swirl flat-teringly with the skirt as the wearer moved.

I ran back up Leone's steps and into the bedroom.

"Here. This is just the thing. I saw it on sale today, and I have no need for it. It was just so darling that I couldn't resist it, and all the while I really didn't know why I bought it. Now I know. It was for you."

"I can't afford a new dress. Not now, especially. They just got that bus driver's strike settled, and it'll take a while to catch up. I simply couldn't."

"You can afford this one. I got it on sale. Try it on. Here, try it on."

I forced her to try on the dress, and as it slipped down over her head, magically, the flaring skirt reformed her figure. When she put on the cape, it covered the twist in her spine.

"See, I told you. How wonderful you look. If you wash your face and put some cold cloths on your eyes, you'll be as good as ever. Really, Leone, it is darling—you're darling!"

"I can't afford it," she repeated. "We've spent so much on me and Bill and the kids need things much more than I do—they go out—"

"I'll lend it to you."

"Bill would never allow me to wear anything I'd borrowed, even if I would, which I wouldn't. We'll stay home, but I feel better now, anyway."

"Leone, you must have this dress. I got it on sale," which was true, "for eleven dollars," which was not.

"Eleven dollars? Are you sure? I've shopped a lot of sales, but this doesn't look like an eleven-dollar sale dress to me."

"It is a sale dress, I swear," I raised my right hand.

"I can afford eleven dollars. Mama always gives me ten for my birthday. That's in a couple of weeks. If you can wait for the money."

"I can wait. I'd *love* to wait. You look just beautiful."

Leone never cried like that in front of me again. I don't know whether it was because she never reached that low ebb again, or if it was because she was too proud to allow me to come up with any more sale dresses.

I GREW BUSIER AND BUSIER in the Church, and we did not need to walk any more because she could get around her house by herself—though she was never able to be out of her wheelchair for very long. I wouldn't tell her fortune after a while. She was disappointed, and I disliked saying no, but she was becoming dependent on what the cards said. I could see that encouragement was strengthening, but dependency was weakening. I stopped reading cards, but she started. After a while, she could do it much better than I could, and the shuffling and flexing of the cards did a great deal for the muscles in her hands, she said.

Even after I moved away from Utah, I went back to see her every time I was in Salt Lake City—until the last time, a month ago. I telephoned, but her line was busy and I didn't call back. I've been so sorry that I didn't try one more time to get her, because Leone died unexpectedly just after my return home. She'd been ill, but didn't want to go to the hospital for the operation she was told she must have. She had spent the holidays in the hospital the year before, and that year she wanted to be with her children and grandchildren for the Christmas season.

With her indomitable courage, she hid her pain from her family, and when she went to the hospital the day after New Year's, it was too late to operate.

I think Leone must have been very surprised to die. She'd overcome so much, she must have been certain that she could do it again. If she hadn't thought that, she wouldn't have taken such a chance.

The last time I saw Leone, I told her I planned to write about her in my next book.

"Whatever for?" she said, shaking her head and laughing at me, but pleased all the same.

"Because you are the most courageous person I've ever known," I told her. "You always make me want to do more—you shame me with all that you accomplish."

And now, I write of her with a pain in my throat and tears running down my cheeks, for not since my grandfather's death have I felt so bereft.

MY SYMPATHY FOR LEONE and my recognition of all the help the Polio Foundation had given her, made me accept with alacrity when Maurine Mugleston asked me to be Salt Lake City chairman for the Mothers' March one year. Maurine was the Salt Lake County chairman and I had met her at the polio clinic when we were learning to hot-pack patients. Maurine told me that the job would be a time-consuming one, full of last-minute headaches, but she said that she would help me all she could.

For six weeks I worked on the campaign organization. I was PTA president of Forest School at the time, and it helped because I called all of the city's PTA presidents, many of whom I had met, and asked them to captain their districts, and to appoint block marchers from among their active PTA mothers.

About the time the work started, Barbara came down with measles and chicken pox simultaneously; when I wasn't caring for her, I was pleading with captains who suddenly decided they couldn't solicit funds, getting replacements for those who had to leave town or who had sick kids or uncooperative husbands.

Maurine took a six-week leave of absence from her job for this drive. She met frequently with Mrs. Brown and Mrs. King

(the two Salt Lake County chairmen) and me, to help us coor-
dinate our work. When we had found captains and marchers
to cover the entire county, we held a big meeting in the Hotel
Utah to give instructions and answer questions. We were also
prepared to spur their enthusiasm for the task with examples
of the Foundation's help to Utah victims, but this wasn't necessary. The women were aware of the polio threat. Fear as well
as organization helped the Mother's March that year. In my
district, Emma Tadje, whose son David had been crippled by
the disease, offered to walk her assigned block and any other
blocks in our district that were not covered.

One of the two state chairmen is now a Congressman. He
did his share of organization and perhaps a little more. He was
one of the speakers at the Hotel Utah meeting and he arranged
for the National Guard to pick up money from the various
districts and bring it to the bank. But his co-chairman, Euphemia Smith-Morrison, didn't show up. I had been looking
forward to meeting this woman, for her name frequently
headed the society columns. She was a daughter of one of the
Church authorities, and was known throughout the state for
her charitable works. I was disappointed that she hadn't come.

By the night of the Mothers' March, we knew that every
house in the county would be visited. Each captain had a map
of her district, and as the women reported in, the block was
checked off. In a few cases where the blocks were missed, the
captains took care of them, and if they could not, they called
us. Maurine went to do it herself.

The captains were to collect the monies from their districts
and bring it to the bank to be totaled. If they were unable to
do this, men from the National Guard picked it up for us. By
nine o'clock all the change counters were busy, and we were
turning and smoothing and stacking the currency for easy
counting by the bank tellers.

Money poured in and we were excited and pleased. We had

not been paid for our time or our expenses, but as the money came in, we were elated, knowing that it would be a great contribution to the county and state polio victims.

Then it was that I had my first encounter with a PRINCESS OF THE BLOOD. I have had them since, but they have not had the sting that this first one did.

About ten-thirty, a woman attired in a dinner dress and furs swept into the bank followed by reporters and cameramen from the city newspapers.

"Oh, oh, that's dear Famia," someone whispered.

"Who's she?" I whispered back.

"That's Euphemia Smith-Morrison. She is the other state chairman," Maurine told me.

While we counted the money we had worked so hard to bring in, I watched "dear Famia" pose for several pictures, all of them with stacks of "our" money before her. She ignored us as she would have ignored flies on the wallpaper. And the next morning I read how once again the marvelous organizational ability of Euphemia Smith-Morrison made the Mothers' March the most successful in Utah history. She was awarded a gold-lettered plaque and a trip to Washington, D.C. for her efforts, and I got a lesson in society politics. At the very bottom of the newspaper story on an inside page, I read the names of Mugleston, Brown, King and my own as district chairmen.

When I took the job, I had not thought of the credit but I did not think the results of my work would be claimed by someone like "dear Famia," either. All in all, it was a valuable lesson.

Chapter II

VIEW FROM
TEMPLE SQUARE

IN THE SUMMER, things in the Ward slow down. The Relief Society sisters still go round the block once a month to do their visiting teaching, but Report Meeting is combined with Work Day and all the rest of the meetings are dispensed with for about four months. The MIA meets once a week, but there are no activities except the summer sports programs which go on rather desultorily. Sunday School is always the same, and there are a few Sunday School picnics and class parties. Primary takes a month's vacation.

Most of the wards hold their annual ward reunions in these warm months. The Relief Society women cook enormous quantities of marvelous food, and everyone who has ever been a member of the ward is invited back for a day of visiting and eating. There is usually a program in the evening and dancing in the amusement, er, *cultural* hall.

There always used to be several Missionary Farewells. These were held during the Sacrament Meeting time and there is still a collection box to help out the missionary. Hundreds of dollars are often left in the little box by ward members before the night is over.

Elaborate programs announcing the leave-taking and the mission field of the missionary, as well as the night's program, used to be printed and mailed out to friends and relatives, and notices of the missionary's departure were printed in the paper. Then when he came home from his mission to give his report, we had his welcome-home gathering, and it was always surprising to see how much the young man had matured in such a short time, and how few of them had ever converted or baptized anyone while they were gone.

Although as many or more missionaries go into the field now as they ever did, the fuss isn't made about their going any more. Not that it isn't considered important, but because the publicity called attention to the fact that many young men avoided serving time in the armed services by going on missions. The criticism is a just one, and there are few of us who do not recognize it. I think that it is a rather furtive treatment for a service supposed to be rendered to God. Now, because of the adverse reaction, the only time you know a boy is going on a mission or returning from a mission is when you read in the hometown newspaper that so-and-so spoke in Church last Sunday night, or when it is announced from the comparative privacy of the ward pulpit.

WHILE ALL THE WARD FUNCTIONS go on in the summer, their pace is slowed in many ways. Weddings take up some of the slack; actually, they are receptions. Few wards allow marriages in the chapel. A church wedding for Mormons must be a Temple wedding. Although the Relief Society room is occasionally used for a wedding, most of the receptions in the wards take place after the wedding has been performed in the Temple.

Because they are exhorted literally from infancy to Temple marriage, Mormon women are simply not fulfilled until it, or the alternate sealing (after civil marriage) is done. Marriage in the Temple becomes a lifetime goal for many women who, in the rush of youth and the desire to get married, don't hold out for the "only proper way." And since many men like a glass of beer on a hot day and a cup of coffee on a winter morning, they don't take their wives to the Temple because they can't get a Recommend. This is the cause of a tremendous amount of marital strife and upheaval.

I've always wondered why women who constantly quarrel in this life with the men they have married, nag them for forty years to marry them for eternity. When the man has a heart attack or a kidney stone, and is forced to face the fact that he will surely die, he sees empty eternity stretching before him. Then he goes to the Temple and has his wife and family sealed to him. If you count the widows and widowers who willy-nilly take their mates through by proxy there must be as many marriages of middle-aged adults in the Temple as there are of young people.

But I understand the compulsion behind it. I have been told all my life that unsealed women can only be servants in heaven. This explains the rush of hundreds of women to be sealed to the early prophets—the greater the man in the Church on earth —the greater the promise in eternal life.

Indeed, the Temple is a lovely place to be married—peaceful, beautiful, dignified—but I can hardly have sympathy with women like the one I met recently, who has married and divorced five men because none of them would take her to the Temple. They all promised her beforehand, but would not fulfill the promise. It seems to me that if Temple marriage was what she wanted from life, she would have insisted on it before the fact, not afterward.

A man can marry as many women as he can get to marry him (one woman at a time, of course, since the Manifesto against polygamy) "for time and all eternity," providing the women have not been married in the Temple previously. If women have been married in the Temple, they automatically belong to their first husband in the next world. If the husband should die, a woman can again marry in the Temple, but only for "time" or this life.

It hardly seems right that a woman must be sealed for eternity to her first husband when she might love the subsequent one more—but then, women, no matter how much they insist that they "share" the Priesthood with their husbands, are *not* considered equals by the Church. Women, like blacks, cannot hold the Priesthood, cannot perform any of the ordinances (except some simple ones in the exclusively female rooms of the Temple), cannot form any of the policies of the Church. A woman cannot ascend to the highest degree of glory—the Celestial Kingdom—except as the wife of a Priesthood bearer. She cannot attain anything by herself. She only shares her husband's glory. So it seems only right that she should be able to choose which ever husband promises the most glorious future for her in the hereafter.

The most powerful motive for Temple marriage is not, I am sure, personal glory. It is the promise of having their children around them. Children born of Temple marriage—the Covenant—belong to the parents for the next life as well as this.

If they aren't married in the Temple, the children are apparently shuffled off somewhere else. However, according to the teachings, it's only the male children whom they can be sure of living with, since women go with their husbands and husbands go with *their* fathers. Also, it is believed that all of a woman's children fathered by a second husband, if she has been married in the Temple and widowed, will belong to the first husband in the next world.

Recently I heard of a young man who called off his marriage to a childless young widow. He loved her, he said, but he did not want his children to belong to another man in the Celestial Kingdom.

It has often seemed to me that many Mormons spend more time thinking about the next world than they do about this one. When I complained, the answer I got was: "And why not? We'll spend more time there."

I wonder sometimes if the hereafter isn't going to be every bit as mixed up a mess as the here.

THERE ARE SPECIAL ROOMS in the Temples set aside for Temple weddings and sealings. These are lovely rooms, of various sizes, but none of them are very large. In some Temples you do not have to wear Temple clothes to attend a Temple marriage. The bride does and the groom does, but guests, although required to produce a Recommend, can wear street clothing except for their shoes. In other Temples, white clothing is required for all. Often the guests go with the bride and groom through the entire endowment rite. They "go through" the Temple. To do this, they must wear Temple robes and act as a proxy (take a name of one dead). If they attend only the wedding ceremony, they do not do this. There are special entrances to the Temples for such guests, who, of course, must have already gone through the Temple. Nonmember relatives who have not been endowed, or relatives who do not have active Recommends are not permitted to be present at the marriage.

Occasionally, special privileges are granted for both civil and Temple ceremonies, but this permission must come from the First Presidency (the President of the Church and his two councilors)and they are usually reluctant to grant such permission. After a civil marriage, the couple may go to the Temple to be sealed, and they are urged to do so, but there is still a waiting period before they are given permission.

In order to obtain a Recommend, you must be interviewed, first by the bishop of your ward and then by the stake presidency. Some bishops and stake presidents ask searching questions, other than those outlined in *The Bishop's Handbook*, which are: Do you keep the Word of Wisdom? Do you pay a full tithing? Are you morally clean? Do you promise to devote yourself and your time and your worldly goods to the building up of the Church? Do you uphold the authorities of the Church? Do you wear the regulation garments? Have you been divorced? Special permission from the First Presidency must be obtained before a divorced person can go into the Temple.

The searching questions asked by the bishop and stake president often elicit surprisingly honest answers. I have known cases where couples have admitted to premarital relations and have been denied Temple Recommends for a period of a year— to give them time to mend their ways. Even the questioning, however, does not eliminate all the pregnant brides who have perjured themselves to obtain the desired Temple wedding.

Unmarried women are not encouraged to go through the Temple so long as there is hope that they will marry—unless they are called on missions. It is suggested that they wait until they wed, although the privilege is not denied any young woman who seems to be sincere in her desires. Once a person goes through the Temple he must put on "garments" while he is there. This is a special type of underwear that he must wear—except for unusual circumstances—for the rest of his life, if he wishes to obtain the blessings that he has gone to the Temple to receive. Upon request, servicemen have been allowed to take them off during their tours of duty, and they can be removed in hospitals to facilitate medical and nursing care (but most often the person wearing them will not remove them). One prominent Church woman wrote to ask for a special dispensation to remove her Temple garments while she was on a vacation in New York. She was shopping for dresses in Saks Fifth Avenue and noticed that all the saleswomen on the floor were making all sorts of excuses to come into her dressing room. Then she realized that they were coming in to get a look at her Mormon underwear—"angel pants," some irreverent Saints call them. She was granted permission to remove her garments on subsequent shopping tours and in situations where they might be ridiculed.

The Mormon garment has always been a curious thing to the gentile who has heard of it, but there is little reason for curiosity. It simply replaces other underwear. It is made of cotton, rayon, or nylon. If worn properly, it insures a certain degree of modesty in female dress: no strapless or sleeveless dresses, and no immodestly short skirts. The garment has a brief sleeve, a reasonably low neckline, and although it is supposed to cover the knee, usually comes to several inches above it, rather like a chemise. Men wear a slightly different design although basically it is the same. Garments are worn as a symbol of promises made and as a reminder of protection to be received.

The garments were designed in the early days of the Church by the Prophet Joseph Smith. When Aunt Tressa lived with me, I made copies of a family diary that she had. I found some of it very interesting:

. . . My grandfather [James Allred] settled in Pittsfield, Pike County, Illinois and in the same year (1839), they moved to Commerce, which was later called Nauvoo, where he was ordained a high priest and a member of the High Council and was chosen as one of the Prophet's body guards in the Nauvoo Legion. He also held several other responsible positions, and helped to build the Nauvoo temple and assisted in giving endowments.

It was while they were living in Nauvoo that the Prophet came to my grandmother who was a seamstress by trade, and told her that he had seen the Angel Moroni with the garments on, and asked her to assist him in cutting out the garments. They spread unbleached muslin out on the table and he told her how to cut it out. She had to cut the third pair, however, before he said it was satisfactory. She told the Prophet that there would be sufficient cloth from the knee to the ankle to make a pair of sleeves, but he told her he wanted as few seams as possible and that there would be sufficient whole cloth to cut the sleeve without piecing.

The first garments were made of unbleached muslin and bound with turkey red [muslin, I suppose] and were without collars. Later on the Prophet decided he would have them [the necks] bound with white. Sister Emma Smith, the Prophet's wife, proposed that they have a collar on as she thought they would look more finished, but at first the Prophet did not have the collars on them. After Emma Smith had made the little collars, which were not visible from the outside, then Eliza R. Snow [a polygamous wife of Joseph Smith, and after his death, of Brigham Young, but she has always been known by Snow in the Church] introduced a wider collar of finer material to be worn on the outside of the dress. The garment was to reach the ankle and the sleeves to the wrist. The marks were always the same.

In the year 1842 my father was ordained a seventy and a member of the Fourth Quorum of Seventies. About this time the saints began to be persecuted very hard and more especially the heads of the Church. The Prophet Joseph and his brother Hyrum were continuously being hunted and persecuted by the mobs. Grandmother often used to put potatoes in the coals in the fireplace at night and leave fresh bread and butter and buttermilk, of which the Prophet was very fond, out on the table so that they could come in during the night and eat.

In the year 1844 in June the Prophet Joseph Smith, his brother Hyrum, John Taylor [later President of the Church] and Willard Richards were taken to Carthage Jail in Hancock County, Illinois. At the jail the Prophet Joseph handed his sword to my grandfather and said, "Take this, you may need it to defend yourself." Grandfather carried this sword with him to Utah, and it is now on display at the Utah state capitol. [I believe it has been moved to the Daughters of the Pioneers building.]

On the 27th of June, the Prophet and Hyrum were murdered in Carthage Jail. The Prophet had previously prophesied that Willard Richards would not be harmed, and true to the prophecy, he escaped without a scratch, but President Taylor was badly wounded by four bullets. [Grandfather Allred was the man who drove President Taylor and Willard Richards away from the jail in his wagon to escape the further wrath of the mob.]

The collars on the garments became a little too fancy and it was then that they were told to take off all the trimming and to wear the collars underneath their clothing. These are the so-called "old-style garments." Nowadays, they are not made of muslin, of course, but this is the style still worn in the Temples and in the grave. Necessary adaptations have been made for everyday wear.

But the fanatics are always with us. In their wild search for greater holiness, they often go to ridiculous lengths. In the Temples, the people are told to wear the garment always, and some of them take this literally. I know people who have never been completely undressed since first visiting a Temple. They bathe themselves while wearing half of the garment, and remove the soiled ones only after they have put clean ones on the half of the body they have bathed. I have never heard any Church authority advocate this, but I have heard that they should be removed in situations where they might be ridiculed. It

could be for this last reason that they can no longer be purchased in retail stores as was possible for many years, or perhaps
they were removed from the stores because they were being
purchased by non-Mormons, like one man, who told me he
always bought Mormon underwear because it was the most
comfortable he'd ever found. Now they can only be ordered
through the Relief Societies.

THERE ARE MANY MORMONS who have made working
in the Temples their life's work. There are special tours only
for Mormons to visit all of the Temples of the Church. While
each of them is different in architecture, there is a basic similar-
ity, and, of course, the rites are the same in each Temple.

I went to the Manti Temple in southern Utah at the desire
and insistence of my husband and his family some time after
we were married. It is an impressive old building, and there is
an almost tangible aura about it. Perhaps the aura comes from
the tales of miracles or the expectation of them. I had never
gone back to that Temple or any of the others, and I was
never stirred by any desire to go through the Temple again
until I met Sister Thompson. I'd been in the Salt Lake Temple
once, a year or two before my visits with Sister Thompson,
but had only entered the area where baptisms for the dead
are performed. I had been shepherding a group of Primary
girls, Sally and Ann among them. I'd seen pictures and read
and heard descriptions of the baptismal font in the Temple
(not to be confused with the one below the Tabernacle where
live baptisms are performed and where Papa had baptized
Sally). But I was unprepared for the baptismal font even at
that.

We entered the Temple through a special entrance, and after
the girls were dressed in their baptismal suits, we went into a
large room where the font dominated. It was a golden oval

basin, large enough to hold two elders and two proxies. (Children were usually used as proxies for the dead because it is easier to baptize them than it is to baptize adults.) At the top of the steps leading into the font was a platform, and a recording clerk sat there, entering the names and other baptismal information.

Inside the gold basin the water was blue and pleasantly warm, but the impressive thing about it was that it was supported on the backs of twelve golden oxen—life-size. I wondered if the first baptismal font like this had been in the ancient Temple of Solomon. There was something so ageless in its design. But then, as I watched the elders lift their hands and intone the rite of baptism before immersing the children, I remembered that baptism is not a Jewish rite—it is a Christian rite performed first by John and then by Jesus. I wondered if the Jews had used such fonts as ceremonial baths, or perhaps it had come out of the antiquities of Egypt, passed down to the designer of the font from one of those who had walked through the division of the Red Sea. I tried to find out something about it, but I couldn't find the right source. Brother Gardiner failed me here. Had no one before me wondered who designed the great baptismal font?

The elders worked alternately, allowing the proxy to catch her breath between baptisms. After each child had been baptized a number of times for dead females, she left the font and went to the curtained rooms where she dressed quietly and came back to wait until the rest of the group had had their turns. Apparently, here, as in the other Temple ceremonies, men and women were separated. There were no little boys in the baptismal rooms that day.

The children seemed to enjoy being baptized, and I heard one slightly older girl say that she had been baptized for the dead 117 times.

Annie Thompson was one of the most faithful of all the

sisters in Lincoln Ward. I noticed her the first time I attended church, for although she was eighty-four at the time, she was one of the most beautiful women I have ever seen.

She was sitting across the aisle from me on that day when I went to Church wearing Chanel #5 and came back wearing oil of wintergreen. I remember staring at her. She seemed quite aloof, and although she hobbled rather than walked, she moved with patrician dignity, her pale gray, gloved hand resting on an ivory-headed cane. Her hair was snowy white and piled on top of her head in much the same way she had worn it at twenty-five. I believed, when I saw her, what artists say about having "good bones." The skin of her face was drawn over bones that were both delicate and strong. Her nose was straight and slender, her eyes large and deep-set, her mouth, from which tiny wrinkles sprayed, was beautifully shaped.

That Sunday she wore a gray silk dress, not much above her ankles, but the length suited her. It had a narrow lace collar and matching cuffs. Around her head and neck she wore a lavender scarf of soft silk or chiffon. The scarf was carefully and beautifully draped, and at the time I wondered that a woman of her age could still retain her vanity to such a degree.

I was wrong about Sister Thompson. She was not vain. She wore the soft silk scarves to protect her head and neck from drafts that plagued her arthritis. The seemingly artful draping was simply a toss and a twist, achieving instantly what a less beautiful woman could not have done in half an hour. She wore gray silk because someone had given her a bolt of it and she had made herself several dresses. She chose the color of her scarves, which she also made, because she loved the colors. That they suited her coloring and the set of her fragile loveliness was more or less incidental.

Annie Thompson never missed a Sunday School or a Sacrament meeting or a Relief Society meeting or a conference. I watched her sitting attentively at meetings and each time I was awed by her beauty. It was almost two years before I became her friend. I'd been assigned with another Relief Society lady as a visiting teacher for Sister Thompson's block. She lived in one of the more modest houses that we visited, which surprised me. I had thought that Sister Thompson was rather well off. She had that air about her—the way she dressed, her way of walking, the aristocratic manner in which she turned her head or placed her palm on her cane, and the soft, cultured voice with which she spoke, but I found that she lived on very little.

The house, not more than four rooms, was painted a soft gray which needed retouching. Her yard was small, but neatly kept. Inside her house there was a busy clutter. There were baskets of scraps from which she was piecing quilts and making patchwork pillows. She had just baked bread the first day we went, and she gave us a slice, cut from a warm loaf and spread with butter and honey. I hated to see her ruin the warm loaf by cutting it so soon, but she insisted.

Her floors were carpeted with hand-woven rugs and the house was heated by a large, brown heater. The kitchen was small and immaculate—its cupboards crowded with jars and canisters. Her windows were filled with flowers in cans and pots, each set on a plate or saucer to catch the overflow as she watered them. I think there may have been two bedrooms, but I could only see one, the bed covered by a pieced quilt that made a colorful coverlet.

Sister Thompson wasn't wearing silk that day. Her dress of faded blue cotton was cut from the same pattern as her Sunday dresses. It, too, was trimmed with bits of lace at the collar and cuffs, and an amber brooch caught the neck at her throat.

After that, whenever my partner was unable to go block-teaching with me, I went alone and always left Sister Thompson's house for last and timed the visit to be the longest one. I found her beautiful within, too: good and kind. She told me bits and pieces of her life during my visits, after we had disposed of the lesson for the month and the routine questions as to her well-being.

She had lived all of her childhood and girlhood in the deserts of southern Utah where her father and mother had been sent by Brigham Young to build up the Church. She had been terrified of the warring Indian chief Walker, who raided the area frequently. He had seen her once with her brothers while she was helping them round up their stock. Two days later the chief appeared at her father's door and asked to buy her for a wife.

Her father refused the munificent offers of horses and blankets in trade for her, and from that time the family worried for fear the Indian would try to kidnap her. Finally driven by a combination of drought and fear, they left Blanding and moved to a small farm north of Salt Lake City.

"Do you have any pictures of you when you were young?"

"Just this one, taken when I was married." She handed me a picture of the wedding pose that was so popular then, the man sitting, the young wife standing by the side of his chair, her hand resting in stylized submissiveness on his shoulder.

"Oh you were absolutely lovely. I thought you must have been, because you are so beautiful now."

"Pshaw," she said, "I was taught that pretty is as pretty does, and I didn't think I was pretty. No one told me that I was."

"But you could see for yourself. You can see that you are now." I waved a hand toward her mirror, an old one in a wide, carved frame that hung above an ancient commode.

"Well, you see, dear, we didn't have any mirrors when I was young. I never saw myself in one until we moved up from the ranch."

"But you surely had seen a reflection of yourself in water or in the back of a pan or something."

"Maybe, I don't remember, but I thought I must be fairly good-looking because the men and boys made over me some."

"Didn't your mother tell you how pretty you were?"

"I had a stepmother, and though she was a good woman, she didn't allow me to think I was anything special. There was too much work to be done to allow a girl to think she was anything special."

"Oh," I said in pity, "to be that lovely and not be able to appreciate it. What about later, when you moved up here? I'll bet you were the prettiest girl in the valley."

"By then it wasn't important. I was married soon afterward, and I was too busy with my family."

"What a shame."

Sister Thompson laughed at me and made me a cup of Postum and gave me a slice from a fruitcake which she unwrapped very slowly, for her hands pained her and the points of her slender fingers were swollen.

"I'll be honest with you, dear. It's been *convenient* to be beautiful, as you say I am. I can look nice on so much less than it takes for many women." Then showing a bit of the pride that I knew so lovely a woman must surely take in herself, she said, "I like looking nice." And she adjusted the brooch at her collar.

During the months I visited her, I learned that more than anything else in the world, Sister Thompson wanted to go to the Temple and do the work for some of her dead relatives. But she was so crippled and so slow that she would not ask to go on the regular Ward Temple excursions.

"I'm always the last, and I won't bother people when they are so busy," she said firmly. All the same, she worried about the salvation of her dead and feared that there was no one except her to do for them. Sister Thompson had one son, but he lived in another state and was not very active in the Church.

I loved beautiful little Sister Thompson, so I decided that I would get a Temple Recommend and go with her through the Temple. Until now, I couldn't have honestly obtained a Recommend, because I hadn't kept the Word of Wisdom—I had drunk coffee since before Ann was born. I drank it because my friends drank it, and I found it very sociable to share a cup of coffee. I could not consider it the sin that good Mormons did. I could not consider it important enough to be embarrassed about—except once.

Papa and I were at breakfast during one of his visits with me. The two older girls were in school, Barbara was sitting in her highchair with a piece of toast, my husband had gone to work. Papa, always trying to be unobtrusive, stayed in his room until the house cleared. I'd prepared his bowl of Germade (which was "good enough, but not like the old grain they used to get"), his dish of apricots, his salt-free buttered toast, his cup of barley coffee, which he still enjoyed although his diet forced him to forego the cream he loved.

I made myself a cup of coffee and brought it to the table to sit with him while he ate.

He spooned his cereal, made the usual comment about it, and then sipped his barley coffee. As he wiped the brown drops off the ends of his mustache, he looked at me as only Papa has ever looked at me. He bent his head as if to peer over the tops of glasses he was not wearing, and stared directly into my eyes.

"Do you drink coffee, girl?"

I had really thought he would assume I was sharing his brew and denial raced around in my head for a moment. Then I answered honestly.

"Yes, I do, Papa." I felt as if I'd just owned up to committing adultery in the Church. I braced myself for a couple of hours' lecture on the Word of Wisdom, but he only sighed and reached over to pat my hand.

"Well, at least you admit it. You don't hide your instant coffee in the Postum bottle." Then I thought what a good idea that would have been and wondered why I hadn't thought of doing it. But it was too late.

I can't remember whether it was because I wanted to get a Recommend to take Sister Thompson through the Temple or whether it was because I couldn't give the lessons on the Word of Wisdom to my Mia Maids without feeling hypocritical, but I gave up coffee for several years and didn't miss it at all. Neither could I see that giving it up was any special benefit to me, and I certainly never felt that I had earned any stars in my crown by storing the coffee pot.

We bought a new car that year, and I called Sister Thompson and told her that if she would like to go, I would pick her up the next Thursday and we would go to the Temple. The Bishop gave me my Recommend without question or comment—and I loved him for it. He had paid me a trustful compliment.

Thursday was a lovely summer morning. Warm, not hot, bright and clear, the mountains which surround the valley stood out clean and sharp. Sister Thompson was radiant with anticipation, and while I rather reluctantly faced the unfamiliarity of the Temple, the delight on her fine old face was more than enough to overcome my doubts. I went in the house to help her out to the car.

"Oh," she said, flustered, "I haven't my clothes packed. Pressing them took longer than I thought."

"That's all right. We have plenty of time. I'm early."

"Look," she said, "I made my Temple clothes by hand. Well, I really made them to be buried in. I never thought I'd get to wear them to the Temple." I looked at the clothes as she laid them out on the table, preparing to fold them. Her dress was of white silk, the same pattern that she wore on Sundays. There were dainty ruffles of lace around the high collar and long sleeves.

"It's prettier than most of the wedding gowns, I've seen."

"My wedding gown wasn't as nice as this, not nearly," she said. I looked at the pleated robes and veil of sheerest chiffon, the delicate, white silk slippers, the long, lace-trimmed slip. Her green moire apron was delicately embroidered in cutwork, the required pattern of fig leaves was backed by another piece of green moire and had satin ribbons for ties. I had noticed that even on Sundays, Sister Thompson wore stockings of fine lisle which were cheaper and lasted longer than nylon, but for the Temple her stockings were of white nylon. There was a fine linen handkerchief trimmed with handmade lace for her pocket, and the brooch fastened at the high neck of her dress was a small bouquet of white roses cut from ivory.

We carefully packed the clothes into her cardboard suitcase on which she had printed her name in large block letters. After she adjusted the pin at her neck and patted her hair, I took her arm to hurry her along a bit, for packing the clothes had taken more time than I thought it would.

"Oh, my," she said when she was seated and I'd started the motor, "this car is brand-new, isn't it?"

"Yes. We got it yesterday. Today is its maiden voyage."

"How nice of you, my dear. Makes me feel like Cinderella in her new coach must have. I've never ridden in a brand-new car before. They smell quite different when they're new, don't they?"

I sniffed. They did.

We drove through the tree-shaded streets to Temple Square and parked in a large lot conveniently located across the street, north of the Temple. People are always walking in the cross-walk there, carrying small suitcases and valises. I wondered what tourists thought of the suitcase parade on North Temple Street. Now Sister Thompson and I joined it.

We crossed the street and walked the wide, winding walk

through the beds of shrubs and flowers to the Temple Annex
where we stood in line to have our Recommends inspected be·
fore being allowed to enter the Temple proper.

Sister Thompson and I were the last of the women ready
for the Session. I had undressed and was wrapped in my "shield,"
waiting for the interminable washings and anointings to be
completed. Sister Thompson appeared long after all the rest
of the ladies had left the dressing rooms. I understand that the
rites of washing and anointing are now done by proxy, as
baptisms and confirmations are done. This would greatly shorten
the time of the Sessions. Then, we waited for the long line
of women ahead of us to step into the cubicles and trail back to
their dressing rooms to don their robes. I read one account of
these ceremonies which implied that the body was exposed. In
the women's section this is not true. The ceremonies are conducted with the utmost—even prudish—modesty and entirely
by women workers. These are the only ordinances that women
are allowed to perform in the Church, for obvious reasons.

The rest of the people going through in the Session were
seated and waiting when we finally found our seats in the
Creation Room, but the workers were patient. They were used
to the aged and the slow. We were also the last to reach the
top of the stairs on the second floor, but Sister Thompson
looked so hurt at a worker's suggestion that she take the elevator,
that I agreed with her that she could make it.

After my first natural impatience, I relaxed and allowed the
hours to slide. Although Temple Square is in the center of one
of the busiest commercial districts in the city, I heard no sound
of traffic, no honking of auto horns. There are many windows
in the Temple, symmetrical rows of them on each floor, but
the world is shut out by heavy glass and hewn stone. I was
constantly amazed by the peaceful quiet. We were in the midst
of the several hundred people which constitute a Session. Be-

hind us and ahead of us were groups just as large or larger than ours, as many as seven or eight hundred in all.

Occasionally, I heard a hymn being sung by the group ahead or behind, but other than that, just the swish of white robes, footsteps, and whispers, which were dulled by the heavy carpeting on the floors and the draperies drawn across the windows. I went through the responses as instructed, but I paid little attention to most of it. It was an oasis of stillness, and for the six or seven hours it took the group to go through, I drifted in the silence.

I've spent a lot of time in the woods, and there is peace there, but it is a noisy peace. Birds sing, squirrels shrill, crows caw, twigs crack, the wind soughs through the trees. Even so, there was much the same feeling in the Temple that one finds alone in the woods. The ceilings were enormously high, the rooms huge, the people all looked alike, moving quietly, pleasantly through the day. Some of these people would finish this Session and then change and have lunch. (Incongruously, there is a lunchroom in the Temple.) Then they would change again and go through another Session, for there were several throughout the day. I could hardly visualize it—thousands of people in groups of hundreds, proceeding through the rooms and rites, dressed all in white, shod in white, with only the green aprons giving color to the congregations. One group never saw another one, even though they shared the same dressing rooms, the same hallways, the same stairs and rooms. The only evidences of other people were the street clothes hanging in the lockers of your dressing cubicle and the occasional sound of singing.

The rooms have furnishings of good quality, with padded and comfortable seats for long sitting. The last room, the Celestial Room, is elegant, royally furnished and decorated— the kind of room you would expect in a palace. I thought that perhaps one of the reasons so many people went there so regularly was that nowhere else they would ever go, except possibly the heaven for which they worked so hard, would offer them such surroundings.

Throughout the day we had been taken on a symbolic journey from the time before Creation and the Word until the entrance into the Celestial Kingdom after death.

We sat first in the semidarkness of the Creation Room where the walls and ceilings are painted with waves and clouds, shapeless shadows, whirling and blending. From there we went into the Garden of Eden, where the walls were vast murals of trees and shrubs, flowers and lions and lambs lying down together. Here was the Tree of good and evil—of knowledge and Eve's downfall.

I wondered if many of the women who sat there felt as I did when I first heard Adam's weak excuse to God: "The woman whom *thou gavest to be with me*, she gave me of the tree, and I did eat." No matter what religious rationale I've heard applied to the scene in the Garden of Eden, I've always thought it set the precedent for men blaming their troubles on women.

Driven out of the Garden of Eden, we found ourselves in the "lone and dreary" world. Actually, it wasn't so lone and dreary. In this room, animals fought in life-size murals on the walls, and there were expanses of desert instead of the lush Garden landscape; still, the world depicted in this room was full of interest and beauty.

From this room to the next was an abrupt change. The room that precedes the entrance into the Celestial Room was decorated to blend walls and draperies and carpeting into a muted aura of waiting. The seats were comfortable. There were large religious paintings on the walls. It lacked the drama of the rooms we had just come through. Here we waited to be individually conducted through the veil, which to me symbolized death, into the Celestial Room. Once there, you could stay and look or visit with friends as long as you liked. Groups of white-robed people were chatting here and there. Most of them, however, hurried through the room they had seen many times and went down to the dressing rooms, either to leave the Temple or to take another name through the ceremonies.

In some of the newer Temples, the time-consuming processional has been eliminated. The people sit in one room and are transported by audio-visual means through the session. Often, they stay for two or three Sessions, but one session at a time was enough for me. It would be dusk by the time I got home and gathered up my children from Mickey Aloia. In return, I sat with Mickey's children when she went to Mass.

I took Sister Thompson to the Temple about eight times at two-week intervals. For her, it meant offering the blessing of her Church to lost souls, and she was pleased with her efforts. I didn't dwell much on any blessings that might accrue to me. The names I walked through by proxy would no doubt be those of people who were hardshell Baptists, Orthodox Jews, or Catholic nuns, and since the dead have a right to accept or refuse the work, they'd probably refuse mine. But it didn't matter. I found that the trips with Sister Thompson gave me joy. If I was worried or troubled about something, I chose those days to take her to the Temple, for I found that I could not dwell on them while I was there. I took my problems with me and prayed about them, and I always came away with enough peace of mind to last for a while.

Strangely, nothing in the Temple brought me closer to Papa as I had hoped it might. I could more easily see him in the Circle Room of the Heber Third Ward.

Our last trip spoiled things for me.

There is a luggage room for the use of frequent Temple workers. It has rows of shelves, alphabetically lettered to hold the suitcases full of Temple clothing so it does not have to be transported every time the worker goes through a Session. I didn't have any clothes, and for people like me, clothing can be rented for about two dollars—nothing like the beauty and quality of Sister Thompson's but serviceable enough. When we were through the session, I returned my clothes to the clothing room desk, but Sister Thompson would carefully fold her dress and robes in thin tissue and pack them into her suitcase. We would leave it in a special place in the "T" section of the luggage shelves.

On our last visit, we went in to pick up Sister Thompson's suitcase, but we couldn't find it. We spent the morning, checking every suitcase and every shelf, thinking that someone in a hurry might have shoved it out of its niche or moved it by mistake. But it wasn't there, and the enquiries we made came to naught. There was much shaking of heads and clicking of tongues that such a thing could happen in the Temple, but it appeared that Sister Thompson's exquisite, hand-wrought clothes had been stolen.

I could not believe it, but one of the regular Temple workers shook her head sadly at our questions.

"Does this happen often?"

"Too often, I'm afraid. Seems impossible that people would steal in the House of the Lord, doesn't it? But I guess they always have—always will."

I felt terrible, much worse than Sister Thompson seemed to, and in my shocked rage, I certainly wished some unpleasant things to fall upon the head of the thief. I wondered if some envious woman had seen the perfection of Sister Thompson's dress and robes and had envied her enough so that she watched where the suitcase was placed. It must have been a deliberate theft—the suitcase was too distinctive and too plainly marked for a mistake.

Sister Thompson stopped my angry words with tears in her eyes, but with a shrug of acceptance.

"I shouldn't have left it there. But I didn't think . . ."

"You shouldn't have had to think."

We did not go any more. My friend lived on a small pension.

She could not afford to rent her clothes as I did, and she would not accept my offer of the rental. My time had been generosity enough, she said.

It was not long after that Sister Thompson died. I wondered what kind of burial clothing she wore, certainly she would not have had time or money to make another set. But I did not go to the funeral.

What kind of person could have stolen Sister Thompson's clothes? Obviously they had obtained a Recommend, but when I took mine out of its little case and read the fine print, it said nothing at all about denying admission to thieves.

I went back to the Temple only twice more, once to witness a marriage, and I watched to see if the bride and groom had the same difficulty stretching to kiss each other across the lace-covered altar that I had when I was married.

The second time, I went to the Logan Temple with Emma Tadje. I really became acquainted with Emma that day. She wanted to go through a Session before the summer was gone. I still had a few weeks left in the life of my Recommend. (They are issued for a period of a year and can be renewed again and again on the condition of continued worthiness.)

We had decided that although the drive to Logan took about four hours, both ways, we would still be able to go through a session in less time than it took to go through the crowded Sessions of the Salt Lake Temple. Neither of us had been in the Logan Temple and we wanted to see it.

The Logan Temple sits high on a hill overlooking the city. Here it was that my grandfather and my grandmother Hicken were married. Then, instead of two hours one way, their trip took two days. They had driven in a white-top buggy from Heber with another couple, and they had stopped with relatives at the halfway mark to spend the night.

The Temple is approached by a beautiful winding drive

around the hill, and atop it, grasses, trees, and flowers make it an Eden.

There is a different atmosphere in the Logan Temple than in the others I have visited. It is sweeter, friendlier, and not so disposed to hurry. The Sessions, which accommodate fewer people, take only two hours or so from start to finish. Brides and bridegrooms and those going through for themselves, or to be sealed in marriage, are given the first few benches. Although a bride may see her husband-to-be all through the journey that the ceremonies symbolize, she is separated from him by an aisle. Women on the left, men on the *right*—wouldn't you know. If the seating is prearranged, it is possible that a bride could pass from room to room at the side of her groom, but usually it is not, and the white-clad male who briefly walks beside you in the march through the Creation Room to the Celestial Kingdom is as faceless to you as you must be to him.

Only at the veil does the bride come close to her groom, who has, by plan, preceded her, and it is only after the journey is done and the Celestial Room has been entered that the marriage party goes to the room assigned for the wedding. Often, the Temple endowments are performed prior to the wedding. In this case the party can proceed directly to where the wedding will take place.

The day in the Logan Temple was even more peaceful than the ones in the Salt Lake Temple. Most Temple workers have kind and patient faces—in the Logan Temple they seem even kinder and more patient. The feeling of love and friendliness is evident there as in no place I have ever been. As the day went on, by some spiritual osmosis, this feeling penetrated deep into me. I suppose it is because these people believe that they are serving God. And if they believe it truly—then they must be.

Chapter 12

TESTIMONY AT ALTURAS

"THERE'S NO NEED FOR women's clubs in Mormon Communities," I've heard more than one zealous Mormon declare. "If you're doing all that you should in the Church, you won't have time for them, anyway."

I had to drop the clubs I joined after Papa died and refuse invitations to rejoin them later because all my spare time was channeled into Church activities. No matter whether Mutual or Relief Society activities slackened in the summer or not— there were other spontaneous ones that arose to crowd the hours of every day.

One night in Officer and Teacher's meeting, the Bishop told

us that he had been offered a loan of the recreational facilities
high in the Sawtooth Mountains of Idaho. The invitation had
come from an enterprising California Ward that had bought
the site at Alturas Lake some forty miles north of Sun Valley.

"There are several cabins, each of which will accommodate
six to eight people—more, if it is necessary. There is a big clubhouse with kitchen and dining accommodations. We've been
counting the Ward's pennies, and if you people are willing to
help with your time and talents, we think we can take all the
young people in our Ward, boys *and* girls up there for three
or four days. We're told that there is a lake for swimming,
fishing, and boating, and that nearby there are riding horses for
rent. What do you say?"

We said, "Wonderful," unanimously, and the Bishop assigned
us our tasks. The Bishopric and their wives would plan the
meals and buy the groceries. Minnie, Veronica, and I would be
assigned the welfare of the girls, and the brethren would take
responsibility for the boys. The Young Women would be given
the responsibility for some sort of entertainment each night, so
that the youngsters would want to stay in the clubhouse after
dinner and during the evening hours until bedtime.

Minnie and Veronica and I went. None of the Young Men
did—as usual.

The members of the Bishopric and two of their wives drove
up in private cars. Minnie and Veronica rode with them. Emma
and I rode up on the bus with the kids. Ida Whiteley couldn't
get away; she had brides' and bridemaids' gowns for two weddings that had to be ready that week. She had made boxes of
what she called "icebox" cookies and sent them in her stead.
There is no recipe for these cookies. She made them out of all
the leftovers that were in her refrigerator: jams, jellies, fruits,
leftover puddings—they were some of the most delicious cookies
I've ever eaten.

"These have peas in them," she told me as she handed the big boxes to us for loading on the bus.

"Peas?"

"Oh, yes. Peas are sweet—very good in cookies." And they were.

The bus driver's name was Joe. I don't know how old he was, but when he wasn't driving the bus, he was one of the kids. He seemed remarkably cheerful to me that early dawn as we gathered on the Church lawn to load ourselves into the cars and bus. He grinned happily as the rowdy kids piled on the bus and then haphazardly piled off again. He nodded attentively while parents who had come to say goodbye to their youngsters gave him instructions for caution.

Joe loaded all the gear and the odd-sized parcels, packages, and baskets carefully. Then he came to my luggage and stopped. I had two suitcases, a vanity case, a large hatbox, and another box. It was this last box that stopped him. My neighbor's bathtub had been shipped in it.

"What's this?"

"It's just things. Things I'm supposed to take." The Bishop and his councilors came over to see what was causing the delay. Most everyone was in their cars, and the kids were in the bus with the windows down, watching us noisily.

"She says this is supposed to go."

"What is it, Sister Hunter?"

"It's a surprise. If I tell you what's in it, the surprise will be ruined."

There was a short, whispered consultation between Clarence, Parky, and the Bishop.

"Do you really have to take this?" the Bishop asked me seriously.

"Yes, I do."

"She says she has to take it," Bishop Trauffer said, with more than a tinge of resignation in his tone. "So load it on. We'll have to get it in there somehow."

None of the brethren were pleased with me as they lifted and hauled and tugged and pushed. But they got the box in the bottom of the bus, after they had unloaded some of the other stuff and put it in the racks above the seats.

The bus eased slowly out onto Ninth East as one of Salt Lake City's unsurpassable sunrises raised its orange, blue, and pink banners and sent them streaming out from behind the Wasatch Mountains. But the bedlam on the bus was so loud that I couldn't see the sunrise very well—to see things like that, you have to have quiet.

Until we reached Ogden you couldn't hear what your seat-mate was yelling at you. I'd typed up some booklets of songs to shorten the boredom of the empty Idaho prairies and I passed them out now and started the kids singing. The bus driver had a beautiful, powerful baritone, and he loved to sing. The ride was bearable while they were singing; we kept them singing all the way to Alturas Lake.

For some of the young people it was the first trip into Idaho and even the sagebrush was interesting. We stopped only when we had to, except that we pulled up in Brigham City and toured the many-spired Tabernacle there. This historic building had been built in the early days of the Church and it had been beautifully kept and preserved.

Tragically, this is not the case with some of the other beautiful buildings of that time. Those who fight to preserve them do so despite the glowering of the Church authorities who have developed endemic status fever, it seems: the newer and bigger the building, the more status for the stake presidency. In Heber City, where the fight to preserve the old Stake Tabernacle has caused internecine warfare, a line of women stood in front of the building and defied the waiting bulldozers. That time they saved it. The stake president had sworn to pull it down. Their cause was helped by the fact that the city, not the Church, owned the land upon which it was built. However, the exquisite, hand-wrought Coalville Tabernacle was gutted in the middle of the night by men called out by the stake president, who had resisted all the pleas of the people, and who was abetted by the higher authorities. The wanton destruction of the Coalville Tabernacle seems to have been without reason, since a generous offer for its purchase had been made. It seems the *only* reason was to pound into the people the belief in the power of authority. I do not know how much longer those who have a love for their pioneer heritage and history can hope to stand against the will of such authorities, for the Priesthood can be and *is* used as an effective intimidating force. I say all of this because it may be that the Brigham City Tabernacle will be one of the next to fall to the ambitious building programs of the Church—and it is by way of warning to those who would fight for it. I can almost predict that it would be a useless fight, as the people of Coalville grievously found. I do not believe that even mass exodus from Church membership would stay the hand of such determined powers.

WE LEFT SALT LAKE between five and six in the morning and we arrived late in the afternoon at Alturas Lake. We made quick surveys of the cabins and clubhouse, and then formed clean-up crews and wood-chopping details before the kids could scatter into the beckoning forest. The cabins had been vacant most of the summer, and they were full of mountain dirt—a collection of squirrel midden, mouse nests, leaves, pine cones and needles, twigs and dust. By nightfall and suppertime, the cabins were swept, in some cases scrubbed, windows washed, mattresses aired and swept, beds made up, woodboxes filled, and a stack of kitchen wood was beginning to pile up on the wide porches which bordered two sides of the clubhouse.

In the clubhouse, built of lodgepole pine, we found two rooms: a kitchen and a very large hall, used for dining, dancing, and the like. At one end of it were stacked folding chairs and tables, at the other end was a huge fireplace, and off to one side of that was an upright piano. At the other side was a ping-pong table. The place was furnished with rustic chairs and couches. We found the kitchen well equipped, with a mammoth wood-burning stove, dishes, cutlery, pots and pans sized to cook for mobs, a large griddle, stacks of trays, even dishtowels. A wide covered wooden porch ran the length of the building, and from there the view of the mountains and the forests which surrounded was superb. So was the weather.

Some of the boys had brought sleeping bags and they slept outside under the trees. They would come in to breakfast in the mornings excited about the things they'd seen and heard, or thought they'd seen and heard, in the night. There were deer tracks and moose droppings on the trails that led down to the lake, and once, Veronica and I surprised a doe who was lying just off the trail in a clump of bushes. She jumped and we jumped, but before we had time to run, she already had.

While the kids played ball and fished or boated and hiked, on foot or horseback, going steadily back and forth to the mountain store to buy pop and candy, all the Young Women were in the clubhouse with the drapes pulled, rehearsing for Saturday night.

I wrote a song and we were working out a dance number to go with it. In the dance line were Minnie, Veronica, Beverly Walker, Clarence's wife, Dorothy Monson, wife of the Ward clerk, and me. Emma, as usual, was at the piano. When she wasn't cooking or taking her turn supervising dish or table crew, Emma was at the piano.

I lugged in the large suitcase and the hatbox and displayed what I had brought in them: feather boas, satin and crepe de chine dresses from the twenties, earrings, beads, bracelets, shoes tied with bows, and my collection of horrible hats. We chose our costumes from these and put them aside to alter in secret before opening night.

At the end of a couple of hours of rehearsing, we were exhausted and Emma was leaning on her arms on the piano. The dancing hadn't sapped us, but our laughing had. As we fell into chairs giggling and gasping, there was a knock at the door. We'd put a NO ADMITTANCE sign on it, but this knock was authoritative.

Minnie went over and opened the door a crack. A forest ranger stood there with his hat in his hand. His pants were dusty and there was an odd look on his face.

"May I come in?"

"Of course," Minnie said. "Did you want to see someone about a fire permit or something? We have one, but I'll go get the Bishop."

"No need for that. I came over to look around. You are in my area. I heard the music in here and," the funny look split into a wide grin, "I've been watching you through a crack in the window curtain, and I laughed so hard I fell off my perch." He brushed himself off and straightened up. "Are you gals rehearsing for something special?"

"We're rehearsing for tomorrow night's program," Veronica said with her usual clipped dignity, and the ranger started to laugh again.

"Then would you . . . is there any way . . . say, would you let me bring the rest of the guys from the ranger station over here for your show? From what I saw through the crack, I sure wouldn't want any of us to miss it."

We said we'd be glad to have him come and bring his friends, and we asked him to stay for lunch.

"Sorry, I'd like to, but I've got to get back to work. I'll be here tomorrow night, though."

While Veronica and I were helping to prepare lunch a little

while later, she came up to me and said quite seriously, "It isn't often that I deliberately set out to make a jackass of myself." She said "ahss," giving the word a singular dignity. "I don't know that I *like* being thought that funny."

"You don't want to do it?"

"Of course, I'll do it. It's in a good cause. I know," and she read my thoughts as so often happened, "that the only reason we are doing it is to set an example for the young people." I laughed happily. So often Veronica tickles my American funny bone without knowing how she has. She usually ignores it, but now she was a bit indignant.

"I mean, I know you think that if we get up there and do the first act, the rest of them will have to follow suit. That is it, isn't it? We are what you call bellwethers for this obstreperous flock?"

"That's it."

"I don't want to be damp, but I do hope we aren't going to be as bloody funny as that forest chap seemed to think we were. What will our daughters think? How can one expect one's daughters to act like ladies when one is acting more than a bit of the fool oneself?"

That night, I guess we were "bloody funny" because the kids howled with laughter and so did everyone else. I thought the "forest chaps" were actually going to roll in the aisle. And someone did fall off his seat in his enthusiasm. One of the older boys had brought a movie camera and there were flash bulbs popping as we did our act. We performed some well executed bumps and grinds (so unexpected that they had enormous and hilarious shock value), along with a combination of the Big Apple, the Eagle Rock, the Lindy Hop, and all the Charleston steps we could remember and manage to do.

We sashayed off stage and out the door to tumultuous applause, and when we went back in, minus hats, paper eyelashes, and beads, but panting from our performance, our audience was still wiping its eyes.

The gist of our song had been that if we had the courage to drop our dignity for one evening and put on our act, the least that the rest of them could do was to follow us on stage and put on the rest of the show.

The Bishop and Clarence brought in the bathtub box.

"In this box is the rest of your evening's entertainment," I told them, and then we took off the lid to reveal the surprise. Inside it were sheets of cardboard, rolls of crepe paper, pencils, paints, fluted paper plates, fur coats, hats, beads, shoes, ribbons, scissors, colored construction paper, stapler, glue, pins, old curtains, the head of a paper maché horse, boots, piles of full petticoats, bundles of paper flowers, scarves, a Peter Pan costume, colored vests, top hats, bowlers, the Ward's makeup kit, and three pieces of sheet music.

We divided the group into three. Each group had a piece of music to work an act around, and they were assigned adult advisers to help. They had fifteen minutes to plan their act, fifteen minutes for makeup and costuming, fifteen minutes to learn their song and dance routine, and fifteen minutes to practice at the piano with Emma. In one hour they had to be ready to present their acts.

Veronica helped in the makeup corner. Emma held forth in one unbelievably noisy end of the room, and Minnie and I circulated. The bus driver and the forest rangers helped, too. I don't know exactly what they did, but everyone was frantically busy, and even though three full-dress rehearsals were going on in the same room at the same time, everyone was greatly surprised by the others' acts. It is unbelievable what an hour of creative frenzy can accomplish.

Afterward we served hot chocolate and plates of Ida's icebox cookies. The rangers wolfed a couple of heaping plates of the cookies, excusing their greediness by saying they'd never tasted anything so good. I wondered what they would have thought if I told them there were peas in them.

On Sunday we held Church services. The Bishop presided. The Sacrament was served, but instead of dividing for classes, we held a Testimony meeting.

I have never been to services that touched me more deeply. One shy young man said that he knew that the Spirit of God was with us that morning. I envied his certainty until I remembered the Scriptures.

"Wherever one or two of you have gathered together in my name, there am I also."

All the rest of Sunday was peaceful, restful. The kids played ping-pong, sang in groups at the piano, and walked on the forest trails. The adults relaxed between their cooking chores. Sunday night we had a big bonfire and held a brief prayer and hymn service under the mountain stars. That was most impressive—the songs coming down from generations through those young throats. They sang, among others, *O, Ye Mountains High* and *Come, Come Ye Saints*. It made our hearts tender and our souls vulnerable—the music of our fathers is often more powerful than all the words of all the priests in their pulpits.

We sent everyone to bed early since we would have to rise at dawn to clean and close up the buildings and still reach Salt Lake City in good time on Monday.

We left reluctantly Monday morning, but even though it was over and we were going home, the fun of the past few days was still with us. The kids sang on the way home, too, and though they must have been as noisy as on the way up, they didn't seem to be. Instead of exhausting my supplies of patience and fortitude as I had thought I surely must, I had restocked them, somehow.

We had accomplished far more than an enjoyable outing in the mountains for sixty or so young people. We had welded our Mutual into a solid unit. After that, everything went better, and we knew that for sure when the next MIA dance was given.

The boys danced!

Chapter 13

WILL SHAKESPEARE
AND THE
RELIEF SOCIETY

I'D BEEN TEACHING the literature lesson for about a
year when the Relief Society General Board of the Church
announced that the course of study for the next two years would
be the works of Shakespeare. The Relief Society bought one
textbook of Shakespeare's best known plays which contained
a brief introduction to Elizabethan times. The *Relief Society
Magazine* provided lesson help, and the University of Utah
gave a special series of weekly Shakespeare classes for Relief

Society literature leaders. The classes were taught by Professor Lewis of the English department and there was a nominal fee charged for them, about ten dollars. The classes were helpful, but much too brief, and the groan of dismay when the course was announced in Relief Society meeting made me realize that keeping the ladies awake with Shakespeare would be a formidable task.

I must have been one of the very few literature leaders who looked forward to the next two years, and there were a rash of resignations. But I loved Shakespeare.

In the parlor of my grandparents' home was a big, golden oak bookcase. It was, I think now, a very odd piece of furniture to find in a small-town Mormon home. It had glass doors and ornate carving, and it was topped with an oblong mirror. On one side, a desk top pulled down to reveal numerous cubbyholes and an ink well. No one opened it much, and the books inside were practically unused. Through the years, my numerous relatives had bought books from book salesmen, or they were assigned to read them in school, and after they had finished with them they were stored in the bookcase. Papa and Mama had the peculiar reverence of the uneduated for books.

Mama read the stories in the *Relief Society Magazine* and *The Young Women's Journal* (before it was combined with *The Young Men's Journal* to form *The Era*) but Papa read only Church books. Once I asked him why he never read anything else, when there were so many good books to read.

"Wellsir," he said, "one time I read a story in your Grandma's magazine. It was continued in the next issue. It was a while before I could get to it, but I got the second magazine and read that story right to the next to the last page. Then I found out that one of those damned kids had torn out the end of it. It made me so mad, I decided that was enough for me. I never bothered with any of that kind of reading again."

Among the most important of those books for me was Shakespeare's complete works, and there was also a copy of *Lamb's Tales from Shakespeare*.

By the time I was in third grade, I knew the characters and plots of most of Shakespeare's plays. When it was my turn to take part in a program, I either sang a song or told a story, and my stories were always from Shakespeare. I thought, even then, that they were the best ones I'd ever read.

Perhaps I was a tiresome storyteller, if so, it was partly my fault and partly Shakespeare's for writing such complicated plots. The kids in the room seemed to enjoy the stories, but they liked the ones that Sumner Hatch told a lot better. Sumner told Penrod and Sam stories.

Shakespeare has never been very popular in Utah—not at all like *The Book of Mormon*, which has sold upward of 20,000 copies a year for the last one hundred years. One of my teachers once said of my stories from Shakespeare that I had the most amazing imagination she'd ever come into contact with. She would have easily recognized the names if they had come from *The Book of Mormon*.

But when I looked over the outline of the first Shakespeare lesson for Relief Society, I realized that I didn't know enough about Shakespeare to teach it.

Classes in Elizabethan history, Elizabethan writers, and the plays of Shakespeare were being taught during the summer quarter at the University of Utah, and I felt I had to attend them. I had no money for tuition, so I prayed about getting some. Since wanting to take the classes was not entirely selfish I thought maybe the Lord would listen to my prayers and He did. By chance, I got a job addressing envelopes for a business firm for 1.5 cents an envelope. I addressed 15,000 envelopes to make enough money for tuition, textbooks, and transportation to the campus.

The Shakespeare class was a big one that year, but it was not because it was swelled by literary leaders—there was only one other in the class. The course was taught by Dr. Edward Chapman, who had graduated from Oxford. He lectured mostly with his eyes closed and his face lifted toward the ceiling. I don't know whether that gave him greater concentrating ability, or if he just couldn't stand the sight of students whom Shakespeare bored stiff. I wasn't one of them though. I enjoyed every minute.

I found that if I listened carefully, the professor was very witty. There were a few times when I was, embarrassingly, the only one in the class who laughed, but the embarrassment was mitigated when Dr. Chapman would open his eyes and look at me with a gleam of approval. He gave me an "A" for the course and relieved me of the term paper assignment on *The Winter's Tale*, which I would gladly have written. He invited me to attend a Shakespeare seminar that he was planning to teach in an upcoming quarter. Before you get the idea that I got the "A" for laughing at Dr. Chapman's jokes, I'd better explain that I think I got it mostly for making a set of characters.

With the idea of preparing for my own classes, I went to Ida Whiteley for scraps of silver and gold lamé, bits of purple, plum, and black velvet, silks and satins, scraps of gold and silver lace and brocade. With these, I costumed eight figures: Hamlet, Ophelia, Othello, Desdemona, Portia, Shylock, Romeo, and Juliet. Sally had a set of soft plastic dolls which were part of a schoolroom game. I expropriated the dolls, and cut off the heads, hands, and feet. I couldn't use the bodies because they had been formed in a sitting position. Using pipe cleaners wrapped with thread, I proportioned arms and legs and bodies. I attached the plastic heads, hands, and feet, and dressed the figures in court gowns and wimples, feathered caps, ruffs, capes and robes. They were not more than three inches tall, but they turned out very well. Hamlet was my favorite. Dressed in black satin and velvet, he wore a tiny medallion on a chain around his neck, and carried a purse at his waist.

When I saw Dr. Chapman's pride in the University scale model of the Globe Theatre which had been made by a student as a thesis project, I boxed up my little people and gave them to him. That is when I got the "A"—he was delighted. Later I was told that they were used in TV educational programs about Shakespeare.

By the time the courses began in Relief Society, I was as well prepared as I could manage to be, and the classes were a joy for me. I built a model of the Globe and constructed painted cardboard figures for my characters. With help from the sisters, we presented bits of the plays.

For the most part, my ladies stayed awake, and I found that if they drowsed a bit, there were lines (not included in the suggested outline given by the General Board) that would wake them up again. There is a vein of earthiness in most Mormons that comes directly from the pioneer soil from which they have been nourished.

WHILE I'M NEVER SHOCKED by words on a page, I'm sometimes shocked by things that other people find humorous or take for granted. There was one incident at which I still shake my head.

The ladies in a ward north of Salt Lake were getting ready for a bazaar and all the sisters were asked to bring samples of their handwork so that patterns might be taken from anything that looked as if it might sell well. One of the ladies brought a pair of pads for hot plates made like miniature underwear. One was a pair of men's shorts, the other a pair of lady's panties.

When you examined them closely, hidden by the fly of the men's shorts and the ruffle of the panties were reasonable facsimilies of what they were supposed to cover.

The ladies clucked in shock and rejected the hot pad idea, but after the meeting, the woman who brought them got 120 phoned orders for sets of the hot pads. And not long ago, I went into a friend's kitchen and hanging on the wall was a pair of those hot pads. I guess, in some places, those hot pads were almost as popular as the plastic grapes.

You can see that I had plenty of earthy material in Shakespeare, but I didn't often use it. Our Relief Society seemed genuinely interested in the lessons, so much so that word got around and I was invited to substitute in other wards when their literary leaders were absent. One month, I gave six lessons in six different wards. The play was Othello, and I remember being surprised by how few women knew that a Moor was a black man.

Most Relief Society leaders, including me, will tell you that they are the ones who gain from giving the lessons, so these jobs are highly valued. The leaders stay on in their positions, if they can, through changes in Bishoprics and Relief Society presidencies when everyone is automatically released. It is treasured work, and this seems to be true of many of the positions in the Church. It was with great reluctance that I gave up teaching Relief Society when I moved from the Ward.

It cost upwards of three hundred dollars to teach that class, considering my University tuition, books, traveling expenses, and visual aids, which I bought to teach my classes; I have never regretted it, nor even counted the cost until now, in order to show how the vast body of members in the Mormon Church *pay* to work.

One of the lessons I gave before beginning the Shakespeare was John Millington Synge's *Riders to the Sea*. It is a poignant one-act play about an old woman who lived in the Aran Is-

lands off the coast of Ireland. She has lost her husband and all
but one of her sons to the sea. The play is about the death of
the last son. There are three main characters: the woman and
her two daughters.

I decided that instead of giving a lesson about the play, I
would perform it, using only a few props and leaving anything
the three of us could not do (like carrying in the dead body of
the boy) to the imagination of the audience.

For my daughters in the play, I cast Ann, who was then
about fourteen, and her friend Joy Seiter. We learned the
script well enough, so that occasional referrals to notes in hand
would prompt us.

The play was the most successful lesson I ever gave. The
ladies not only stayed awake all through it, but they wept. And
I had so much empathy for the old woman that I did, too. The
point when they carry the dead body of the young son, dripping with sea water, into the cottage on a slab was a three-
handkerchief scene.

It was a great success, so we were asked to present it in Stake
Relief Society Conference. We did the play on the dais of the
Granite Stake Tabernacle, and even though we had no stage,
no curtains, and the choir seats and the pulpit were slightly in
our way (I think we used the pulpit for a cupboard), we didn't
have a dry eye in the house—and that's always an accolade.

Ann was marvelous. That was the first and last play she has
ever been in, but that afternoon I thought a Duse had emerged.
Joy was superb. Somehow we even came through with an accent. It was fairly easy when no one knew what sort of accent
we were supposed to have. I think ours was a mixture of Scottish
and Swiss. I don't really know how we managed to do so well,
unless it was because I spent a lot of time praying about it, and
somehow I'd gotten through to the powers-that-be.

Chapter 14

CANS AND CANA

WILMA WETZEL ASKED ME to wait for a few minutes after Relief meeting. She said she had something she wanted to talk with me about, so I declined Veronica's offer of a lift home and waited until the room had cleared.

Wilma's voice was a shade apologetic when she approached me.

"I'm sorry to keep you waiting. I know you want to get back before your children get home from school, but the Bishop and I have been talking. We have a problem. You know that the Church has been advocating a two-year supply of food in every home. It is hard for most of us to keep ahead of the grocery bills, let alone store a two-year supply, but the Church has found a way to help us do it."

I waited wearily.

"In order to take part in the program, we have to have a Custom Canning Chairman in our Ward."

"You're not thinking of me!"

"We were reluctant to ask you. We know that you're busy, but we thought you would be the best one to do it; for one reason, you drive, and a car would be necessary—so many of our older ladies don't drive, you know."

"Wilma, I don't think . . . ," but she rushed in before I could refuse.

"We were wondering if you'd take over the job of Custom Canning Chairman?"

"What is custom canning?"

"Custom canning isn't welfare canning. It is canning by the people of the ward for their individual benefit."

"What would I have to do?"

"Supervise a group of canners from this Ward who would use the facilities of the Pioneer Regional Cannery on Thirteenth South to can food for themselves at cost. You've been down to the cannery several times to help with welfare canning, I know."

"Yes," I said, "I think it's interesting, but I don't know enough to supervise any of it."

"Oh, you'd have help from Ida, the supervisor down there. The method is about the same as for welfare canning. Only you'd keep track of orders, the number of cases you can, and how much they cost. You'd have to collect the money for the cases and turn it over to the Bishop. The Ward will advance the canning costs at the beginning of a project. You'd have to set up the projects with the supervisor down there."

"Wilma, I'm doubtful about this."

"We wouldn't ask you to do it, but we can't think of anyone else for the job. Most of our sisters are either too old to do the work, work all day, or they have very young children."

"If I could arrange the times to suit me, then I could probably manage it," I heard myself saying to my dismay. "And
I'd like to get my own cellar stocked," which was true.

"Then you agree?" Wilma was quick to snatch at the affirm-
ative tone.

"I'll do it, or try to," I said, all the time wishing they hadn't
asked me, and that I wasn't saying yes.

I didn't believe for a moment that I was the only person in
the Ward who could do the job. Offhand, I could name a
dozen who were far more experienced, but I thought that perhaps for some reason or another they had refused.

Well, I *was* the only one in the Ward who could have done
that job—BECAUSE I WAS THE ONLY ONE WHO WAS DUMB
ENOUGH TO DO IT! All the rest of the people they must have
asked had refused because they *were* experienced—but not
me. I'm not a person who can learn from the experience of
others. I'm one of those who always learns everything firsthand. It took years for me to learn how to say no.

When I think back on the two summers that I was Custom
Canning Chairman, it is with utter disbelief. If, at this moment,
I could not go down to my basement and touch a few cans of
apricot purée, all that is left from the vast store of canning, I
would not believe it had happened at all. When I read of people
accomplishing the impossible, I know now how it is done—by
not realizing that it *is* impossible.

My first canning project was plum pudding. The cannery
furnished all the ingredients: flour, sugar, spices, nuts, raisins,
suet, everything. The Bishop gave me a blank check. I paid
the cannery with this after the project was completed and
collected the money for the cases of pudding from the people
who had ordered it and who had worked on the project.

However, the pudding was not sold by the case except in
rare instances. It was sold by the can. It cost the ward $227.38
for 714 cans of pudding. Bishop Trauffer had to wait for the

Ward's money until I could collect. I made a firm rule that no cans left the storeroom, which the Ward provided, until they were paid for. I knew that I was not very good at keeping books, but I was no good at all at collecting debts. It had to be cash and carry. I was given one of the two keys to the storeroom; the Bishop had the other.

The pudding project went very well. "Cannery Ida" (I never knew her last name) was the supervisor of the actual canning processes. She must have worked terribly long hours because no matter when our project was scheduled, early morning or after work at night so the men could help us, Ida was always there. I thought at first that she was dry and soured toward us, but I learned that she was none of these—only experienced. After she learned that our group cleaned up after itself thoroughly, she softened considerably, and she was a steady rock of assistance and encouragement. I grew very fond of her, and when we canned our last cases, I sent her a gift and a letter of thanks. The note I got back was pathetic. She had become so used to being thought of as a fixture in the cannery that to be considered a person almost undid her.

I asked Cannery Ida about projects for our Ward. She said that the cannery had all the stuff for the puddings if we wanted to can them. Some of the ladies in our Ward had tried them and thought they were nice to have on hand. The pudding sold for 32 cents for a 2½-size can. When all the money was collected, the Ward made a profit of ten cents. The Bishop had said nothing to me about whether I was to charge anything extra on the cases. Where the ten-cent profit came from, I don't know—probably from some people who told me to keep the change.

Pudding is easy to can. You simply take the ingredients and measure and mix them according to a printed cannery recipe. The mixed pudding is automatically put into cans, which are automatically sealed. Then the cans are loaded into huge baskets which are mechanically lowered into huge vats of water where they are cooked at temperatures high enough to ensure preservation and purity. At that juncture, you wash out the big, stainless steel basins, scrub the sinks, clean the conveyor belts, haul out the refuse, and sweep and hose down the floors. Then you go home to wait for the pudding to cook.

The day after that I went to the cannery again, counted the cases with Ida and paid for them. Parky, who ran a small grocery store, brought the cans back to the Ward in his pickup truck. I had announced the project in Sacrament meeting. People who wanted pudding called me. They came to the cannery, worked about three hours, and went home. I thought, "This isn't going to be much of a job—a few hours once a month or so."

But after the pudding I ran into trouble. Although the pudding was delicious, it was hardly a staple item for a two-year disaster supply, so I thought I had better be more practical.

I called Cannery Ida and she suggested that we can beef. The cannery could furnish the beef, too, she said. We didn't have too much trouble with the beef. Hamilton Wilson, who was a meatcutter, and a few other men from the Ward, showed up— some with wives, some alone. The men cut while the women packed and watched the machines. The beef cost 62 cents a can. We also made beef gravy; those were 8 cents a can. The Ward paid $384.52 for the beef project. Somehow I had figured wrong, and I didn't charge enough for the cans. The Ward went in the hole $5.60.

Bishop Trauffer didn't say much about the loss. The cans of beef sold rapidly, and when I apologized for the discrepancy, he just said that since the custom canning projects were going so well, $5.60 wasn't much for the Ward to contribute to its members' two-year supplies.

I didn't expect to make money, but I decided that I was not going to lose money, either. This was supposed to be a project at cost. I didn't want people to pay a cent more than necessary, but I decided to round out the prices to the nearest half dollar per case, and while this would only add a half cent or so to the price of a can, it would be enough, I hoped, to allow the Ward canning fund to break even.

The beef project was so popular, the beef so good, that more people wanted to can it, and I set up another project for the next month. This time, I thought I might improve the cannery's cost of the beef, and I went to Ham Wilson to see if I could get it cheaper through his butcher shop. I didn't know anything about beef, but the sides he showed me looked better and beefier than those that had come into the cannery before. Buying it from Ham saved a little money, too. I sold the second lot of beef at the same price as I did the first (which was only fair), but by getting the meat cheaper, I made $18.06, giving the Ward a profit of $12.50 for the three canning projects.

The people who canned the beef were very pleased. The meat was tender and tasty. It was packed so tightly in the cans that one can would feed a family of four. One of the differences between custom canning and welfare canning or retail canning was that the cans were packed more solidly—people wanted as much as they could get for their money. Like many other people in the Ward, I liked to see my storage shelves filling up with something besides dust and empty bottles.

After that, there weren't any projects for a while. I couldn't find anything to can. Produce that was in excess of the cannery's needs for welfare had already been spoken for by canning directors who knew what they were doing. I went to the farmer's market and to the produce houses and arranged for some tomatoes when the season started, but I soon realized that in order to can the foods, I had to ensure my source of supply.

Early the next year, I visited farmers all over the valley. I had to buy crops before they were planted and fruits when they were still in blossom. I bought a field of beans, one of

corn, and arranged for a truckload of tiny, new potatoes. I
bought tomato and pea crops and the yield of a bountiful vine-
yard. I bought chickens and beef. I bought salmon from the
West Coast and pineapple from Hawaii. Plainly it was a ter-
rific gamble. But not for me! I didn't know one damn thing
about crops or beef or orchards or anything else, so how could
I know it was a gamble?

I had to trust my intuition about the farmers when I talked
to them, or rather, I trusted that intuition after I had prayed
about it. And I left many an amazed farmer who had offered
me a "bargain." I don't know why I didn't buy. I had one rule:
I had to feel "right" about it.

Most of the time, when I talked to growers, I obtained
promises of delivery when the fruit was harvested. In exchange,
my word was good enough for nearly all of them. They took
my name and phone number and that of the cannery and they
were to be paid upon delivery of the produce. In these cases
Bishop Trauffer gave me two blank checks, one for the farmer
and one for the cannery.

I was not so lucky with the peaches. People who were interested in the canning program had been really upset to find that
there were so few peaches to can when they were harvested
that first fall. It had been the usual late-frost spring, and the
apricots, cherries, and peaches were in short supply. We
canned only a fraction of what people wanted, and I didn't
want a repeat of that.

I spent three days cruising about the orchard lands in Davis
and Salt Lake Counties and I prayed all the time I was driving.
I asked to be led to a good orchard, and I was. I found it in a
rather hidden place, over a couple of small, rolling hills and
tucked behind a swerve in a graveled road. I didn't know any
more about peach orchards than I had known about pea vines,
but I picked my peach orchard because it seemed about the
right size to produce the number of peaches we wanted to can.

I had no idea how many peaches came off a tree, but this little orchard sat trustingly on the side of a hill. Its trees were evenly pruned and there was not a broken limb, or a piece of trash, or an old peach pit lying among the rows of trees. I thought that if I were a peach tree, this was the sort of place I would have chosen to grow in, so I knocked at the door, told the orchard-man what I wanted, and he agreed to sell his crop—tree run, ungraded, for 1,500 dollars.

But my peach farmer would not contract for his crop unless he was paid in advance. He said that fancy packers usually bought his crop, but he hadn't sold it as yet, though he expected to, soon. I knew this was my peach orchard, so I bought it in advance. This was the latter part of February. Spring had come early to the valley and things were leafing out. When this happens, it is more usual than not that we have a late-killing frost and everything in blossom is frozen—that's one reason that peaches were such premium canning produce. But I never gave a thought to the frost that could wipe out my peaches and the Ward's 1,500 dollars.

The Bishop honored my word to the farmer and wrote out the check, and the farmer said he would deliver the ripened crop to the cannery. Then I added the peach crop to the things I prayed for nightly.

Even when the papers came out with the usual spring head-lines—SEVENTY PERCENT OF THE UTAH PEACH CROP LOST TO FROST—it didn't enter my mind that my peach orchard would be one of those hit.

The Bishop worried about it, though. He called me into the office one morning before Sunday School.

"What is it you wanted to see me about, Brother Trauffer?"

"Sister Hunter, are you worried about anything? Would you like to talk anything over with us?" This was about as indirect as I've ever known the Bishop to be. I thought about the question for a moment.

"No," I said, "I'm not particularly worried about anything. Should I be? Have I hurt someone's feelings without knowing it. If I have, I'll apologize . . ."

"No, it's nothing like that." The Bishop glanced at Parky and Clarence. "No, Sister Hunter, if you aren't worried about anything, we won't be, either." Then they rose to go out to the foyer to shake hands with people who were coming to Sunday School, and I went into the chapel trying to figure out what *that* little conference was all about. It took me a while.

While I was waiting for my peas to fill their pods, I went down to Rudd's poultry and bought four hundred chickens. I'd already prayerfully visited a couple of other poultry houses and Rudd's seemed to have the plumpest, whitest chickens. They also took time to conduct me on a tour through the place and explain to me how they killed the chickens.

I didn't ask them to do this. I was quite inured to my grandmother's going out into the barnyard and grabbing one of the roosters she raised for Sunday dinners, chopping its head off, and flinging it down to flop bloody and headless all around the barnyard. But I guess my face didn't show my callousness, so Mr. Rudd took time to tell me how they killed the poultry quickly and painlessly by ramming a specially designed needle through the chicken's throat and into its brain. This, he assured me, was humane. As I'd undertaken to have four hundred chickens slaughtered, I at first liked the idea that it wasn't going to hurt them. But after the long lecture, I wasn't so sure. I said if I were a chicken and had my choice, I'd prefer the ax at my throat to a needle in my brain.

I think Mr. Rudd was a little upset at the seeming waste of his lecture tour, but he was very happy about selling the chickens. They were delivered to the cannery picked and drawn; we had only to cook them in huge vats and then bone them. Everything seemed to be going well and by the time the chickens were cooked, everyone who had ordered chicken had shown up to work on the project. They were waiting at their stools beside the conveyor belts. Their hair was neatly confined under the law-prescribed net. They were protected by their biggest aprons, and they were smiling and happy. It was a daytime project, so there weren't any men from the Ward there to help us.

The first chickens went through rapidly. There were two pans in front of each woman, one to receive bone and gristle, which was discarded, and one to receive the meat as it was removed from the carcass. As I worked, I noticed that my fingers were getting sore, and pretty soon there were complaints running all up and down the belt. The sharp bones of the chicken made minute cuts all over the tips of our fingers. But worse than that! As I looked at the pans, I saw that only a small amount of chicken was mounded in the pan while each lady had dumped her refuse pan two or three times already.

It seemed that at least three-quarters of every chicken was waste. How could that fact have escaped me all those years? Worry began clutching at me as I inspected the pans of chicken. At this rate, there wouldn't be enough meat to be worth canning. I'd paid $378.18 for those chickens, and judging from how much beef it took to fill a can, and the way that the chicken packed in, I wasn't going to have a hundred cans. With the cannery charges, my chicken was going to cost about $450. Oh, Lord! Who was going to pay $4.50 for a 2½-size can of chicken? And then I knew why the Bishop had called me into his office.

With all the money he had been paying out, and still had to pay out through my deals with the farmers and growers, I had the Ward many hundreds of dollars in debt. I was suddenly overcome by nausea, and I went outside on the loading dock for a moment. It was hot and the sun beat down on me. I went back into the steaming cannery. It was noisy and wet. I looked at the tables where my ladies were sitting with pained looks on their faces. On some faces! Many faces that had been there when I went outside were missing when I went back in.

"Where did Sister Blackmore go, and Sister Shipworth and Sister Esterhazy?" I asked Ida Whiteley, who I noticed had put tiny pieces of tape over the tips of her fingers. (Oh, poor Ida, with all the delicate stitching that she had to catch up with at night because she worked in the cannery during the day.)

"Some of the ladies had to go home. Sister Esterhazy was expecting her daughter from California. Sister Rugge said to tell you she was sorry, but she and a couple of the other ladies had headaches, and they decided to go home. Sister Blackmore's babysitter could only stay for a couple of hours. I don't know about the rest of them."

As I counted the empty stools, I saw that half of the ladies whose help I had counted on had disappeared. I supposed that they all had excuses. I wished I had known that so many of them could not stay long since I would have recruited more help. But there was nothing to be done about it now, except pray, and pull the chicken off the bones. I noticed the women who had stayed did not complain of their sore fingers. They were working cheerfully. Now they would have to stay longer, but no one said anything about that, either.

There was Emma Tadje, who worked efficiently, doing as much as possible as fast as possible so that she could get back to the switchboard of her answering service. There was Aurta Rigby, who had seemed rather formidable to me when I first met her. Aurta's face could not be described as a cheerful one; she always seemed to be looking at the world with a slightly jaundiced expression and an inner worry. But I was beginning to suspect that Aurta was a crusted jewel, for whenever there was work in the Ward, Aurta was there, not laughing and joking about it, but *getting it done*. She was getting it done today. Faye Rosvall was there. She and Aurta had just been put into the Relief Society presidency. Beverly Walker, Clarence's wife, was there, and Hermione Trauffer and Veronica. Neil would be down to help as soon as he got off work. There was Sister Remington and Connie Berger, and Beverly's mother, and old Sister Wood. She was the only one whose fingers did not seem to feel the splintery chicken bones. There were others whose names are hazy now.

Whenever I passed any of them, they smiled encouragingly at me, although I knew that Ida Whiteley, as sharply tuned to things as she was, had realized that the chicken was not going very far.

"What do you think?" she asked me, as she rose and stretched her aching back and went to empty her pan.

"Nothing. I'm just praying."

"I'll help," she said.

That day was a long one. We worked into the afternoon and early evening. I made some of the older ladies go home. They were getting visibly weary, and I didn't want them to get sick. That stretched the hours of those who stayed. Throughout those hours, as the Bible says to do, I prayed unceasingly—and not for nothing.

Out of the pitifully few pans of chicken—it seemed to me they were few indeed—we got 321 cans of chicken, 29 cans of giblets, and 320 cans of chicken and rice soup, with sizable pieces of chicken floating in it. I charged 92 cents a can for the chicken, 40 cents a can for giblets, and 10 cents a can for the soup. There was more than one chicken in each can. I bought a case of it and wished for more, but never mustered enough courage to can it again. I served it often, added a couple of cans of cream-of-chicken soup, some diced carrots and peas, and poured it over steamed brown rice or into crisp pastry shells. It was a favorite dish of my children and company exclaimed because there was a special flavor about that chicken. I have never tasted any before or since to compare with it.

My chicken project cost the Ward $426.89. I turned in $444.65, providing $17.76 on the credit side of the ledger.

More important than the profit was something I had begun to believe—somehow I had established communication with the higher powers. If I was doing my best and it wasn't good enough, then I could pray for help and get it. My prayers had been immediately and directly answered.

I canned for two years. Name it, I've canned it. I noted in my little black book (that turned up miraculously when I needed it for this manuscript, although I thought I'd thrown it away) that we canned corn, kernel and cream style, peas, beets, potatoes, tomatoes, tomato juice, pork and beans, catsup and chili sauce. I bought the pork from Ham Wilson, whose wife Estenna helped us can.

I bought beans from Parky and tomatoes from Aoki's who sent me beautiful ripe, firm ones. These were in addition to the tomato crop I bought for $380.07. The total cost of the tomato project to the Ward was $643.15, and the return was $717.42.

We canned prunes and apricots and both grape jelly and grape juice, all sorts of other jellies and jams, and as a late project in December, we canned applesauce. And we made a profit, sometimes just a few cents, usually a few dollars on each project, and the people who worked and bought, saved themselves a great deal of money.

Sometimes I wondered what Parky thought. Parky made his living out of a small grocery store. He never complained, and he would often help us with a project on the evenings when he could get out of his store. Occasionally, he would haul the cans from the cannery to the Church—which was in direct competition to his own livelihood. However, Mormons are used to competition from the Church in all types of businesses. They do not complain about it; they dutifully pay tithes and offerings to what is, in essence, their own competition.

Parky didn't have to work for the competition too often. Norma Greensides taught in MIA. She and her husband owned a moving and transfer business in Sugar House, and Brother Greensides faithfully came down to the cannery loading dock when our cans were ready, loaded them up, and delivered them to the Church from whence they were sold.

The corn project was one of the most difficult ones. We had to husk the ears and then shuck the kernels from the cobs. Cannery Ida told me I'd have to get a big crew because my farmer's crop had been an extra large one. I began to notice that the crops I had contracted for in the spring were all bumper ones. I don't know whether it was a bumper year all over—I had nothing with which to make comparisons—or whether it was because my crops were prayed for so frequently. But while my big crops brought down the cost of our product, our canning projects were lengthened.

The corn took all night long. The stalwart few who saw me through until the last kernel was canned were the same ones who always saw me through. They were the ones who held several positions in the Church at one time, yet who were always available to help with a funeral dinner, a Ward banquet, or the annual magazine drive to sell *The Era*. These were the ones who always had time to bake a cake or make a casserole or prepare dinner for the eight children of a neighbor who was down with the flu.

I tried to show a little favoritism to those who always helped by allowing them to get their orders first, and if they wanted extra cases, I tried to see that they got them, but I couldn't do much—there was always enough to go around for everyone. Except once.

That project was the worst—and the best.

Cannery Ida called me from the cannery about six o'clock one evening.

"Sister Hunter, the farmer is bringing in your beans tomorrow at two, but you'll have to get a lot more people to work. He had a heavy crop. Instead of the truckload you expected, he estimates there will be about three or four loads."

"Lord," I asked after hanging up, "what am I going to do with three truckloads of string beans?"

"Can them." The answer was clear.

So I called the Relief Society president of a couple of neighboring wards and asked if they would be interested in a string-bean project. They were. My crew met at the cannery, a hundred-strong. As usual, most of them were women, shrouded in aprons and heavy hairnets. They arranged themselves on the stools along each side of the long conveyor belts. The beans began pouring down the chutes.

In a few moments there was an audible feminine buzz above the clank of the machinery and the rattle of the cans being swirled into their slots. I went over to the tables to inspect the produce.

As the beans trickled onto the belts, the women were supposed to cut off the ends, pull the tough "string" from the sides, and snap those that were extra long into a uniform canning size.

"There's something awfully wrong with these beans," one woman informed me. I picked one up to see. There *was* something wrong. They were the toughest, wiriest, meanest beans I've ever seen. They wouldn't snap, and they resisted cutting. The beans piled up in the chute and the processed beans merely dribbled off the ends of the belts. It was obvious that we wouldn't be through in the estimated seven or eight hours.

The women from the other wards began whispering among themselves, and then they began leaving the belts. One of the ladies came to tell me that they had decided that the beans were so tough that they would not be edible, so the sisters from those wards were canceling their case orders, and thus did not feel they should help any more with the project.

I watched as two-thirds of my canning crew left. This time they self-righteously marched out. It was not the usual cannery sneaking that I had grown accustomed to. And there I was with a couple of tons of beans and thirty people to can them. Some of these, the older women, would have to be taken home in the early evening. They could not be expected to work long hours, and some of the younger women only came for the afternoon. They would have to go home to take care of their children at bedtime. There were always the promises to return if it was possible, but I'd learned never to count on them.

By this time, I'd learned to control the frantic despair that could descend on me in the cannery. I slipped away from the table and went upstairs where the cans automatically spiraled down their iron pathway.

I stood on the wooden platform out of human sight and bent my head. My prayer began as it usually did there.

"Well, Father, what am I going to do about this one? This is worse than the beef, maybe worse than the chicken. I can't see how even You could make these beans easier to process. But You could touch the hearts of my workers so they would come back and help. It's going to take the rest of us all night, you know. Maybe You could give each of us the strength of ten? Please listen, Lord, You know it's not *my* fault these beans grew so prolifically. And it's not my fault that Sister Ellison has a mean mouth and talked all the ladies at her belt into quitting. I'll go on the rest of the night doing what I can, but it's really up to You. They're Your children and Your beans and this is Your cannery, so it's really not my responsibility, is it? Please help me to know what to do and how to do it. And thank you again for helping with the corn and the chicken. Amen."

I left the stairs with the task before me not diminished by a bean, but the bitterness toward the ladies who had left was not dragging at my energy, and I had a feeling of warmth and calm acceptance. I knew that I could work untiringly and cheerfully through the night, and while the beans waited in vast piles for processing, I did not fret about them. They were simply not my problem. They were the Lord's and it was evident to me and to everyone else that He was the only one who could cope with it.

It was after six in the morning when the few of us who were left (always the same blessed women) finished our task. The moving van would transport the cases to the Ward later in the afternoon. The stack of boxes filled the dock and I should have looked at them with despair—hundreds of cases of beans that I wouldn't be able to sell. But I was only relieved that every one of those damn beans was in a can. There were a few cans sitting atop one of the cases and I distributed them among the women in my car.

My children were still asleep when I got home, and without thinking, I turned on the stove, opened the can of beans I carried, and heated them. I drained off the juice, put a dab of butter on them and a sprinkle of salt and pepper and sat down to breakfast.

That was the finest breakfast I have ever eaten. Those beans were delicious. Tender, nonfibrous, delicate-tasting. I figured the cost of a can. About 7 cents. I could sell a case of 24 cans for $1.75 and make a few dollars profit for the Ward canning kitty. As I sat there, I realized that I'd had another miracle.

"Thanks, Lord," I was humbly matter of fact. I wasn't surprised. I didn't know what I'd expected, but I had expected something. The children slept later than they usually did on Saturday mornings and it was ten before I was awakened by the ring of the telephone. I was amazingly refreshed.

"The beans," said Ida in her quick, soft voice, "have you tasted them?"

"Oh, yes," I said, "aren't they wonderful?"

"I want six cases. I only ordered one, but these are so good, and they'll be so cheap." Her chuckle was girlish and she did not sound tired, but I did not ask her if she was because I knew that she hadn't gone home to bed—she had gone home to finish the bridesmaids' dresses that she'd promised for five that afternoon.

I have never eaten beans as good as those, not even freshly picked from my grandfather's garden. By the end of the week, every case was gone. Every order had been increased by five and ten cases. The women of the other wards began calling to see if I could fill their orders.

"But you canceled them," I said. "You said that you didn't want any of the beans, so I've sold them all."

In my private *Book of Saints* I call this chapter "The Miracle of the Beans," and at least to me, it ranks right along with the Miracle at Cana.

My last big project was the peaches, but there was no worry about this one. It went more smoothly than any of the rest. My crew showed up and stayed since everyone wanted as many peaches as they could get. Utah peaches, when they are good, are unsurpassable. The orchardman knew his work and these had been picked only hours before canning. They had been carefully packed and carefully delivered. Out of the entire crop, there was only one half of a peach that was bruised and was not canned.

The grower had called me just before picking.

"I'll buy the peach crop back from you, Sister Hunter. I'll give you a little to boot if you want."

"What do you mean?"

"This is the best crop of peaches I've ever raised. With the shortage this year they're worth a lot more than I charged you. But it's more than that. Every peach on the tree is a prize peach. These are the kind we wrap individually in purple paper and put into gift baskets. I'll buy any or all of them back."

"No," I said, "the people in the Ward are counting on them, and I learned from last year that I won't be able to get enough to can from anywhere else. You'd better deliver them." I didn't count the bushels of peaches that we canned, although it seemed that every available inch of floor space in the cannery had a basket on it. I didn't pray that night in the cannery, except a prayer of thanks at the end of the project because it had gone so well and we were home before ten o'clock. I'd put that orchard on the tag end of my night prayers for eight months, and it was apparent that it had been beautifully blessed.

After canning, those peaches were incomparable to any I've ever eaten, and I've even canned them big and tree-ripened from my own trees, picked and canned all within an hour or two. Those home-canned ones were good, but not like the ones I'd prayed over.

I had a young friend who worked where I did. He was a bachelor who loved to cook and frequently gave small dinner parties. When these were special parties, he would come to me.

"Could you possibly part with another can of your peaches? My guests are from out of town and I want to serve them something that they've never had before. I'll pay you anything you want for a can of them."

Of course, I never charged him. I think they cost a fraction more than 12 cents for a No. 3-size can, and to see his pleasure at the success of his dinner was payment enough.

At the end of my projects, we had canned more than 5,000 cases of food. Most of the families in the Ward had a large portion of their two-year supply stored away, and my basement shelves were filled. Of course, it cost me a little more than it did most of the canners when you think that I had driven a couple of thousand miles for the project. I suppose I could have bought my cans retail and saved money—if you figure that way—but I wouldn't have taken the trouble to buy them and haul them home from the store. The food would not have been so good, either, and I would not have had the pride of canning it.

I learned a great deal about people, too; maybe even enough to write a little truth about them. I learned that you can socialize with someone for years, you can go to school with him, you can be his next-door neighbor or his best friend, but you don't really know him until you work—in physical labor—with him. I had some heartbreaking disappointments in people and I made some heartwarming discoveries.

I found to my disappointment and sorrow, after I got over being angry about it, that the same people sloughed off all the time. It was a shock to find that a former MIA president would sneak out when she thought I had my back turned, and that many of the women I had thought were the most faithful and admirable would work until the easy part was done and then leave—always when I was in another part of the cannery.

I learned on whom I could depend and it was seldom the gracious lady who bore her testimony so touchingly on Fast Sunday. I'm sure that knowing these things colored any relations I had with these people afterward. But—joy!—I also found some who I could count on until the Millenium.

Even more important, I learned that prayer is so powerful that a good pray-er had better be sure he wants what he prays for—he's most likely to get it.

Chapter 15

MATTERS FOR
THE PRIESTHOOD

In Utah when someone mentions the President, nine
times out of ten he is referring to the President of the Church,
not the President of the United States. In Mormon hearts, the
President is next in line to God, Jesus Christ, and the Holy
Ghost. He is Prophet, Seer, and Revelator, the Voice of God
to His people on this earth. The President's picture is displayed
in thousands of devout Mormon homes much as a bearded
Christ or a crucifix hangs in the homes of pious Catholics.
When he, or any of the apostles, preface or end a statement
with the words, "Thus sayeth the Lord," the Latter-Day Saint
accepts that statement as God-spoken revelation.

My grandfather had met all of the Presidents from Brigham Young to the present one. He seemed to have his favorites among them, although he would never criticize any of them—not even President Grant who seemed to have more critics than most.

"He has his mission," Papa would say. "I think that Heber J.'s mission is to put the Church on its feet." And time has proved him right, for President Grant certainly showed the Church his financial acumen.

I have seen only three of the Presidents at close range, although all of the authorities are present in the Tabernacle at conferences and are usually available before and after meetings for handshaking if you should so desire. I saw President McKay there. I stood on the steps at the rear of the Tabernacle and watched him. He was a tall, dignified man with a shock of white hair and a pleasant, photogenic face. During his lifetime he preached love, marital faithfulness, and family solidarity.

I saw President George Albert Smith as he lay in state after his death. He had been a most tenderly loved man. Among other reforms, he demanded that the portable liquor setups for room service in the Hotel Utah be removed, and that the Hotel, which belongs to the Church, be run as nearly as possible according to Church standards.

I stood among the lines of people, my first and last time for such a thing, to bid him goodbye, and his face was that of an ascetic, calm and dignified. It was the face of a just man who had known adversity, I thought. I do not really know much firsthand of George Albert, only that I have heard from all sides from people who did know him well that he was a man who truly practiced what he preached. He was an elderly man when he succeeded President Grant, and he did not live many years afterward. He was not the handsome, photogenic man that President McKay was, and one time, I understand, the

Church bought up all the copies it could find of a magazine which they felt carried an unflattering pose of President Smith on its cover. I cannot believe that this was at his instigation, for from what I can learn from those who knew him, this was a man from whom the commandment to "uphold the Authorities" was an easy one to keep.

The other President I have seen at close range was President Heber J. Grant, who was President when I was born and until after I was married. The circumstances were unusual.

I was editor of my school paper and, often as not, the mimeograph would break down and the staff had to go back to school on Thursday nights and work for a few hours to see that the paper was ready for Friday morning distribution.

It was a lovely, fall evening, warm but with a snap in the air that crisped the Jonathan apples on the trees and made walking down a Heber sidewalk a stimulating delight. Right then, I wasn't enjoying my walk as I might have, for I'd stopped briefly and visited with a friend. While we were talking, I'd answered yes to something she'd asked, and it was a tacit lie which I could not correct without embarrassing explanations. I walked down the sidewalk which ran along the Church block in front of the Wardhouse. (The other three sides were grassy walks worn bare. Alongside of them the irrigation ditches flowed.) The sidewalk was pitted and scarred from the weather and the weight of thousands of churchgoing feet.

I was troubled, and I couldn't enjoy the sunset which flamed over the peaks of the Wasatch mountains. I had lied without any real reason, and I felt in some queer way that the lie would follow me.

As I approached the foot of the long flight of stone steps that led into the Third Ward, I noticed that a car had parked in front of them. Two men, who looked remarkably like pictures I'd seen of J. Reuben Clark and David O. McKay of the

First Presidency, were about a third of the way up the steps. A third man was taking a briefcase from the back seat. As he turned and straightened, I drew abreast of him. I stopped and stared. It was President Grant, and he stared right back at me —or rather, he looked all the way through me. It was not a kindly look, it was an appraising one, deep, clearly penetrating. I thought, "He knows I'm a liar!"

The President said, "Good evening," and I said, "Hello"; he turned up the Church steps and I kept on walking, feeling absolutely damned.

When I reached the high school, I told the rest of the paper staff who I had just seen, and they very vocally didn't believe me. What was the President doing at the Heber Third Ward? No one knew he was coming. They scoffed when I said that the President had been alone—no one to meet him—no delegation. It would have been easier to convince them that Jesus Christ had just bid me good evening—they weren't so sure of what He might do.

"They were just there, alone on the steps," I said, "but it was the First Presidency, and I did see them." It is most frustrating to tell the truth and not be believed, but I thought that I had it coming for telling the lie that had gone unquestioned.

I had seen the First Presidency though. They had come to Heber without entourage, without a chauffeur, without fanfare. They met with the Stake presidency, the Stake High Council (of which my grandfather was a member), and certain other members of the Priesthood. The meeting was already in session when they arrived, and I don't believe even the Stake president knew they were planning to come.

It was always hard to pry out the reasons for Priesthood meetings, because my grandfather honestly believed, as he had been taught, that no woman could comprehend these affairs, and because he resented a female even questioning such things. However, from the things I picked up here and there—and I was good at that—I think the meeting was about Church welfare. This was at a time when the Depression had put a vast number of Mormon families on the government "dole" (which I grew up thinking was a dirty word), and the authorities of the Church were casting about for some sort of plan to remove as many Mormon names from the relief rolls as was possible.

I will never be able to accept such words as "welfare," "social worker," "relief," "aid to the poor," and "charity," with any degree of equanimity, for as Papa pronounced them, they had the ring of obscenity. For an able-bodied man to accept charity when he could work was disgraceful to the point of being sinful. My grandfather quoted Brother Brigham often: "If a man will not work, he shall not eat." And while I flay myself now and then about my stiff attitude toward "welfare" programs, it does no good. I am militantly opposed to the weakening process of a political philosophy which "gives them bread and circuses."

I DO NOT BELIEVE THAT it has ever been the aim of the Church to give anyone something for nothing. As the welfare program developed over the years, if people could work for part of the help they receive, they have been expected to work. There are exceptions: the sick and the afflicted, the widow and the orphan have always been charges of the Priesthood even before the Church welfare program grew to its astonishing proportions.

Papa used to load a wagon full of garden produce and take it around to the widows of our Ward every year. He and John Hanson would go into the hills time after time when their own wood was hauled, to bring in the winter wood for women who

had no husbands to do it for them. Whenever I think of Mr.
Hanson, always it is with nostalgia. His wife was the first
non-Mormon that I knew very well.

"I don't know what Dave would do without John, or for that
matter, what John would ever do without Dave," Mama would
say. "He's always been such a good neighbor."

John Hanson, rotund little John Hanson with his round,
smiling, perspiring face, and his clean, blue shirt and his faded
bib overalls. Papa called him John. Nearly everyone else called
him Pig. John Hanson killed pigs for a living, and he did it
with neatness and dispatch. I watched him more than once,
staying carefully out of the way so that Papa wouldn't send me
inside. Mr. Hanson knew why I waited, his eyes twinkled at me
as he passed.

Pigs are intelligent animals, far more than most people
realize. And they always know when they are going to die.
They run from their doom squealing frantically. Mr. Hanson
brought with him a huge, handmade wooden wheelbarrow
when he came each year. The boards of the barrow were
scrubbed to spotlessness with lye and the repeated scrubbings
had bleached the inside almost white. Inside the barrow were
two wooden barrels, each large enough to hold a big pig, a
rope with a block and tackle, some vicious-looking hooks and
a polished .22 caliber rifle.

Mr. Hanson knew that the pig knew why he had come, and
almost as soon as the rumble of the cart stopped in the barnyard, the crack of the rifle came—just once. He always hit
them in the head, a tiny black hole, dead center between the
eyes. Then, remarkably fast for a man of his bulk, he was over
the fence, had slit the animal's throat and had emptied the
body cavity preparatory to hanging it from a two-by-four
which extended from the barn for such purposes.

The carcass was scrubbed, washed, and rinsed in the barrels
that Papa had filled with water, which had been heating in

tubs on our kitchen range since early morning. Then Mr. Hanson scraped off every vestige of the pig's bristly hair. When he finished, the pig was hung out to cool in the night air, wrapped in a cotton bag against the flies.

Before Mr. Hanson left, he always blew up the pig's bladder which he had carefully washed and rinsed.

"Here, girl, here's your ball," he would say and bob his head shyly at my thanks.

For his labor, he charged two dollars and the pig's head and feet. His wife, Mary Ellen, made a most remarkable head cheese, and she pickled the pigs' feet. She was as spotlessly clean as her husband and as spare as he was plump. They lived in a two-room log house, without the conveniences of running water or electric lights. I never went into their house—no matter how early before school my grandmother sent me— when everything was not astonishingly immaculate.

I went to their house frequently to carry messages for my grandfather, always verbal messages because Mrs. Hanson couldn't read. She was terribly embarrassed about it, so much so that she would not associate with the ladies of the Ward, who might discover her secret. She had a Bible prominently opened on her kitchen table next to a kerosene lamp, but not *The Book of Mormon.*

Papa never preached to John Hanson. They helped each other haul their winters' wood for years, and this meant hours in the mountains alone together, but Papa, with great difficulty I am sure, held his tongue.

"I know what you do, Papa," I teased him, "you take it all out on me. I can tell every time you've spent the day with Mr. Hanson because you preach to me all evening." That was after Papa had told me that Ellen Hanson wasn't a Mormon and resented any Mormonism being talked with John, who *had* been baptized when he was a boy. Papa respected her wishes, knowing that his friendship with John rested on this unspoken

agreement with Mary Ellen Hanson. If John had asked something about the doctrine, Papa would have been hard put, but
I guess John didn't. Mary Ellen questioned her fat, little
husband sharply and knew that in his goodness he could not
possibly have lied to her.

"Well, Miss," Papa said, "John is a good man. The Lord will
take care of him, but you, now, you're my responsibility." And
he turned to the next section in *The Pearl of Great Price*.

Both Mary Ellen and John Hanson died before Papa. He
preached the funeral sermons for both of them, as they requested, at services which were held in the Third Ward, where
neither one had ever gone to Church. And after John Hanson
died, Papa hauled no more wood nor raised any pigs. They were
among the people Papa visited most frequently, taking a bouquet
of flowers, a big yellow squash, or a basket of vegetables or
fruits. Ellen Hanson died first, and Papa visited John even more
often then. I remember that Papa cried when old Mr. Hanson
died.

"Pig Hanson," he said, with a grief that brought tears to
my eyes, too. "People called him Pig."

The Hansons were the poorest people I have ever known,
but John Hanson would not accept welfare even though it
was offered—not as long as there were pigs to kill. And Papa
would not accept it either, even when Sylvan Rasband, Papa's
nephew who headed the Relief Office in Heber City, came to
our house.

"Uncle Dave," he said, "my office is set up to help people
like you. You can't work—"

"Who says I can't work? I can work with the best of 'em!"

"Let's say," said Sylvan diplomatically, "that you're a little
past the age for it. We can't hire men past seventy-five to
wield a pick and shovel. I know your life savings went down
the drain when the bank closed. Uncle Dave, you need some
help, and we'd like to give it."

"Thanks, my boy," said Papa to Sylvan, who was old enough to have gray hair plainly showing on his head, "but you take the help to those who need it. We don't owe a dime, and we get by. Ann and Ward send us enough to pay for our lights and taxes. We have plenty to eat. You just give it to people who need it."

Papa turned down proffered help from the Church, too, although Brother A. Y. Duke argued fruitlessly that Papa had more than paid into the Church any monies he might get out of it—and he had.

A member of the Latter-Day Saints Church is expected to give much more of his income to the Church than the 10 percent tithing. He also gives fast offerings, he contributes to the Church building fund, he pays into the missionary fund, and he pays his budget, which is used for the maintenance of the ward buildings and the expense of ward activities. This amount is levied on the income the Bishopric thinks the family has. It is remarkable how closely they can estimate the actual dollar-and-cents income of any family. And then there is the assessment for the Welfare Plan.

This assessment threatened to be the straw that would break many Mormon backs, until communal welfare projects were established. Sometimes these are ward welfare projects, sometimes they are stake projects. Many of the outlying small towns have welfare farms. These are planted, worked, harvested by the men of the ward who donate their time and equipment in lieu of money. In one Ward in which I lived, the women divided into two groups, alternately providing lunch and dinner for the workers and delivering it to the fields.

There are manufacturing projects, dairy farms, beef- and sheep-raising projects, fruit farms and many more, thousands more. All of the profits go to the Church to pay the heavy welfare assessment levied on all wards and stakes.

In Granite Stake and Lincoln Ward, the welfare project was a bakery. The six Wards of the Stake had combined their efforts and the bakery slowly became successful. For awhile it was staffed with volunteer help from the Relief Societies, but before too long, help could be hired from the profits and there would still be enough to meet the assessment. Members of the Wards were constantly urged to buy from the Stake bakery, and their refreshment and banquet needs were furnished (at retail prices) by the bakery.

The Church built large canneries in order to can foods for welfare. Vast quantities of produce were becoming available from Church farms. Labor was furnished by quota from each ward, and the cost of the canned foods was minimal. Recipients of welfare were required to give as much of their time as the state of their health permitted to the canneries or to other welfare enterprises, such as Deseret Industries (secondhand stores where the stock is donated, refurbished, and sold). The paid help of the canneries was almost entirely limited to supervisors and special equipment operators, and judging from other Church operations, they were never paid a cent more than the minimum required by law.

For as long as I can remember, Mormons have been urged to put away a supply of food against catastrophe and emergency. It used to be that the supply was for one year, then during the last twenty years or so, it has become a two-year supply. At first it was just foodstuffs, but now I understand that water kept in plastic chlorine bleach jugs should be part of this supply.

The members of the Church have always interpreted this storing of supplies as something near a commandment. "For in the last days, there will be wars and rumors of wars, there will be earthquakes in diverse places, and calamities, and people will flee to the tops of the mountains for safety."

Sometimes those who have heeded this advice have benefited in the face of natural disasters, but I have also seen a great deal of waste. When Papa died, we hauled out a wagonload of foodstuffs. Cans were bulged, fruit spoiled in bottles, jellies and jams were dried up. The dried fruits and vegetables, which will last longest, hung waiting for emergency use until they crumbled at a touch.

Zoa and Zola, my twin aunts, died last year, and in both their basements, there were not two, but more nearly ten years of supplies, put away in faithful obedience, bought out of meager incomes, and most of it wasted. So many times there is not much thought given to the storage—food has to be rotated, used, and replaced. Wheat, which will last in airtight barrels for five years without harm, will not last fifty.

The disasters to come must be beyond the scope of mortal imagination if we are to judge them by the preparation that is being made for them. At times, the Church's vast storage houses have meant succor for its members. When the great floods of a few years ago struck Yuba City, California, the Church was on the scene almost immediately with all manner of things. It is at such times that the great Welfare Program is blessed.

WHEN YOU ARE YOUNG, growing old seems impossible, but though Mama had always seemed old to me, Papa never did. His youth came bubbling up from some irrepressible source. I used to listen to some of Papa's worried conversations and wonder why he worried. Still, I was always weighted down by his worries somehow.

"Growing old is hell." Papa would say out of the blue. And I could see that it was for Mama because her faculties were dulled, but not for Papa.

"I hear the Church is asking old people to sign over their homes in return for old age assistance," Papa said to A. Y. Duke. "I don't think I like that much." The living room door was ajar, and I was sitting at the kitchen table studying. I could hear them clearly.

"Well, the state has been doing it for quite a while, and I guess the Church feels it has as much right as the state."

"Maybe so, but I think I'd go without an awful lot before I'd sign over my house. It's all I've got to show for about seventy-five years of living."

"Well, it isn't taken over as long as you are alive."

"No, but if the state or the Church takes it, there's nothing left for your children."

"If children honored their parents and helped them as they should, there would be no need for either the Church or state to take the property."

"Not always," Papa said, considering. "My married children would help me if they could. They're having a hard go as it is. If it weren't for my two unmarried ones, maybe I'd have to go on the dole, too. Not now. When I'm older. But to give up my house—hell, I hope I never get that old." Papa said fervently. He never did. Although he didn't live in it the last few years, he kept it for his children. But his worry about it stayed dormant in my memory.

It was revived one afternoon when I took Leone Curley to visit an old friend of her mother's, a Mrs. Erlich, a woman who had been one of Leone's childhood favorites. Leone had been worrying about her because the woman was widowed, childless, and blind, and she had just been released from the hospital.

The old lady lived in a very nice home in one of the better residential areas of Salt Lake City. She was pathetically glad to have us visit.

"How are you getting along?" Leone asked her.

"Fine now. The Church paid all of the hospital bills and they bring me everything I need. I guess I'm not going to have to worry about things any more."

"That's wonderful for your Ward to help you like that," I said.

"Well, it isn't exactly one-sided, you know," she said drily. "I had to sign over my home to the Church. I can't but see how they'll come out on top—you can see it's a good house, and it should be worth more money than I'll use up. But then, you never know. That's why I didn't sell it. I had offers, but then I'd have had to go to a home, and I can manage here in this house and in this neighborhood. I'm used to it and I can get around easily. This way, at least, you can live in your house until you die."

"You had to sign over your house to the Church? Really?" I couldn't believe it. I thought that true charity was giving without strings, as it had been preached to me.

"Yes, I did. I signed the papers a couple of weeks ago. There wasn't anything else to do. I had hospital bills and doctor bills, and I'll no doubt have more."

On the way home, Leone said thoughtfully, "That house is worth money. There's a huge lot with it. The Church will do very well on this deal." Distressed, I agreed. It did not seem right to Leone and it didn't seem right to me, and it hadn't seemed right to Papa, either. It bothered me so much that I went to Bishop Trauffer and told him the story.

"I think it's terrible," I said. "The Church is wealthy beyond the belief of most of its members. It has an enormous income, and it seems detestable to me that they would take the homes of their faithful old members as security for caring for them in their old age. Besides, Sister Erlich is past seventy. In her lifetime she has paid in a lot more tithing than any help she'll ever take out."

"Well, Sister Hunter, I don't know the circumstances of the Sister you are concerned about, and you only know one side. But I do know that the care of the helpless aged is one of the big problems for bishops. Such things are usually left to the discretion of the bishop of the ward. It may be that her Ward simply did not have the money to help her, or maybe they

have a number of similar cases in the Ward. I don't know. I'm
going to show you something that I want you to keep in confidence. I would never tell you this except that you are so
upset. You know old Brother and Sister Heath?"

"Yes," I said. The Heaths were among the oldest people in
the Ward. They lived in a modest, but comfortable house, and
they came to Church whenever their health allowed, which
wasn't as often as they would have liked.

The Bishop brought out a set of books and stabbed with his
long finger at certain entries.

"This Ward has paid nearly all the payments on the Heaths'
home for the past several years. They have children who could
have helped, but did not. We provide them with food, clothing,
utilities, and a small income. We have for a long time. We pay
for their doctor and hospital bills and for their medicine. We
will care for them until they die. No one but the Bishopric
knows very much about this. The Relief Society president
knows that we help them with food and clothing—that is her
job. But to save the Heaths' pride, none of us would ever
mention it."

"Who holds the deed to their property?" I asked suspiciously.

"They will when the final payment has been made, which
thanks be, will be soon. It's been a load for the Ward to carry.
But the decision was up to the Bishopric, and we could not
ask the Heaths to sign over their home. It would have crushed
them. When they die, the property will go to their children, who
have never paid a cent for the old folks' upkeep. It upsets me
more, though, that they don't even write very often or come
home to visit them. The Ward is their family. This is what we
chose to do—whether it was fair to the other members of the
Ward, I don't know. Now Sister Hunter, when they die, do
you think that the children should inherit what they have."

"No," I said, "that doesn't seem right. But it doesn't seem
right that the property should go into the General Fund of the

Church, either. It seems that it should be the property of this Ward."

"The Ward is Church property—it makes no difference."

"I guess not," I said slowly.

"And what's more, the children won't even be told of their parents' indigence. The Heaths wanted it this way, and we agreed. They desperately need help. It was our privilege to give it."

"Why didn't the Bishop of the other Ward do the same thing for Sister Erlich?"

"I don't know, of course. Each bishop has to judge—and it is hard—especially when good sisters like you question our judgment so bitterly."

The Heaths have long since died, and the children came to the funeral that, I assume, was also paid for by the Ward. I am violating no breach of confidence now. The children inherited, and I felt no better about that than I did about Sister Erlich.

Sister Erlich lived only six months. She did not go back to the hospital. She was found dead in her bed by a neighbor who called each morning. The Church profited. But I could see, on the other hand, how it had lost with the Heaths, for though each case was a ward problem, no ward could bear all of the burden alone—they would have to have assistance from the General Welfare Program.

Brother Trauffer's telling me that such things were at the discretion of the bishops made me alert to their personalities. Sometimes these men are chosen to make the ward into a family unit with their warmth and love. Other times they are chosen because their business sense is well known. In these cases, they are seldom loved, but they are respected, and the ward has become financially stable when they leave the Bishopric. Personally, I prefer the bishop of brotherhood over the bishop of business, but I have come to the painful conclusion that the latter would most likely be the choice of the authorities. I am experienced enough, however, to know that alms cannot come from empty pockets.

One other time, Brother Trauffer talked to me confidentially, and I've never been able to find a parallel for that interview.

"Sister Hunter," he leaned back in his chair, rubbed his chin, tapped his pen on the desk, and began abruptly, "you know that Sister Wetzel hasn't been feeling so well. She has asked that she be released from the Relief Society presidency." He did not allow the moment for me to think that he was perhaps asking me to take the position. He went swiftly on.

"The Bishopric has considered you for the position, and because you have been such a strength to this Ward, we want you to know that you have been passed by for what we feel are reasons for your own good. This is the first time I've ever explained to anyone why they weren't chosen for a position, but we know that you are worthy, and you are capable. And *you* know that," he looked at me keenly in a way that suddenly reminded me of Papa, "so we didn't want you to have any wonder in your heart about our decision. We have decided to give the position to another sister who I'm sure you will agree is certainly worthy, too. But we are not asking you to consider the position because you already have more of a load than many women could carry."

I listened to him quietly. I think that most active women of the Church consider that the honor of being Relief Society president is about the highest a Bishop has to bestow, and perhaps there have been women who were hurt by being passed over. Perhaps Bishop Trauffer had known of such women who were hurt and he was taking no chances.

"You work in nearly all the auxiliaries, you are the Canning Chairman, and you cannot know the extent of our gratitude for the job you are doing, and you are PTA president. We felt that any addition to your load would harm your health and your family relationships, and so we are not asking you to be Relief Society president."

"That's perfectly all right, Bishop," I said and laughed, but perhaps he had known me better than I thought, for I felt a twinge of regret. Being a Relief Society president might help one become worthy of Second Endowments. That was the first time I realized that I had such righteous ambitions. "Well," I thought, "I have some dark spots in my character anyway, and the Bishop probably knows best."

He did know best. For that year was the year of the Mother's March, Sally came down with hepatitis, my father-in-law died of congestive heart failure, my mother-in-law tragically succumbed to a swift and deadly melanoma (her death was terrible for me—I loved her very much), and for the first and only time in my life, the pressures of living reached the point where I thought one more thing would break me. If I had been Relief Society president, I would have collapsed—I almost did, as it was. In what had been, I am sure, a prayerful decision, Bishop Trauffer had shown a wisdom greater than both of us realized.

I am sure that there are many Walter J. Trauffers in the Church, there must be for the grass roots to stay so green. But he was a rare man who certainly deserved the positions he was later given. He was called to the presidency of the Swiss Temple where he stayed for many years, and he was recently released, came home, and was reassigned to the Arizona Temple, and the flowers will grow there, too. I think perhaps the thing that makes Bishop Trauffer "my" Bishop was that he was slow to judge people. He simply accepted them. I wish that were true of all the authorities.

MANY MORMONS WOULD DENY POLYGAMY if they could, sweep it under the rug, hide it in their dusty closets—

not me. When Mormons write of polygamy they feel tangible disproval from within the Church. I do not understand this, really, although I know the avowed reasons for the "better-not-mentioned" policies.

I am not at all ashamed of my polygamous background. I find it intriguing. It doesn't bother me that my grandmother was the daughter of the second wife. But I know that being from the "second family" irked her because she made frequent references to the first wife. Once: "Oh, that family thinks they are tonier than us—they are the offspring of the first wife." In fact, I felt a little soiled by her feelings sometimes, and it was not until I was grown that I could rationalize my own responsibility and become objective about polygamy.

It is obvious that some lusty old goats took advantage of the peculiar privileges of Deseret, but in many cases it was no privilege. It took endurance to live in polygamy.

Both my great-grandfathers on my father's side were polygamists. My great-grandfather Murdoch had two wives of whom he seemed equally fond, but, of course, he chose his first wife to live with when the Manifesto separated the three. That "of course" cast a shadow on my great-grandmother. She came to live out her days with Papa, who was kind to all those who needed kindness, and Mama, who was her daughter.

My great-grandfather Hicken had three wives. His first wife was my grandfather's mother. His second wife was a "duty" wife, quite typical of many cases of polygamy. According to Papa, his father was called in to see President Young.

"Thomas," said President Young, "you are a respected man in your community. The Lord has blessed you. You have a prosperous farm, and yet you have only one wife. There is a deserving widow in this city who has a family to support. She needs the help of a good man to help her raise her family. I want you to marry her."

So Grandfather Thomas Hicken married Mrs. Clotworthy

who was known thence forth in Heber as Mrs. Clotworthy. He built her a house at the other end of town from his own and cared for her and her family in friendship. He did not live with her, and, of course, there were no children.

Then, only three years later, Grandfather Thomas took a third wife—this was evidently a "privilege" wife because he had five children with her. Papa was very fond of the third wife and her five children. When my great-grandmother Hicken died, Grandfather Thomas didn't take any more wives, but he lived the rest of his considerably long life with his third one. That there was some adverse feeling between the second and third wives seemed evident from a quote I found in a published history.

"In 1862, as polygamy was being practiced, Thomas Hicken married Mrs. Jane Clotworthy, a widow with four children, and helped her raise her family. Her children had great respect for him and his *first* wife, and his children respected the Clotworthy family" (my emphasis).

Both Papa and Mama considered polygamy a trial rather than a privilege, yet both were exceptionally fond of their half brothers and sisters. I'm certain that they were glad about the Manifesto, which was announced before my grandfather was required to take another wife. As faithful Latter-day Saints, they would not deny the "principle" as it was taught, and which Mormons understand will be practiced in the Celestial Kingdom again. As faithful Latter-day Saints, I am sure that had the President of the Church asked it, they would have lived in polygamy. But if they had, I cannot imagine their home would have been the one it was—so peaceful that people noted that peace and remarked about it when they came into our front room.

I cannot imagine Papa loving another woman as he loved Mama. I remember when she was almost eighty, he told her she had the best-looking legs he had ever seen on a woman.

"Oh my, Dave!" she remonstrated, but she was as pleased as she was abashed.

I cannot imagine any other woman being able to live in any sort of harmony with my grandmother's quick, spiced tongue. I don't think that Papa knew she had such a tongue—she was too well drilled in the duties of a Mormon wife—but another woman would have felt its edge, I am sure of that.

I suppose that there are those who fear the adverse criticism of the Church for its one-time practice of polygamy, but Mormons are among the first to admit the evils of the practice. I know of one man, a son of a polygamous marriage, who was born in Mexico. To gain citizenship in this country, he had to swear to his own bastardy. The experience was bitter and one which helped sour him against the Church. It would take more than that for me. I am a firm believer that while "the sins of the fathers can be visited on the heads of the children unto the third and fourth generations," I am not responsible for those sins. It is something I cannot help and without which I would not have a heritage half so colorful.

Chapter 16

SMALL BUZZ
IN ZION'S HIVE

CONTRARY TO THE OPINIONS of most of the authorities
of the Church, all of them male, I think that women are the
backbone of the Church. That some of the men may be afraid
of this "petticoat power" seems to have been demonstrated by
a recent arbitrary slicing away of the *Relief Society Magazine*
and the Church bazaars, by which the women of the Relief
Society stayed financially independent. They may raise money,
but all of it must be turned over to the bishops of the wards.
The women no longer have any financial control—the greatest
part of any control—over their affairs.

Even the Relief Society building, which was erected by five-dollar contributions from almost every woman in the Church, has for the most part been taken over by the authorities. It has been a difficult thing for women to accept, but accept it they are trying to do—with varying degrees of meekness. That the degrees aren't as meek as could be desired is shown quite plainly in some of the explanatory excerpts from one of the last issues of the doomed *Magazine*.

We realize, sisters, that the discontinuance of the Magazine after fifty-six years during which it has served the Society well and been a source of inspiration, instruction, enlightenment and interchange of ideas, as well as providing an outlet for the creative writings of the women of the Church, brings feelings of sadness to our hearts. We must remember, however, that with the growth and expansion of the Church, changes must be anticipated, accepted, and adjustments to new ways and new programs made with willingness and faith in the inspiration that guides our leaders. . . .

Women who have questioned that inspiration have been soundly rebuked. One woman wrote a letter to the Salt Lake *Tribune:* ". . . For taking away the women's voice, the women's work [the bazaars which they have given for years to raise money for their needs] and their building, the powerful few with absolute authority who are responsible for this act of discrimination against women should be rewarded with separate beds in a separate room. And, if this please them, they are wished an eternity of the same." I don't think the temporal threat would bother the powers that she speaks of greatly—most of them are too old, but the spiritual threat might—it is a Latter-day Saint teaching that they'll go on populating other worlds with spirits ad infinitum.

For her direct and very feminine threat, she was severely criticized by subsequent writers in the same newspaper: "As mortal men, possibly those 'powerful few' she [the above writer] refers to are not in a position to tell the women 'what they are interested in.' But as prophets, seers, and revelators— and members proudly sustained them as such only last April— they are in such a position. I would not want to be so foolish as to go on record as being in opposition to the prophet of God. I sustain the General Authorities of the church in their calling, in their work, and in their decisions, and my observations lead me to believe that the greatest majority of the women in the church share that confidence."

I think the last writer has a point. Most of the women *will* go righteously trailing their husbands and kings into eternity. Which leads me to think that there's going to be a huge new industry in the afterlife—building thrones for all of these heavenly Mormon kings and queens.

However, if *any* women sit on thrones up there, the wives of the bishops and stake presidents should be among them. Other than the reflected glory of their husbands' positions, being wife to one of these men gives them only a lot of hard work, responsibility, and lonely child-raising. Bishops' wives are a most unsung group. They have to set perfect examples; they must be good housekeepers—they have hordes of unexpected callers and can never allow a mess in the living room or dirty dishes in the sink; they are alone much of the time, for I doubt that a bishop can count on many uninterrupted evenings at home; their children are always on display as they are themselves; they must never lose their tempers, nor reveal the delicate secrets they know; they must always be first with a roast chicken or a salad or a cake for the ill or bereaved; and they must always be kind and gracious to everyone they meet. Unbelievably, most of them fulfill their difficult roles most beautifully.

Sometimes, however, being a bishop's wife is more than the poor woman can handle. She starts claiming her queenly rights even before she's walked through the pearly gates.

I know of one instance in which a young woman was working with the bishop's wife and pointed out a mistake that the older woman had made. The next day the young woman was called to the bishop's home where she was furiously denounced. The girl ran out to her car carrying her sobbing baby who had been upset by all the screaming. The older woman followed her out, threatened physical violence and made the girl come back into the house. She responded meekly as she had been taught to do all of her life.

After another round of vituperation, with tearful apologies which were not in any way due, the bishop's wife sullenly allowed her to go with a parting shot.

"If you did what you were supposed to, you'd kneel down and kiss my feet." And she meant it!

"Did you kiss her feet?" I asked curiously.

"No, but if the baby hadn't been screaming so loud that the woman wanted us to get out of the house, she'd probably have made me do it. Oh, it's funny now," she giggled, laughing with me, "but yesterday, the tears were running down my face in a fieldstream. It wasn't funny then."

An incident like that, however, is so rare that it is hilarious. I never see that particular bishop's wife that I don't smile, but she never smiles back. And I wonder if it is because royalty does not smile at serfs or if it is because she senses my mean thoughts. I must try to do something about my thoughts—I have a lot of them that don't follow along the charted paths. I wonder what Papa would say to me. And then I suddenly know. He would listen to my story and then he would throw back his head in the peculiar soundless laugh he had. After he had thoroughly enjoyed himself, "Ah, humpf," he would say and wipe his eyes, "well, I'll be danged—it takes all kinds, don't it, girl?"

It does, but all of the kinds are affected by the Word that pours out from Church headquarters in Salt Lake City, and yet much of the strength of the Church comes to it from outside its stronghold, from the rural areas surrounding Salt Lake City, the mission fields, and states like Idaho, Wyoming, Arizona, New Mexico, and California, which are heavily populated with Mormons. All of the important decisions of Mormon lives are made within the guidelines of the Church. Good Mormons base their feelings of pride and guilt on the approval and disapproval of the Church authorities. Books that are given for gifts are those recommended in Church magazines —usually written by General Authorities. Family planning is influenced by the teachings of the Church and marriage out of the Church is assiduously discouraged.

Only a few months ago, I had a conversation with a woman who, along with her husband, had forcefully talked their daughter out of her engagement. I had thought the girl fortunate indeed to find some promising young man, and I listened resignedly as the mother talked.

"He was a nice enough young man," she said. "We couldn't find any fault with him, really, except that he was a Catholic, and we couldn't have that. My daughter is having a hard time getting over him," she said, then added righteously, "but in the long run, I know that we were right."

I wondered about that. The girl was not attractive. Viewing it realistically, as most women are realistic about other women's children, I did not think that the girl would have another opportunity to marry as well—if she had any opportunity at all.

"Would you rather have your daughter marry a good man of another religion or a bad man who is a Mormon," I asked of no one in particular one day, while I was at a quilting. At least half the group opted for the Mormon, so I stirred my troubled waters a little more. "Would you rather have your daughter marry a good Negro or a bad white man?" And except for one woman who wavered indecisively, they chose the white man unhesitatingly—for any male offspring of a black person could not hold the Priesthood.

I thought back to a conversation with Papa when I was seventeen and had received my first proposal from a personable, gentle young man.

"Papa, J.B. asked me to marry him when I graduate. What do you think about that?"

"He's a nice, young man. You could do worse. What do you think about it?"

"He's not a Mormon."

"No, he's not," Papa hid a smile between his hand and his mustache. Usually I was quite astute about his smiles, but I've never quite figured that one out. "But I think he's a fine boy. I think he'd make a good and kind husband. And," he said rather quizzically, "he'll never be a Mormon, either, unless you marry him."

"I'm not going to marry anyone just to bring him into the Church. Besides, that doesn't work a lot of the time. I can name as many women who are still going to Church all alone or who have dropped out altogether, as I can whose husbands were finally converted."

"I don't expect you to marry just to make him into a Mormon. I expect you to marry him because you loved one another and thought you could make a good life together. It's a long row to hoe, and it's a most lucky woman who finds herself hoeing it with a good companion."

"You're not upset?" I asked him. I had really thought he might be, and I had worried.

"No. I've been upset too often for naught. Look at Bessie. She didn't marry in the Church and it hurt me. It hurt until the first time I saw her man help her bathe those two little ones who tumbled into life one right after the other. She married a good man. He doesn't believe like us, and he doesn't talk as much as most, but he takes good care of her and his family. He may never join the Church, something tells me that he won't— not until he's old—maybe not even then. But she'll have had a good marriage, and that's about the best I can ask for any of you."

I'd expected a lot more and a lot different than I'd got. Papa once told me sincerely, that he'd rather see one of his daughters dead than drunk. I still can't figure out why he wasn't at least as strong for Temple marriage.

"Then it's all right for me to be engaged?"

"Not until I talk to the young feller, then I think it will be fine—but you don't need to tell him that beforehand."

J.B. talked with Papa and came away from the talk smiling and pleased. I don't know for sure whether they talked about the Church. I think that they did, because some time later, J.B. said he'd be willing to join if it would make things nicer for me. I said I didn't think he should join for that reason—and he didn't. So we were pleasantly engaged, and then he went away to school, and I went into nurse's training, and we pain-lessly drifted apart.

I think Papa knew that we wouldn't marry. And as I go over this fragment of the past, I am certain that he also knew that if he had objected, I might have rushed into something. He knew long before I did about my propensity for learning everything the hard way.

My grandfather lived what he preached, but he was a Saint with a broad mind, like Brother Trauffer, and like I'm told Clarence Walker has become. There are not too many of those around.

It seems that abstaining from all the little things—drinking, smoking, tea and coffee, keeping the little laws, going to Church, paying tithing—has set up entitlements. "Because I do these things I am entitled to more than my share of some-thing else." And I have been dismayed to find that drinking or smoking calls forth more head-shaking than fornication, adul-tery, or theft. I wonder if it is because doing the little things, the things so often preached about, is comparatively easy, and the big things take too much moral courage, or maybe it is the entitlements again.

I know of one woman who glares stonily when her neighbor buys a can of coffee in her presence, and yet she kept her elderly mother cruelly tied to her bed for about two years before it was discovered. I can name dozens of the little commandment keepers—those who bear their testimonies with fervor and weeping, though they turn their cattle out on another man's field to graze, or steal a little stream of water out of turn, or cause a hit and run accident, or neglect their children or their parents, or frequent the hideaway motels, or who are cruel and negligent of their wives, or who knowingly accept the wrong change if it is in their favor.

I know of one man who questioned my fitness as a speaker in a ward for no other reason that I know of except that I had remarried out of the Church. This man, not long afterward, boldly propositioned one of the ward's poor widows. I cannot understand this kind of thinking—and yet it is widespread. All of the hypocrites are not New Testament pharisees—many of them are in the Mormon Church!

Papa said, "You can't judge the Church by its people." And perhaps that is so, but then the reverse must also be true. You can't judge a people by their Church. They are no worse than people anywhere, and they are no better—it is only that they claim to be.

IN MORMONDOM THERE IS a great striving to belong. The gregariousness of human nature fits into the structure of the Church like flesh into its skin. I asked one woman why she had gone to the Temple after she had been married many years, and she told me honestly, "Because I felt left out of things." There are circles within circles in Zion, and no gentile can belong. He may penetrate the outer ring of pleasant acceptance, but unless he is interested in joining the Church, he will find himself unconsciously rejected because he does not speak the Mormon language. And this language is every bit as provincial and peculiar as it would have been had the Mormon alphabet devised in the early days of the Church replaced the English one.

This great need to belong is evident at the General Conference times when the Latter-day Saints flock to Salt Lake City. April Conference is usually the big conference of the Church, although all three of the General Conferences have become so vast that I cannot see much difference in attendance.

In October, windy blasts can blow, but the city is a mass of late fall blooms, and the warmth of Indian summer lies in sunny puddles on the streets. Attending the conferences, you will usually find a full complement of Utah's United States Senators and Representatives sitting on the stand, rendering their obeisance to the power of the Church.

No Utah politician could be elected if the power of the Church was turned full against him. Occasionally it is, and I have been in Sacrament meetings at election times when voting for particular candidates was encouraged or discouraged. Church and State are still as intertwined as they were in the days of Brother Brigham, when the people voted so unanimously that there could be no two-party system in Utah. The Church authorities took care of this by dividing the congregations down the middle, making Republicans of the right half, Democrats of the left. Either party was fine so long as they ran Mormons for office.

In one recent survey, it was found that 98 percent of the Utah State Legislature was Mormon, and though this heavy majority may be somewhat smaller at times, it is not reduced enough to make any difference. It is always a vast campaign boost to be able to include on the campaigner's vote-for-me brochure: "Active Latter-day Saint Church member, former

Bishop of Highspring Heights Ward, father of eight children."

All the conferences (even MIA Conference which may not have such a heavy influx of outside visitors) draw enough people to crowd the motels and hotels and fill the Tabernacle on Temple Square.

But it is in April that Joseph Smith organized the Church and it is believed by many Mormons that Christ was born in April, much nearer Easter than Christmas. The Conference always occurs around April 6th, the day of the Great Organization, and on April 6th, it rains—nearly always. I can only remember one or two sunny April Conferences, but April in Salt Lake City is still beautiful.

Except for unusual years, the weather has been warming for the two months preceding the Conference, and the fruit trees are in blossom. Hyacinths and daffodils and masses of tulips brighten every yard. The carefully landscaped Temple Square, on which the great, domed Tabernacle is built, is a pleasant and colorful garden even if the flowers are dripping rain and the grass is soaked with it. The trees are newly, brightly green and the leaves glisten.

Salt Lakers have planted and preserved their trees. From vantage points on the high rim of the city, much of it looks like a forest with the tops of the higher buildings spiking through. There are fragrant lilacs, snowball trees, flowering fruit trees, and flaming japonicas in bloom.

The brick wall that Brigham forced upon the early Saints to keep them working so that they would not have time to think and complain of their privations, still surrounds the Temple, the Tabernacle, and the Assembly Hall (where overflow crowds watch the Conferences on television screens). Visitors' centers have also been built on the spacious grounds. Surrounding the walled square are the cars of visitors from every state of the Union. The windshields of these vehicles seldom bear a traffic ticket for overtime parking. It is the gift of the city to the out-of-state visitor.

Five types of Mormons throng Temple Square at Conference times. There is the curious Mormon who goes to see what's going on—how frail the President has become, and if some of the General Authorities are as senile as he has heard. He goes for one session and fidgets in boredom, but he can always say, "I went to Conference this time. Didn't watch it on TV. The spirit doesn't come through." And among the city Mormons, he is commended because they know the press of the traffic and prefer a little less spirit and a little more comfort themselves.

There is the self-seeking Mormon. He goes because he wants to be seen. He sits near the stand so he can identify the dignitaries and make a point of shaking hands with as many of them as he can before they finally break away from congratulatory hands and voices. The self-seeker is not always found in the general assembly. He is quite often found in those seats which are reserved for the "very elect."

There is the SUPERIOR Mormon. He is most obnoxious to me. He is the man who goes to the aid of those in an automobile accident, saying loudly, "We are Mormons—now what can we do for you?" He is the man who is the epitome of mediocrity, and who sits in judgment upon better men because they are not Mormons. He has a wife, whose smiling face is radiant with self-approval because they are Mormons. He is the man who says, "*We* are God's Chosen."

And then there is the great majority—those for whom the Conference of Jesus Christ of Latter-day Saints is a joy and a privilege to attend. While some of the speakers are bound to be boring, repeating the same banal phrases made meaningless by a hundred and forty years of repetition, the faithful wait for the sentences that feed their souls. And it is true that if you seek you will find.

Mormon speeches can be fitted into one of three categories, or most of them can, and sometimes one speaker will cover all three in his talk. There is the *praise* category. The Church is praiseworthy, the people who belong to it and support it are praiseworthy, and the authorities are praiseworthy. All are praised highly. There is the *push* category. Push the payment of tithing, push obedience to authority, push Church solidarity, push the Word of Wisdom. And last, most rare, is the kindly and loving lift of *things to live by*. Of all the authorities in the Church, the one who gave the most succinct and uplifting messages was J. Golden Kimball. He is now long dead and forgotten by many, and it is a shame that we do not have more speakers of his kind in the pulpits. But Brother J. Golden, though loved by the congregations, was the despair of his brethren in the Council of the Twelve—for Brother Kimball swore—to the delight of all who were privileged to hear him. Perhaps his most quoted line is: "The Church must be true— if it weren't, the missionaries would have destroyed it."

Sadly, there aren't many speakers of the caliber of J. Golden Kimball and the best comment upon this is the number of people who doze through the speeches—including those who sit on the dais.

The simple eloquence of Richard L. Evans was always enjoyable. His philosophies may have been timeworn, but they were also time-proven. His phrases were well chosen, but more than that, they carried truths that the heart recognizes. And he was blessed with the voice to deliver them.

I cannot enjoy the clipped tones of the business-like authorities. Their speeches fall on ears that do not hear because they are only prepared to be read, to fill a prestigious spot in the speaker's roster, not an empty space in some troubled heart.

I have recurring thoughts during these addresses. I wonder if I am really considered a human being by these speakers, a person to be led into a good and gentle way of life which will ultimately give me peace in this life or in the next, or perhaps in both. Or—I wonder if I am but a blob in the blobby expanse of faces looking up at them. Is there a statistical report somewhere in the Church files that shows just how much money I will pour into the Church coffers if I live a certain length of time and work actively in the wards in which I live?

It has become apparent to even the most naive believer that the Church is big business, and most of those believers are proud of this. I've heard that pride expressed again and again: "The Mormons are the richest Church in the world, per capita." Whether that is true or not, whether its income exceeds a million or two each day as I have also heard, whether it is listed as the third or fourth largest business in the United States by Dun and Bradstreet, or if it is really the second-largest owner of real estate in the *world*—all this does not impress me. I would much rather have the Church be one of more love and less loot.

Papa frequently used to read a passage from St. Matthew: "No man can serve two masters: for either he will hate the one and love the other; or else he will hold to the one and despise the other. Ye cannot serve God and Mammon." But it seems to me the Church is trying hard to do just that. I can be more explicit. In one meeting, held for the express purpose of excommunicating a man who had flagrantly and frequently been caught in adultery, I have been told that the plea which saved him was, "We can't excommunicate *him*. He's the biggest tithepayer in the Stake."

Only the fanatically faithful can say that they enjoy the sustaining of the General Authorities. This procedure is the same as it is in the wards. The soporific voice drones on and in the pauses, hands are automatically raised, swearing oaths of allegiance to words they have not even heard.

Just once, I would like to see a hand raised in reasonable dissent. That would no doubt cause pandemonium. At times of sustainment, I think of sheep who mindlessly follow one another off a high ledge and into the gorge below, piling body upon body in their disastrous tradition of follow-the-leader.

The Great Tabernacle Choir of the Church of Jesus Christ of Latter-day Saints has sung all over the world and it is respected by musicians everywhere. The musicians make up the fifth group that comes to the Tabernacle at conference times. As one hard-shelled Baptist told me, "I felt terribly out of place, but I was most willing to stand in the back all through the meeting just to hear that Choir. It lifts me to the skies." And an erudite Jew once said in a lecture I attended: "I have long been having a love affair with your mountains and the music from your Tabernacle—both are incomparable."

Nowhere is the Choir more honored or acclaimed than it is in Utah. Its rigid rehearsal schedules are attended with eagerness. It never lacks for voices and there are waiting lists of people who are hoping to fill any seat that is abdicated. To be a member is considered a great privilege. And the state as well as the Church honors the Choir. One woman whom I worked with was given annual leaves of absence for the extended Choir tours. These leaves were in addition to her vacation time. It was simply her right as a member of the Choir.

The massive Tabernacle organ fills one end of the oval building. It is majestic to see and marvelous to hear. Choir and organ, together, make music that does indeed lift the soul. I remember the first time I heard *Come, Come Ye Saints* sung in the Tabernacle. I wept then; I weep even now when I hear it sung as it should be sung—as I think it should be sung.

The song was written by William Clayton, an early Mormon, who left his sufferings and his hopes to be engraved into the heart of every Mormon by the stark power of his words.

Come, come ye Saints, no toil nor labor fear,
But with joy wend your way

Tho' hard to you, this journey may appear
Grace shall be as your day
'Tis better far for us to strive
Our useless cares from us to drive
Do this, and joy, your hearts will swell
All is well! All is well!

Why should we mourn, or think our lot is hard?
'Tis not so; all is right
Why should we think to earn a great reward
If we now shun the fight?
Gird up your loins, fresh courage take
Our God will never us forsake
And soon we'll have this truth to tell
All is well! All is well!

We'll find the place which God for us prepared,
Far away in the West
Where none shall come to hurt or make afraid
There the Saints will be blessed
We'll make the air with music ring
Shout praises to our God and King
Above the rest these words we'll tell
All is well! All is well!

And should we die before our journey's through
Happy day! All is well!
We then are free from toil and sorrow too;
With the just we shall dwell.
But if our lives are spared again
To see the Saints, their rest obtain
O, how we'll make this chorus swell
All is well! All is well!

For me, this is the great song of the Mormons. It tells the whole story of the fears and faiths of the early Saints. When it is sung, I see them: ragged and weary and dirty. Tired women holding babies over their shoulders, babies that they could not keep as clean as babies should be kept. Sore-footed women and children who trudged along, often hungry, always tired, and cross and whining as tired children will always be. I see men, bearded and dirty, their strength coming entirely at the last from their faith in God.

And then they hear Brother Clayton's song which gave hope to the perishing and which, as much as the protestations and promises of the prophets, brought the people to their destiny. It is a song that is never dated. It fits our sorrows and trials today as it fitted them over a hundred years ago, and it rings with its promises.

Lately, I've been hearing a modern, fancied-up version of this song. It is a travesty of the early arrangements. Again, someone has gotten an idea that truth and simplicity have to be pounded and thumped into the ears of the listener. As Mama used to say, "It's a wise man who knows when to leave well enough alone." I was appalled the first time I heard the new arrangement with the full complement of organ and choir. Now, when it begins, I snap off the radio or TV until they are done tearing it to pieces—and I think that it is the same way they have treated the Coalville Tabernacle.

But when I hear the clear and simple notes of *Come, Come Ye Saints*, sung as it has been sung for over a century—appealing, pleading, exhorting, comforting, and confidently accepting the will of God as it does in the fourth verse—I am shaken with my response to it. As the song rises to a paean of triumph and gratitude, then my heart swells and tears come to my eyes and I am humbled before the courage of my forebears. "All is well! All is well!" Those final, clear high notes of the sopranos have more than once lifted me out of the mire of discouragement and set me atop Mount Olympus.

And sitting atop Mount Olympus is a good, safe place to be

according to the prophecies of the Church. From the time a Mormon child begins to understand what his elders are saying, he has heard of the prophecies of the Last Days. I grew up with the threat of the sun darkening and the moon turning to blood because of all the smoking and drinking that was going on.

I was well into my teens before I realized that there was a little more to sin than this, but I learned to watch for the signs of the times just as every other Mormon does. While Mormons will not put themselves on the spot so far as to tell you the day or the hour of His coming, there are certain prophecies that are deeply burned into every Mormon heart that will alert us all—active Saint, backsliding jack, and hardbitten apostate—to the Great and Dreadful Day of the Lord.

If I am alive at the time when the Last Great War begins, I will know that it is the last great war. According to the prophecies my grandfather read to me, it will begin in the east and will center around Jerusalem. (I have uneasy qualms about this Arab–Israeli conflict.)

It will be in fear and trembling that Mormons receive the news that work on the Great Temple in Jackson County, Illinois has begun. For this Temple is to be built in preparation of the imminent coming of Christ and the ushering in of the Millenium—the thousand years of peace before Satan is to be "loosed for a season," followed by the utter destruction of the earth by fire.

If I am alive when we hear that the building has begun (and word will run rampant throughout all of Zion), then you will see me in the forefront of all the runners to repentance.

But if I die before the "hearts of men fail them, and they flee to the tops of the mountains for safety" (and because we all have two-year supplies of food in our basements) then happy day—all is well!

When either of these two events occur, I will, like Papa, "find out . . ." Until then I guess I'll just go on living and wondering about things and maybe writing down some of the things I wonder about.

THE UTAH STATE ROAD COMMISSION decided to widen Seventh East, and so all of the property owners on the west side of the street were forced to move.

We were among the last to go, and by then the neighborhood had almost completely changed from what it had been when we first bought the house ten years before.

We moved to a beautiful split-level near Mount Olympus, but happiness doesn't depend on the kind of house you live in, although a lot of women seem to think so. It wasn't to be found in this one. My husband and I separated and then divorced when Barbara was in her last year of high school. Sally had married and Ann had graduated from the University of Utah.

Then, sort of all of a sudden, I remarried—"a writer feller," Papa would have called him—and moved to Wyoming. This morning I woke to the burbling, liquid notes of a red-winged blackbird.

I have never been active in the Church after I left Lincoln Ward. I decided when we moved from Seventh East that I would not become engulfed in ward activities again. There is no end to them once you start, leaving time for nothing else. Perhaps that is one reason why there are so few creative artists, writers, or philosophers of note who come out of Mormondom, though I do not believe that the Church especially wants artists and writers and philosophers and thinkers. It wants churchgoers, tithepayers, baby-getters, and time-givers. It wants those people who will meekly abide by the thundering words of the last speaker in a recent conference, "BELIEVE AND OBEY!"

I have come to that point in life where I am either brave enough or foolhardy enough to publicly say that I will believe what study and research and serious thought prove to me is truth, and I will obey the laws of the land, but not those set forth by a theological authoritarianism, unless my conscience and intelligence first agree.

I wonder what Papa would have said to that? It would have been the basis for a week-long argument at least. And then I hear him as if he were sitting in an easy chair across the room.

"A man ought to do what he's cut out for. Now me, I should have been a musician. There's nothing I can't play if I have a mind to, from a tin whistle to a fiddle. But I just didn't have a chance to learn music. Now, you girl, you go on with your writin'. I'm right proud of you. Imagine, I didn't even know you had it in you!"

And so I will, for most certainly Papa is a Son of Zion, and I, though perhaps wayward, *am* his loving daughter.

Rodello Hunter's first book, *A House of Many Rooms,* was a kind of first volume to her story about life among the Latter-day Saints. In that book she told of her childhood in a Mormon family. Educated in the public schools of Heber City, Utah, before she attended the University of Utah, Rodello Hunter's interest turned to conservation, for which her writing won her several state and national awards. She served for nine years as Associate Editor of Publications of the Utah State Department of Fish and Game. Rodello Hunter is the wife of Frank Calkins, himself a writer and professional game-management expert. They live in Freedom, Wyoming close to the scene of her last book, *Wyoming Wife.*

A NOTE ON THE TYPE

This book was set on the Linotype in Janson, a recutting made direct from type cast from matrices long thought to have been made by the Dutchman Anton Janson, who was a practicing type founder in Leipzig during the years 1668–87. However, it has been conclusively demonstrated that these types are actually the work of Nicholas Kis (1650–1702), a Hungarian, who most probably learned his trade from the master Dutch type founder Dirk Voskens. The type is an excellent example of the influential and sturdy Dutch types that prevailed in England up to the time William Caslon developed his own incomparable designs from them.

Composed, printed, and bound by The Haddon Craftsmen, Scranton, Pennsylvania.

Typography and binding design by CLINT ANGLIN.